SOCIAL WELFARE
Politics
and
Public Policy

Diana M. DiNitto / **Thomas R. Dye**

Florida State University *Florida State University*

PRENTICE-HALL, INC. Englewood Cliffs, New Jersey 07632

Library of Congress Cataloging in Publication Data

DiNitto, Diana M.
  Social Welfare.

    Includes index.
    1. Public welfare—United States. 2. United
States—Social policy. I. Dye, Thomas R.
II. Title.
HV95.D56 1983   361.6'13'0973   82-15113
ISBN 0-13-819474-2

Editorial/production supervision: Linda Benson
Cover design: Ray Lundgren
Manufacturing buyer: John Hall

© 1983 by Prentice-Hall, Inc., Englewood Cliffs, New Jersey 07632

Printed in the United States of America

10   9   8   7   6   5

ISBN 0-13-819474-2

Prentice-Hall International, Inc., *London*
Prentice-Hall of Australia Pty. Limited, *Sydney*
Editora Prentice-Hall do Brasil, Ltda., *Rio de Janeiro*
Prentice-Hall Canada Inc., *Toronto*
Prentice-Hall of India Private Limited, *New Delhi*
Prentice-Hall of Japan, Inc., *Tokyo*
Prentice-Hall of Southeast Asia Pte. Ltd., *Singapore*
Whitehall Books Limited, *Wellington, New Zealand*

For Vincent, Mary, and Daniel DiNitto
From Diana

Contents

2

GOVERNMENT AND SOCIAL WELFARE   20

3

DEFINING POVERTY: WHERE TO BEGIN?   45

4

PREVENTING POVERTY: THE SOCIAL INSURANCE PROGRAMS   62

5

HELPING THE "DESERVING POOR": AGED, BLIND, AND DISABLED   78

8

FIGHTING HUNGER: FEDERAL FOOD PROGRAMS   148

9

WARRING ON POVERTY:
VICTORIES, DEFEATS, AND
STALEMATES   169

10

IMPROVING HEALTH CARE:
TREATING THE NATION'S ILLS   186

Preface

Social Welfare: Politics and Public Policy is intended to introduce students to the major social welfare programs in the United States and to stimulate them to think about major conflicts in social welfare policy today. By focusing on "issues," we hope to emphasize that social welfare in America involves a series of *political* questions about what should be done about the poor, the near-poor, and the nonpoor—or whether anything should be done at all.

Social Welfare: Politics and Public Policy describes major social welfare programs—their histories, trends, and current problems and prospects. But, more importantly, it tackles the difficult conflicts and controversies which surround these programs. Social welfare policy is *not* presented as a series of solutions to social problems. Instead, social policy is portrayed as public conflict over the nature and causes of poverty; over what, if anything, should be done about poverty; over who should do it; and over who should decide about it.

Major public programs—

Social Security (OASDI)
Unemployment Compensation
Supplemental Security Income

Aid to Families with Dependent Children
General Assistance
Food Stamps
School Lunches
Community Action
Comprehensive Employment and Training
Mental Health
Care of the Elderly
Child Welfare Services
Legal Services
Vocational Rehabilitation
Medicare
Medicaid

are described and analyzed, and alternative proposals and "reforms" are considered.

This book is designed for undergraduate and beginning graduate courses in social welfare policy. It does not require prior knowledge of social work, nor does it attempt to introduce students to all aspects of the social work profession.

Many books on social policy treat social insurance, public assistance, and social service programs *descriptively;* by so doing they tend to obscure important conflicts and issues. Other books on social policy treat these programs *prescriptively;* by so doing they imply that there is only one "right" way to resolve social issues. *Social Welfare: Politics and Public Policy* views social policy as a *continuing political struggle* over the issues posed by poverty and inequality in society—conflicting goals and objectives, competing definitions of problems, alternative approaches and strategies, multiple programs and policies, competing proposals for "reform," and even different ideas about how decisions should be made in social welfare policy. A distinguishing feature of the book is that it discusses the relationship of Reaganomics to the social welfare scene and provides an up-to-date discussion of Reagan's welfare reforms for each of the major social welfare programs.

We would like to acknowledge the reviewers who commented on this book at its various stages: Stephen M. Aigner, Iowa State University; Creasie Finney Hairston, University of Tennessee, Nashville; David Hardcastle, University of Kansas; Karen S. Haynes, Indiana University; Lawrence S. Root, University of Michigan; and Theodore Walden, Rutgers University.

1

Politics,
Rationalism,
and Social Welfare

POLITICS AND SOCIAL WELFARE
POLICY

No one is really happy with the nation's welfare system—not the working taxpayers who must support it, not the social work professionals who must administer it, and certainly not the poor who must live under it. Since the Social Security Act of 1935, the federal government has tried to develop a rational social welfare system for the entire nation. Today, a wide variety of federal programs serve the aged, the poor, the disabled, and the sick. "Income maintenance" (social insurance and public assistance) is the largest single item in the federal budget, easily surpassing national defense. The Department of Health and Human Services is the largest department of the federal government, and many additional welfare programs are administered by other departments. Yet even after nearly fifty years of large-scale, direct federal involvement, social welfare policy remains a central issue in American politics.

Social welfare policy involves a series of *political* issues about what should be done about the poor, the near-poor, and the nonpoor—or whether anything should be done at all. The real problems in social welfare are not problems of organization, administration, or service delivery. Rather, they are political conflicts over the nature and causes of poverty and inequality, the role of government in society, the burdens to be carried by taxpayers, the appropriate strategies for coping with poverty, the issues posed by specific social insurance and public assistance programs, the relative reliance to be placed on cash versus services for the poor, the need for reform, and the nature of the decision-making process itself. In short, social welfare policy is a continuing political struggle over the issues posed by poverty and inequality in society.

Policy-making is frequently portrayed as a *rational* process, in which policy-makers identify social problems, explore all of the alternative solutions, forecast all of the benefits and costs of each alternative solution, compare benefits to costs for each solution, and select the best ratio of benefits to costs. In examining social welfare policy, we shall explore the strengths and weaknesses of this rational model.

More importantly, we shall portray social welfare policy as a "political" process—as conflict over the nature and causes of poverty, and over what, if anything, should be done about it. Social welfare policy is "political" because of disagreements about the nature of the problems confronting society; about what should be considered "benefits" and "costs"; about how to estimate and compare benefits and costs; about the likely consequences of alternative policies; about the importance of one's own needs and aspirations in relation to those of others; and about the ability of government to do anything "rationally." We shall see that the *political* barriers to *rational* policy-making are indeed very great.

SCOPE OF SOCIAL WELFARE POLICY

Social welfare policy is anything government chooses to do, or not to do, that affects the quality of life of its people. Broadly conceived, social welfare policy includes nearly everything government does—from taxation, national defense, and energy conservation, to health, housing, and public assistance. More elaborate definitions of social welfare policy are available;[1] most of these definitions refer to actions of government which have an impact on the welfare of citizens by providing them with services or income.[2] For practical purposes, however, let us limit our concerns to the policies of government which *directly* affect the income and services available to the aged, sick, and poor. We would discourage lengthy discussions of the definition of social welfare policy. These discussions are often futile, even exasperating, since few people can agree on a single definition of social policy. Moreover, these discussions divert attention away from the study of specific welfare policies.[3]*

Note that we are focusing not only on government action, but also on government *inaction*—that is, what government chooses *not* to do. We contend that government inaction can have just as important an impact on society as government action.

The boundaries of social welfare policy are fuzzy. But this should be viewed as a challenge, not an obstacle. Specifically, we will be concerned with major government programs in

Income Maintenance
    Aid to Families with Dependent Children (AFDC)
    General Assistance
    Social Security
    Supplemental Security Income (SSI)
    Unemployment Compensation

Nutrition
    Food Stamps
    School Breakfasts
    School Lunches

Health
    Medicaid
    Medicare
    public health

Social Services
    Community Action programs
    community mental health
    Comprehensive Employment and Training (CETA)
    legal services
    social services for children and families

---

* This definition implies a difference between governmental actions and an overall plan of action toward a specific goal. The problem, however, in insisting that government actions must have *goals* in order to be labeled as "policy" is that we can never be sure what the goal of a particular government action is. We generally assume that if a government chooses to do something there must be a goal, objective, or purpose, but often we find that bureaucrats who helped write the law, lobbyists who pushed for its enactment, and members of Congress who voted for it all had different goals, objectives, and purposes in mind! The stated intentions of a law may also be quite different from what government agencies actually do. All we can really observe is what governments choose to do or not to do.

Political scientists Heinz Eulau and Kenneth Prewitt supply still another definition of public policy: "Policy is defined as 'standing decision' characterized by behavioral consistency and repetitiveness on the part of those who make it and those who abide by it" *Labyrinths of Democracy* [Indianapolis: Bobbs Merrill, 1973], p. 465). Now certainly it would be a wonderful thing if government activities were characterized by "consistency and repetitiveness"; but it is doubtful that we would ever find a public policy in government if we insisted on these criteria. As we shall see, much of what government does is *in*consistent and *non*repetitive.

social services for the elderly
vocational rehabilitation

Some of these programs are labeled *public assistance* programs because people must be poor (according to legal standards) in order to receive benefits; benefits are paid out of general revenue funds. Public assistance programs include AFDC, Food Stamps, Medicaid, SSI, School Lunches, and General Assistance. Other programs are labeled as *social insurance* programs because they are designed to prevent poverty; people pay into these programs during their working years and are entitled to their benefits whether poor or not. Social insurance programs include Social Security, Medicare, and unemployment compensation. Still other programs are labeled *social service* programs because they provide care, training, and assistance to children, the elderly, the poor, sick, or disabled. Social service programs are included in children and family services, care for the elderly, community action, CETA, legal services, mental health, public health, and vocational rehabilitation.

We shall endeavor, first of all, to *describe* these programs. But we shall also be concerned with the *causes* of social welfare policy—why policy is what it is. We want to learn about some of the social, economic, and political forces that shape social welfare policy in America. We shall be concerned with how social policies have developed and changed over time. We shall also be concerned with the *consequences* of welfare policies—their effects on target groups and on society in general. We shall consider some alternative policies—possible changes, "reforms," improvements, or phase-outs. Finally, we shall be concerned with *political conflict* over the nature and causes of poverty—and conflict over what, if anything, should be done about it.

SOCIAL WELFARE POLICY:
A RATIONAL APPROACH

Ideally, social welfare policy ought to be rational. A policy is rational if the ratio between the values it achieves and the values it sacrifices is positive and higher than any other policy alternative. Of course, we should not measure benefits and costs in a narrow dollars-and-cents framework, while ignoring basic social values. The idea of rationalism involves the calculation of *all* social, political, and economic values sacrificed or achieved by a public policy, not just those that can be measured in dollars.

Rationalism has been proposed as an "ideal" approach to both studying and making public policy.* Indeed, it has been argued that

---

* Other major theoretical approaches to the study of public policy include institutionalism, elite theory, group theory, system theory, and incrementalism. For an introduction to these approaches, see Thomas R. Dye, *Understanding Public Policy*, 4th ed. (Englewood Cliffs, N.J.: Prentice-Hall, 1981), especially chapter 2.

rationalism provides a single "model of choice" that can be applied to all kinds of problems, large and small, public and private.[4] We do *not* contend that government policies are in fact rational, for they are not. Even so, the model remains important because it helps us to identify barriers to rationality. It assists us in posing the question: Why is policy-making not a more rational process?

Let us examine the conditions for rational policy-making more closely:

1. Society must be able to identify and define social problems and agree that there is a need to resolve these problems.
2. All of the values of society must be known and weighed.
3. All possible alternative policies must be known and considered.
4. The consequences of each policy alternative must be fully understood in terms of both costs and benefits, for the present and for the future, and for target groups and the rest of society.
5. Policy-makers must calculate the ratio of benefits to cost for each policy alternative.
6. Policy-makers must choose the policy alternative that maximizes *net* values— that is, the policy alternative that achieves the greatest benefit at the least cost.

Because this notion of rationality assumes that the values of *society as a whole* can be known and weighed, it is not enough to know the values of some groups and not others. There must be a common understanding of societal values. Rational policy-making also requires *information* about alternative policies and the *predictive capacity* to foresee accurately the consequences of each alternative. Rationality requires the *intelligence* to calculate correctly the ratio of costs to benefits for each policy alternative. This means calculation of all present and future benefits and costs to both the target groups and nontarget groups in society. Finally, rationalism requires a *policy-making system* that facilitates rationality in policy formation. The Israeli political scientist Yehezkel Dror provides a diagram of such a system in Figure 1–1.

Identifying *target groups* means defining the segment of the population for whom the policy is intended—the poor, the sick, the disabled, dependent children, or others in need. Then the desired effect of the program on the target groups must be determined. Is it to change their physical or economic conditions—for example, to increase the cash income of the poor, to improve the housing condition of ghetto residents, to improve the nutrition of children, or to improve the health of the elderly? Or is the program designed to change their knowledge, attitudes, or behavior—for example, to provide job skills, to improve literacy, or to increase awareness of legal rights? If several different effects are desired, what are the priorities among them? What are the possible *unintended consequences* on target groups—for example, does public housing improve the physical environment for many poor blacks at the cost of increasing

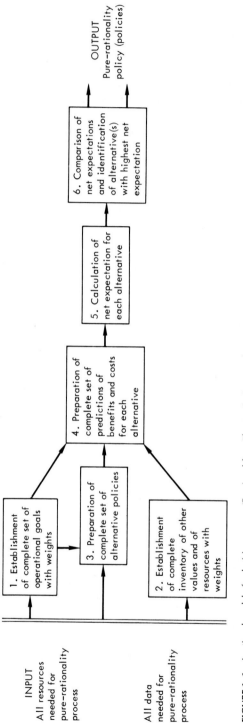

FIGURE 1–1 A rational model of a decision system. (Reprinted from Thomas R. Dye, *Understanding Public Policy*, 4th ed. Englewood Cliffs, N.J.: Prentice-Hall, 1981, p. 33.)

INPUT
All resources needed for pure-rationality process

All data needed for pure-rationality process

1. Establishment of complete set of operational goals with weights

2. Establishment of complete inventory of other values and of resources with weights

3. Preparation of complete set of alternative policies

4. Preparation of complete set of predictions of benefits and costs for each alternative

5. Calculation of net expectation for each alternative

6. Comparison of net expectations and identification of alternative(s) with highest net expectation

OUTPUT
Pure-rationality policy (policies)

housing segregation between blacks and whites? What is the impact of a policy on the target group in proportion to that group's total need? A program that promises to meet a recognized national need—for example, to end poverty altogether—but actually meets only a small percentage of that need, may generate great praise at first but bitterness and frustration later when it becomes known how insufficient the impact really is, relative to the need.

Policies have different effects on various segments of the population. Identifying important *nontarget groups* for a policy is a difficult process. For example, what is the impact of welfare reform proposals—such as a guaranteed annual income—on groups other than the poor (government bureaucrats, social workers, working-class families, taxpayers)? Rational policy-making requires consideration of "spill-over effects." These non-target effects may be benefits as well as costs—for example, the benefits to the construction industry from public housing projects or the benefits to farmers from Food Stamp programs.

When will the benefits or costs be felt? Is the policy designed for short-term emergency situations or is it a long-term, developmental effort? If it is short-term, what will prevent bureaucrats from turning it into a long-term program, even after immediate needs are met? Many studies have shown that new or innovative programs have short-term positive effects—for example, Head Start and other education and job-training programs. However, the positive effects sometimes disappear as the novelty and enthusiasm of new programs wear off. Other programs experience difficulties at first—for example, in getting physicians and hospitals to accept Medicaid patients—but turn out to have "sleeper" effects—as in the widespread acceptance of Medicaid today.

Rational policy-makers must measure benefits and costs in terms of general social well-being. Government agencies have developed various forms of cost-benefit analysis to identify the direct costs (usually, but not always, in dollars) of providing aid and assistance to the *average* family, worker, or job trainee. It is more difficult to identify and measure general units of social well-being. We need to know, for example, how to measure improved health, improved job skills, better nutrition, and greater employment opportunities. We are still struggling with better ways to measure these social values.

Actually *comprehensive* rationality in public policy-making may not really be rational. This apparent contradiction was noted many years ago by Herbert A. Simon, a Nobel Prize winner for his studies of the decision-making process in large organizations. It is so costly and time-consuming to learn about all of the policy alternatives available to decision-makers, to investigate all of the possible consequences of each alternative, and to calculate the cost-benefit ratio of each alternative, that the improvement in the policy selected is not worth the extra effort required to make a comprehensive rational selection. Simon developed a theory of *bounded rationality* which recognizes the practical limits to complete rationality: "It is impossible for the behavior of a single isolated individual to reach *any high degree of rationality*. The number of alternatives to be explored is so great and the information to evaluate them so vast, that even an approximation of objective rationality is hard to conceive."[5]

In contrast to completely rational decision-making, the notion of "bounded rationality" means that policy-makers consider a limited number of alternatives, estimate the consequences of these alternatives using the best available means, and select the alternative that appears to achieve the most important values without incurring unacceptable costs. Instead of maximizing the ratio of benefits to costs, policy-makers search for a "satisfying" choice—a policy alternative that is good enough to produce the desired benefits at a reasonable cost. This means that policy-makers do not try to create the best of all possible worlds but rather seek to get by, to come out all right, to avoid trouble, to compromise.

Rationalism, then, presents an ideal model of policy-making—in social welfare and in other policy fields. But policy-making "in the real world" is not usually a rational process. Policy-making occurs in a political context which places severe limits on rationality.

SOCIAL WELFARE POLICY:
A POLITICAL APPROACH

Social welfare policy is "political." By *political* we mean that social welfare policy arises out of conflict over the nature of the problems confronting society and what, if anything, should be done about them.

Politics has been described as "who gets what, when, and how";[6] it is an activity through which people try to get more of whatever there is to get—money, jobs, prestige, prosperity, respect, and power itself. Politics, then, is conflict over the allocation of values in society, and this conflict is central to politics and policy-making. "Politics arises out of conflicts and it consists of many activities—for example, reasonable discussion, impassioned orating, balloting, and street fighting, revolution—by which conflict is carried on."[7]

Why do we expect conflict in society over who gets what? Why can't we agree on "a theory of justice" according to which everyone would agree on what is fair for all members of society, particularly the poor, the aged, and the sick.[8] Why can't we have a harmonious, loving, caring, sharing society of equals? Philosophers have pondered these questions for centuries. James Madison, perhaps the first American to write seriously about politics, believed that the causes of "faction" (conflict) are found in human diversity—"a zeal for different opinions concerning religion, concerning government, and many other points ... [and] ... an attachment to different leaders ambitiously contending for preeminence and power." More importantly, according to Madison, "the most common and durable source of faction has been the various and unequal distribution of property. Those who hold and those who are without property have ever formed distinct interests in society" *(The Federalist,* No. 10). In short, differences among people, particularly in the sources and amount of their wealth, are the root cause of social conflict.

It is the task of government to regulate conflict. It does so by (1) establishing and enforcing general rules by which conflict is carried on, (2) arranging compromises and balancing interests in public policy, and (3) imposing settlements which the parties to a dispute must accept. Governments must insure that conflicts are channeled into elections, legislatures, bureaucracies, or courts, rather than into street fighting, terrorism, or civil war. Governments must arrange settlements in the form of public policy— settlements that allocate values in such a way that they will be accepted by both "winners" and "losers" at least temporarily. Finally, governments must impose these settlements by enforcing public policy and by promising rewards or threatening punishments.

From a "political" perspective, public policy is the outcome of conflicts in government over who gets what, and when and how they get it. A policy may be considered *politically* rational when it succeeds in winning enough support to be enacted into law, implemented by executive agencies, and enforced by the courts. Or it may be considered *politically* rational if it is supported by influential groups and believed to be popular among the voters. But this is not the same type of rationality that we described earlier in the rational model.

Indeed, the political approach raises serious questions about rationality in policy-making. It suggests that:

1. There are no *social* values that are generally agreed upon, but only the values of specific groups and individuals, many of which are conflicting.

2. Problems cannot be defined because people do not agree on what the problems are. What is a problem to one group may be a benefit to another group.

3. Many conflicting costs and values cannot be compared or weighed; for example, how can we compare the value of individual dignity with the cost of a general tax increase.

4. Policy-makers, even with the most advanced computerized analytic techniques, cannot predict the consequences of various policy alternatives or

calculate their cost-benefit ratios when many diverse social, economic, and political values are involved.

5. The environment of policy-makers, particularly the political system of power and influence, makes it virtually impossible to forecast the consequences of public policy or accurately weigh many social values, particularly those that do not have active or powerful proponents in or near government. The poor and the sick may have little access to governmental representation.

6. Policy-makers are not necessarily motivated to make decisions on the basis of social values. Instead they often seek to maximize their own rewards—power, status, reelection, money, and so on. Policy-makers have their own needs, ambitions, and inadequacies, all of which can prevent them from performing in a highly rational manner.

7. Large, segmented, government bureaucracies create barriers to coordinated policy-making. It is difficult to bring all of the interested individuals, groups, and experts together at the point of decision. Governmental decision-making is "disjointed."

How can we bridge the differences between an ideal model of *rational* policy-making and the realization that policy-making is a *political* activity? Political scientist Charles E. Lindblom first presented an "incremental" model of policy-making as a critique of the rational model. Lindblom observed that government policy-makers do *not* annually review the entire range of existing and proposed policies, or identify all of society's goals, or research the benefits and costs of all alternative policies to achieve these goals. They, therefore, do not make their selections on the basis of all relevant information. Limits of time, knowledge, and costs pose innumerable obstacles in identifying the full range of policy alternatives and predicting their consequences. Political limitations prevent the establishment of clear-cut societal goals and the accurate calculation of cost-benefit ratios. The incremental model recognizes the impracticality of comprehensive rational policy-making and describes a more "conservative" process of public decision-making.

Incremental policy-making considers existing policies, programs, and expenditures as a base. It concentrates attention on newly proposed policies and programs and on increases, decreases, or other modifications of existing programs. Incrementalism is conservative in that policy-makers generally accept the legitimacy of established policies and programs. The focus of attention is on proposed *changes* in these policies and programs. This narrows the attention of policy-makers to a limited number of new initiatives, increases or decreases in the budget.

There are important *political* advantages to incrementalism in policy-making. Conflict is reduced if the items in dispute are only increases or decreases in existing budgets, or modifications of existing programs. Conflict would be greater if policy-making focused on major policy shifts involving great gains or losses for various groups in society, or "all or nothing," "yes or no" policy decisions. To have existing policies reconsidered every year would generate a great deal of conflict; it is easier politically to continue previously accepted policies.

Policy-makers may also continue existing policies because of uncertainty about the consequences of completely new or different policies. Forecasting is never perfect. It is safer to stick with known programs when the consequences of new programs cannot be accurately predicted. Under conditions of uncertainty, policy-makers continue past policies or programs whether they have proven effective or not. Only in a "crisis" do political decision-makers begin to consider new and untried policies as preferable to existing ones. Thus, groups and individuals who seek more than incremental change in public policy usually try to generate a "crisis" atmosphere.

Policy-makers also realize that individuals and organizations—executive agencies, congressional committees, interest groups—accumulate commitments to existing policies and programs. For example, it is accepted wisdom in Washington that bureaucracies persist over time regardless of their utility, that they develop routines that are difficult to alter, and that individuals develop a personal stake in the continuation of organizations and programs. These commitments are serious obstacles to major change. It is easier politically for policy-makers to search for alternatives which involve only a minimum of budgetary, organizational, or administrative change.

Finally, in the absence of generally agreed-upon social goals or values, it is politically expedient for governments to pursue a variety of different programs and policies simultaneously, even if some of them are overlapping or even conflicting. In this way, a wider variety of individuals and groups in society are "satisfied." Comprehensive policy planning for specific social goals may maximize some people's values, but it may also generate extreme opposition from others. A government that pursues multiple policies may be politically more suitable to a pluralistic society comprising persons with varying values.

ILLUSTRATION: PUBLIC OPINION AND SOCIAL WELFARE

Public opinion toward social welfare policy is ambivalent. Most Americans want to help the truly needy, but they believe that too many people on welfare are able to work and that too many cheat. Most Americans believe that the criteria for getting on welfare are "not tough enough," but they also believe that "many women whose husbands have left them with several children have no choice but to go on welfare." At the same time, most Americans believe that welfare recipients "could get along without it [welfare] if they tried."

THE HARRIS SURVEY (*The New York Times,* August 3, 1977)

	AGREE	DISAGREE	NOT SURE
It is not right to let people who need welfare go hungry.	94%	4%	2%
Too many people on welfare could be working.	89	6	5
Too many people on welfare cheat by getting money they are not entitled to.	85	9	6
Many women whose husbands have left them with several children have no choice but to go on welfare.	74	22	4
Criteria for getting on welfare are not tough enough.	64	23	13
The welfare system allows no dignity for the poor.	45	46	9
Most people go on welfare only as a last resort.	39	54	7
People on welfare should just be given the money and end all the red tape.	16	77	7

Most Americans say they approve of food stamps for the poor, aid to poor families with children, and health care for the poor. Food Stamps, Aid to Families with Dependent Children, and Medicaid are the nation's largest welfare programs. Yet most Americans say, in apparent contradiction, that they disapprove of most government-sponsored welfare programs.

THE NEW YORK TIMES/CBS POLL (August 3, 1977)

	NEED HELP	COULD GET ALONG	NO OPINION
Do you think that most people who receive money from welfare could get along without it if they tried, or do you think they really need this help?	31%	54%	15%

	YES	NO	
Do you approve of most government-sponsored welfare programs?	32	58	10
Do you approve of a guaranteed minimum income?	44	50	6
Do you approve of a national health care program?	60	33	7
Do you approve of food stamps for the poor?	81	13	6
Do you approve of aid to poor families with dependent children?	81	13	6
Do you approve of health care for the poor?	82	13	5

> Public opinion does not necessarily decide public policy, even in a democracy. But even if it did, these inconsistencies, contradictions, and disagreements would generate an abundance of political conflict over social welfare policy. In order to reduce these conflicts, social policy-making in the United States has been an incremental process.

THE POLICY-MAKING PROCESS

Policy-making involves a combination of processes in society. These processes are not always clear-cut and distinguishable in the complex world of policy-making. But we can identify them for purposes of analysis.

Identifying Policy Problems: the identification of policy problems through publicized demands for government action.

Formulating Policy Alternatives: the formulation of policy proposals through political channels by policy-planning organizations, interest groups, government bureaucracies, and the president and Congress.

Legitimizing Public Policy: public statements or actions by the president, Congress, or courts, including executive orders and budgets, laws and appropriations, rules and regulations, and decisions and interpretations, which have the effect of setting policy directions.

Implementing Public Policy: the implementation of public policy through the activities of public bureaucracies and the expenditure of public funds.

Evaluating Policy: the evaluation of policies by government agencies, by outside consultants, by interest groups, by the mass media, and the public.

This is a formal breakdown of the policy-making process used by many students of public policy.[9] What it says is that some groups succeed, usually through the help of the mass media, in capturing public attention for their own definition of a problem. Various government bureaucracies, private organizations, and influential individuals, then, propose solutions in terms of new laws or programs, new government agencies, or new public expenditures. These proposals twist their way through the labyrinths of government and eventually emerge (generally after many alterations and amendments) as laws and appropriations. Government bureaucracies are created to carry out these laws and spend these funds. Eventually, either through formal evaluation studies or informal feedback, the successes and failures of these laws, bureaucracies, and expenditures are examined.

All of this activity involves both rational problem-solving *and* political conflict. This is true whether we are describing Social Security or the Food Stamp program, employment training or free school lunches, Medicaid or legal services. Both rational and political considerations enter into each stage of the policy-making process.

Agenda-Setting

Deciding what is to be decided is the most important stage of the policy-making process. We might refer to this stage as "agenda-setting." Societal conditions not defined as problems never become policy issues. These conditions never get on the "agenda" of policy-makers. Government does nothing and conditions improve, remain the same, or worsen. On the other hand, if conditions in society are defined as problems, then they become policy issues and government is forced to decide what to do.

Policy issues do not just happen. Creating an issue, dramatizing it, calling attention to it, and pressuring government to do something about it are important political tactics. These tactics are employed by influential individuals, organized interest groups, policy-planning organizations, political candidates and officeholders, and, perhaps most importantly, the mass media. These are the tactics of agenda-setting.

Non-Decisions

Preventing certain conditions in society from becoming policy issues is also an important political tactic. "Non–decision-making" occurs when influential individuals or groups act to prevent the emergence of challenges to their own interests in society. According to political scientists Peter Bachrach and Morton Baratz:

> Non–decision-making is a means by which demands for change in the existing allocation of benefits and privileges in the community can be suffocated before they are even voiced; or kept covert; or killed before they gain access to the relevant decision-making arena; or failing all these things, maimed or destroyed in the decision-implementing stage of the policy process.[10]

Non–decision-making occurs when powerful individuals, groups, or organizations act to suppress an issue because they fear that if public attention is focused on it, something which may not be in their best interest will be done. Non–decision-making also occurs when political candidates, officeholders, or administrative officials anticipate that powerful individuals or groups will not favor a particular idea and therefore do not pursue the idea. They do not want to "rock the boat."

The Mass Media

The power of the mass media is its ability to set the agenda for decision-making—to decide what problems will be given attention and what problems will be ignored. Deciding what is "news" and who is "newsworthy" is a powerful political weapon. Television executives and producers, and newspaper and magazine editors, must decide what people, organizations, and events will be given public attention. Without media coverage, the general public would not "know" about many of the conditions or government programs affecting the poor or about alternative policies or programs. Without media coverage, these topics would not likely become objects of political discussion, nor would they likely be considered important by government officials even if they knew about them. Media attention can create issues and personalities. Media *in*attention can doom issues and personalities to obscurity.

The Budget

The budget is the single most important policy statement of any government. The expenditure side of the budget tells us who gets what in public money, and the revenue side of the budget tells us who pays the cost. There are few government activities or programs that do not require an expenditure of funds, and no public funds may be spent without legislative authority. The budgetary process provides a mechanism for reviewing government programs, assessing their costs, relating them to financial resources, and making choices among alternative expenditures. Budgets determine what programs and policies are to be increased, decreased, allowed to lapse, initiated, or renewed. The budget lies at the heart of all public policies.

In the federal government, the Office of Management and Budget (OMB), located in the Executive Office of the president, has the key responsibility for the preparation of the budget. OMB begins preparation of a federal budget more than a year before the beginning of the fiscal year for which it is intended. (For example, work began in January 1982 on the budget for the fiscal year beginning October 1, 1983, and ending September 30, 1984.) Budget materials and general instructions go out from OMB to departments and agencies, who are required to submit their budget requests for increases or decreases in existing programs and for new programs to OMB. With requests for spending from departments and agencies in hand, OMB begins its own budget review. Hearings are held for each agency. Top agency officials support their requests as convincingly as possible. On rare occasions a dissatisfied department head may ask the OMB director to present the department's case directly to the president. As each January approaches, the president and the OMB director devote a great deal of time to the budget document which is by then approaching its final stages of assembly. Finally, in January, the president sends "The Budget of the United States Government" to the Congress. This will be the budget for the fiscal year beginning October 1 and ending on September 30 of the following year. After the budget is in legislative hands, the president may recommend further amendments as needs dictate.

Congress has established separate House and Senate budget committees and a joint Congressional Budget Office to review the president's budget after its submission to Congress. These committees initially draft a concurrent resolution setting target totals to guide congressional actions on appropriations and revenue bills considered throughout the year. Thus, congressional committees considering specific budget appropriations have not only the president's recommendations to guide them, but also the guidelines established by the budget committees. If an appropriations bill exceeds the target set by the earlier resolution, it is sent back to the budget committees for reconciliation.

Consideration of specific appropriations is a function of the appropriations committees in both houses. Each of these important committees has about ten fairly independent subcommittees to review the budget requests of particular agencies or groups of related functions. These subcommittees hold hearings in which department and agency officials, interest groups, and other witnesses testify about new and existing programs and proposed increases or decreases in spending. The appropriations subcommittees are very important because neither the full committees nor the Congress has the time or expertise to conduct in-depth reviews of programs and funding. Although the work of the subcommittees is reviewed by the full committee, and the appropriations acts must be passed by the full Congress, in practice most subcommittee decisions are routinely accepted.

In overall programs and expenditures, however, it is rare that Congress ever makes more than a 5 percent change in the budget originally recommended by the president. Most appropriations are determined by executive agencies interacting with the OMB. Congress usually makes only minor adjustments in the president's budget.

Implementation

Policy implementation includes all of the activities which result from the official adoption of a policy. Policy implementation is what happens after a law is passed. We should never assume that the passage of a law is the end of the policy-making process. Sometimes laws are passed and *nothing* happens! Sometimes laws are passed and executive agencies, presuming to act under these laws, do a great deal more than Congress ever intended. Political scientist Robert Lineberry writes:

> The implementation process is not the end of policy-making, but *a continuation of policy-making by other means.* When policy is pronounced, the implementation process begins. What happens in it may, over the long run, have more impact on the ultimate distribution of policy than the intentions of the policy's framers.[11]

Specifically, policy implementation involves:

1. The creation, organization, and staffing of new agencies to carry out the new policy, or the assignment of new responsibilities to existing agencies and staff
2. The development of specific directives, rules, regulations, or guidelines to translate new policies into courses of action
3. The direction and coordination of personnel and expenditures toward the achievement of policy objectives.

The best laid plans of policy-makers often do not work. Before a policy can have any impact, it must be implemented. And what governments *say* they are going to do is not always what they end up doing.

Traditionally, the implementation of public policy was the subject matter of public administration. And traditionally, administration was supposed to be free of politics. Indeed, the separation of "politics" from "administration" was once thought to be the cornerstone of a scientific approach to administration.

But today it is clear that "politics" and "administration" cannot be separated. Opponents of policies do not end their opposition after a law is passed. They continue their opposition in the implementation phase of the policy process by opposing attempts to organize, fund, staff, regulate, direct, and coordinate the program. If opponents are unsuccessful in delaying or halting programs in implementation they may seek to delay or halt them in endless court battles. In short, conflict is a continuing activity in policy implementation.

The federal bureaucracy makes major decisions about the implementation of public policy. There are over two million civilian employees of the federal government. This huge bureaucracy has become a major base of power in America—independent of the Congress, the president, the courts, or the people. The bureaucracy does more than simply fill in the details of congressional policies, although this is one power of bureaucratic authority. Bureaucracies also make important policies on their own by (1) proposing legislation for Congress to pass; (2) writing rules, regulations, and guidelines to implement laws passed by Congress; and (3) by deciding specific cases in the application of laws or rules.

In the course of implementing public policy, federal bureaucracies have decided such important questions as the safety of nuclear power plants; the extent to which blacks, women, and minorities will benefit from affirmative action programs in education and employment; whether opposition political parties or candidates will be allowed on television to challenge a presidential speech or press conference; and whether welfare agencies will search Social Security Administration files to locate nonsupporting fathers.

The decisions of bureaucracies can be overturned by Congress or the courts if sufficient opposition develops. But most bureaucratic decisions go unchallenged.

SUMMARY

Although there are elements of rationalism in policy-making, the policy process is largely political. Our abilities to develop policies rationally are limited because we cannot agree on what constitutes social problems and on what, if anything, should be done to alleviate these problems. We also hesitate to make drastic changes in our current welfare system because we fear making large, costly errors that may be difficult to reverse.

Public opinion about welfare in the United States provides an excellent example of the inconsistencies and ambivalence that are typical of the way social problems are addressed. Americans believe that aid should be provided to the deserving poor, such as the elderly, but do not support taxes that would make these programs possible. Many Americans believe that there is too much welfare in the United States, that many people receiving welfare do not deserve it, and that the welfare system is in need of major revamping.

Social welfare policy development is much more a political "art and craft"[12] than a rational science. It is not enough for human service professionals to know the needs of people and to want to provide services to help them. Policy advocates must both understand the political process and be adept at working within it if they are to have a voice in shaping social policy.

NOTES

1. David A. Gil, "A Systematic Approach to Social Policy Analysis," *Social Service Review* 44 (December 1970): 411–426; also cited in Neil Gilbert and Harry Specht, *Dimensions of Social Welfare Policy* (Englewood Cliffs, N.J.: Prentice-Hall, 1974), p. 3.
2. T. H. Marshall, *Social Policy* (London: Hutchinson University Library, 1955), p. 7. The distinction between *social policy* and *social welfare policy* is discussed in George Rohrlich, "Social Policy and Income Distribution," *Encyclopedia of Social Work*, ed. Robert Morris (New York: National Association of Social Workers, 1971), pp. 1385–86.
3. See Carl T. Friedrich, *Man and His Government* (New York: McGraw-Hill, 1963), p. 70; Harold Lasswell and Abraham Kaplan, *Power and Society* (New Haven: Yale University Press, 1970), p. 71.
4. Edith Stokey and Richard Zeckhauser, *A Primer of Policy Analysis* (New York: W. W. Norton & Co., Inc., 1978).
5. Herbert A. Simon, *Administrative Behavior* (New York: Macmillan, 1945), p. 79. See also his *Models of Man* (New York: John Wiley, 1957), and *The Sciences of the Artificial* (New York: John Wiley, 1970). Simon was trained as a political scientist; he won the Nobel Prize in economics in 1978.
6. Harold Lasswell, *Politics: Who Gets What When and How* (New York: Free Press, 1936).

7. Edward C. Banfield and James Q. Wilson, *City Politics* (Cambridge: Harvard University Press, 1963), p. 7.

8. John Rawls, *A Theory of Justice* (Cambridge: Harvard University Press, 1972).

9. See Charles O. Jones, *An Introduction to the Study of Public Policy* (North Scituate, Mass.: Duxbury, 1977); Thomas R. Dye, *Understanding Public Policy,* 4th ed. (Englewood Cliffs, N.J.: Prentice-Hall, 1981).

10. Peter Bachrach and Morton S. Baratz, *Power and Poverty* (New York: Oxford University Press, 1979), p. 7.

11. Robert L. Lineberry, *American Public Policy* (New York: Harper & Row, Pub., 1977), p. 71.

12. Aaron Wildavsky, *The Art and Craft of Policy Analysis* (Boston: Little, Brown, 1979).

2

Government
and Social Welfare

HISTORICAL PERSPECTIVES
ON SOCIAL WELFARE

Social welfare policy as we know it today dates back to the beginning of the seventeenth century in Elizabethan England. English welfare traditions were adopted by colonists who settled in the New World. At first, families, friends, and churches were the major sources of welfare aid for the destitute; state and local governments came to intervene only as a last resort. However, the twentieth century brought an increasing number of social welfare problems for Americans. The magnitude of these problems caused the federal government to enact its own welfare legislation during the New Deal Era of the 1930s. From that point on the federal government's role in social welfare has continued to grow with the Great Society programs of the 1960s bringing another large-scale attempt on the part of the federal government to alleviate poverty and suffering.

In the 1980s, however, a different response to hardship in America is emerging. Concerned with growing costs and disillusioned with the perceived failure of many welfare programs, President Reagan's administration has moved to limit the federal government's role in social welfare and to increase reliance on state governments in providing social welfare services.

Elizabethan Poor Law

The first sources of welfare assistance were family, friends, and the community. These forms of assistance were called *mutual aid*. Aid was mutual because people relied on one another. If a family's food crop failed or the breadwinner became ill and unable to work, brothers, sisters, or neighbors pitched in, knowing that they would receive the same assistance if they should need it one day. Later, it became the duty of the church and of wealthy feudal lords to help the needy.[1] During much of the Middle Ages emphasis was placed on doing charitable works as a religious duty.[2] Attitudes toward the poor were benevolent. Those destitute through no fault of their own were treated with dignity and respect and were helped through the hard times.[3]

These early systems of aid were informal systems. There were no formal eligibility requirements, no application forms to complete, and no background investigations. But as the structure of society became more complex, so did the system of providing welfare assistance.

The first laws designed to curb poverty were passed in England during the fourteenth and fifteenth centuries. In 1349 the Black Death drastically reduced the population of the country. King Edward III responded with the Statute of Laborers to discourage vagrancy and begging; all able-bodied persons were ordered to work, and the giving of alms was forbidden.[4]

Changes in the structure of society eventually forced the Elizabethan government to intervene in providing welfare. The Industrial Revolution that occurred in England meant a shift from an agrarian-based economy to an economy based on the wool industry. People left their home communities to seek industrial employment in the cities. The feudal system of life fell apart as the shift away from agriculture and toward industry was completed. Government was becoming more centralized and played a stronger role in many aspects of society, including social welfare, while the role of the church in welfare was diminishing.[5]

The interplay of new social forces—the breakdown of the feudal system, the Industrial Revolution, and the reduction of the labor force—brought about the Elizabethan Poor Law of 1601,[6] the first major event in the Elizabethan government's role in providing social welfare benefits. The law was passed mostly as a means of "controlling" those poor who were unable to locate employment in the new industrial economy and who might cause disruption.[7] Taxes were levied to finance the new welfare system, but rules were harsh. Children whose parents were unable to support them faced apprenticeship. Able-bodied men dared not consider remaining idle.

Distinguishing the "deserving" from the "nondeserving" poor was an important part of Elizabethan Poor Law. Affluent members of society did not want to be burdened with assisting any but the most needy. The deserving poor were the lame, the blind, orphaned children, and those unemployed through no fault of their own. The nondeserving poor were vagrants or drunkards—those considered lazy, shiftless, and unwilling to work. "Outdoor" relief was help provided to some deserving poor in their own homes. "Indoor" relief was also provided to those unable to care for themselves, but such relief was generally provided in "almshouses," which were institutions that housed the poor. The nondeserving poor were sent to "workhouses" where they were forced to do menial work in return for only the barest of life's necessities.[8]

Stringent residency requirements had to be met by all recipients. Welfare aid was administered by local units of government called parishes. Parishes were clearly instructed to provide aid only to persons from their own jurisdictions. There was little sympathy for transients.

Early Relief in the United States

Many aspects of the Elizabethan welfare system were adopted by American colonists. For example, residency requirements were strictly enforced through the policies of "warning out" and "passing on."[9] Warning out meant that newcomers were urged to move on to other towns if it appeared that they were not financially responsible. More often, "passing on" was used to escort the transient poor back to their home communities. These practices continued well into the nineteenth century. In one year alone, 1,800 persons were transported from one New York community to another as a result of these policies.[10]

Life was austere for the colonists. The business of making America livable was a tough job and the colonists were by no means well-off.[11] "Many of them were paupers, vagrants, or convicts shipped out by the English government as indentured servants."[12] Life in the colonies, while better for many, still brought periods when sickness or other misfortune might place a person in need.[13]

The colonists used four methods to "assist" the needy.[14] "Auctioning" the poor to the family that was willing to care for them at the lowest cost was the least popular method. A second method was to put the poor and sick under the supervision of a couple who were willing to care for them at as little cost as possible. The third method, outdoor relief, was provided to most of the needy. And the fourth method was the use of almshouses. Many claimed almshouses were the best method of aid because of the quality of medical care they provided to the sick and elderly.[15] Almshouses in the cities provided a much higher level of care than rural almshouses, which were often in deplorable condition and little more than run down houses operated by a farm family.[16] Politicians, almshouse administrators, and doctors seemed pleased with the progress they had made in assisting the needy during the eighteenth and nineteenth centuries.[17]

The Great Depression and the New Deal

From 1870 to 1920, America experienced a period of rapid industrialization and heavy immigration. Private charities, churches, and big city political "machines" and "bosses" assisted the needy during this period. The political machine operated by trading baskets of food, bushels of coal, and favors for the votes of the poor. To finance this primitive welfare system, the machine offered city contracts, protection, and privileges to business interests which in return paid off in cash. Aid was provided in a personal fashion without red tape or delays. Recipients did not feel embarrassed or ashamed, for, after all, "they were trading something valuable—their votes—for the assistance they received."[18]

As social problems mounted—increased crowding, unemployment, and poverty in the cities—the states began to take a more active role in welfare. "Mothers aid" and "mother's pension" laws were passed by state governments to assist children in families where the father was deceased or absent. Other pension programs were established to assist the poor, aged, blind, and disabled. Federal government involvement in welfare was not far away.

The Great Depression, one of the bleakest periods in American history, followed the stock market crash in October 1929. Prices dropped dramatically and unemployment was rampant. By 1932 one out of every four persons had no job and one out of every six persons was on welfare. Americans who had always worked lost their jobs and depleted their savings or lost them when banks folded. Many were forced to give up their homes and farms because they could not continue to meet the mortgage payments. Economic catastrophe struck deep into the ranks of the middle classes. Many of the unemployed and homeless were found sleeping on steps and park benches because they had nowhere else to go.[19]

The events of the Great Depression dramatically changed American thought. The realization that poverty could strike so many forced Americans to consider large scale economic reform. President Franklin Delano Roosevelt began to elaborate the philosophy of the "New Deal" that would permit government to devote more attention to the public welfare than did the philosophy of "rugged individualism" so popular in the earlier days of the country. The New Deal was not a consistent or unifying plan; instead it was a series of improvisations which were often adopted suddenly and some of them were even contradictory. Roosevelt believed that the government should act humanely and compassionately toward those suffering from the Depression. The objectives of the New Deal were "relief, recovery, and reform" and Roosevelt called for

full persistent experimentation. If it fails, admit it frankly and try something else. But above all try something. The millions who are in want will not stand by silently forever while the things to satisfy their needs are in easy reach.[20]

Americans came to accept the principle that the entire community has a responsibility for welfare.

Included in the New Deal were a number of social welfare provisions. The Social Security Act of 1935, the cornerstone of social welfare legislation today, included Social Security retirement benefits financed by the federal government. Work programs established through projects such as the Works Progress Administration and the Civilian Conservation Corps provided jobs for many Americans. Federal grants-in-aid programs to states and communities were initiated to fund assistance programs for dependent children, the elderly, and the blind. Other programs included unemployment compensation, employment services, child welfare, public housing, urban renewal, and vocational education and rehabilitation programs.

Declaring War on Poverty

From 1935 through the 1950s, welfare programs really did not change very much. Eligibility requirements were loosened, payments were increased, and a few new categories of recipients were added, but there were not many major changes to the system of providing welfare benefits. But the 1960s brought unusual times for Americans. The beginning of the sixties was a time of prosperity for most Americans, but civil rights issues and the depressed condition of minorities came to the foreground. Most Americans were relatively affluent, but there were 25 million people who remained poor. President John F. Kennedy, influenced by the writings of economist John Kenneth Galbraith who directed attention to the existence of poverty in the midst of this affluent culture, began to address the problem of poverty prior to his assassination in 1963.

President Lyndon Baines Johnson, following in the tradition of his predecessor, when on to "declare war on poverty" in March 1964. The War on Poverty comprised many social programs designed to "cure" poverty in America. The goals of the "war" were to allow ghetto and poor communities to develop their own programs to arrest poverty and to root out inequality in the lives of Americans. Model cities programs, community action agencies, and other devices were tried, but many of these strategies failed. As the 1970s approached, the new presidential administration of Richard Nixon began dismantling the agencies of the War on Poverty. The "welfare rights movement" had come and gone.

President Nixon, determined to clean up the "welfare mess," attempted another type of reform in 1970—a guaranteed annual income for all poor persons. Parts of the plan were adopted, notably the Supplemental Security Income (SSI) program in 1972. But for the most part, the concept of a guaranteed annual income was rejected by Congress. Some members of Congress were concerned that Nixon's proposal was too much welfare and others were concerned that it was too little welfare.

Meanwhile, another type of welfare movement had arisen as social services designed to address problems other than poverty grew increasingly popular in the 1960s and 1970s. Consequently, legislation was passed to assist abused children, to provide community mental health services, and to develop social services programs for the elderly.

"The Revolution No One Noticed"

While Americans were preoccupied with the turmoil of the 1960s— the civil rights movement and the war in Vietnam—a revolution no one noticed was taking place.[21] For many years, the argument on behalf of social welfare in America had followed clear lines: The United States was spending the largest portion of its budget for defense; programs for the poor, the sick, the aged, and minorities were underfinanced. In order to be more responsive to the needs of its citizens, it was argued in the 1960s that the nation should "change its priorities" and spend more for social programs to reduce poverty and less on wars like Vietnam. The argument ended with a call for a revolution in national priorities.

In a single decade America's national priorities were reversed. In 1965, national defense expenditures accounted for 41 percent of the federal government's budget, while social welfare expenditures (social insurance and public assistance) accounted for less than 19 percent. While the mass media focused on the war in Vietnam and on Watergate, a revolution in national policy-making was occurring. By 1975, defense accounted for only 25 percent of the federal budget and social welfare expenditures had grown to 38 percent of the budget (see Figure 2–1).

Social welfare is now the major function and major expenditure of the federal government. This reversal of national priorities occurred during both Democratic and Republican administrations and during the nation's longer war.

> The mid to late 1960s were quite prosperous years. The unemployment rate fell under 4 percent, real income rose briskly. In the flush of affluence, new programs could be introduced with minimal fiscal strain, even as the Vietnam War expenditures were swelling.[22]

In short, ideas that welfare expenditures are not likely to increase during Republican administrations or during times of war turned out to be wrong. America's commitment to social welfare was growing.

But not everyone was comfortable with this revolution in public spending. There was fear that the nation was sacrificing national defense in order to spend money on social welfare programs which might not work. As

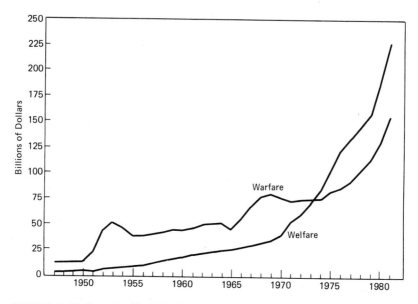

FIGURE 2–1 Warfare and welfare federal spending.

the 1970s ended and the 1980s emerged, a more cautious attitude toward social welfare spending had developed.

Social Welfare in the 1980s

In some respects social welfare has come a long way. We are spending more for social welfare and reaching more people than ever before. But in other ways social welfare in the early 1980s is not much different from social welfare in Elizabethan and colonial times. The expansion of social welfare programs has resulted in a mixture of public policies and programs which are often inconsistent, conflicting, and overlapping. Critics of the welfare reform continue to focus on low payment levels and other demeaning aspects of American welfare.

The liberal ideas and hopes of the 1960s are being altered by the more conservative political philosophies of the early 1980s. These philosophies suggest that (1) government spending for welfare should be kept to a minimum; (2) government, especially the federal government, should minimize its role in welfare policy and programs; (3) only those in extreme circumstances—the "truly needy"—should receive welfare assistance; and (4) welfare assistance should be provided on a short-term rather than on a long-term basis whenever possible. Disagreement about welfare policies and programs continues to represent a struggle between those who support a conservative and selective approach to assist those in need of public assistance and social services and those who believe in a more open, generous, universal system of aid. In the early 1980s we were still in a turmoil over what to do about the "welfare mess."

Today federal expenditures for social welfare (including social insurance and public assistance) far exceed federal expenditures for national defense. In the 1982 federal budget, social welfare spending accounted for about 35 percent of the total budget; if we add the costs of health care (mostly Medicaid and Medicare), this accounts for an additional 11 percent of the federal budget. This means that a total of 46 percent of the federal budget is devoted to welfare and health. Only 27 percent of the 1982 federal budget is devoted to national defense.

Until a few years ago, the relationship between federal spending for "welfare" and "warfare" was reversed: Before 1973 the federal government spent more on national defense than on social welfare. Figure 2–1 shows the changing trends in spending for welfare and defense. Note that defense spending jumped up at the beginnings of the Korean War (1950–1952) and the Vietnam War (1964–1968), and recently in the military build-up begun under President Carter and continued under President Reagan. In contrast, social welfare spending rose slowly for many years and then "exploded" in the 1970s after the Great Society programs were in place.

SOURCES OF INCREASED WELFARE SPENDING

Several factors have contributed to the increase in the number of social welfare programs, the number of people receiving assistance, and, consequently, the amount spent on welfare programs. Some of these factors are (1) the rural to urban migration; (2) the elimination of residency requirements; (3) cost of living increases; (4) the welfare rights movement; (5) the aging of America; and (6) the increase in single-parent families.

The Rural to Urban Migration

During the late 1800s and early 1900s America experienced some of its sharpest growing pains as the Industrial Revolution reached its peak. America changed from a rural agrarian society to an urban industrial society. People migrated from poor rural farming communities hoping to find jobs and a brighter future in the cities. In addition, foreigners were also emigrating to American cities seeking an improved standard of living. The dreams of many persons were shattered. Those who found jobs were often forced to work long hours for low pay under poor working conditions. Housing was often crowded; sanitation and health problems were common. Persons who had come to the cities to "make good" were often far from their families who could provide financial and psychological support. Social problems became more and more a problem for governments. As the Great Depression unfolded, the cities and states were no longer able to cope with worsening social problems. The response to this major economic crisis was the Social Security Act of 1935, by which the federal government assumed its role as the major financier of social welfare programs.

Residency Requirements Eliminated

Residency requirements were traditional means for restricting the number of persons eligible for welfare assistance. These requirements were not based on the belief that the poor and needy are best served in their home communities. Instead residency requirements have been used by states and communities to limit the number of persons dependent on welfare by making means tests (eligibility criteria) difficult to meet. Requiring that a potential recipient reside in the city or state for six months or a year or even requiring that they intend to reside in the city or state were ways of keeping welfare caseloads small. Following a number of court challenges, the Supreme Court declared residency requirements unconstitutional in 1969.[23] Since then it has become easier to qualify for assistance and caseloads have continued to grow.

Cost of Living Increases

Some of the welfare spending increases of recent years have been due to congressional approval of cost of living increases designed to keep welfare benefits in line with inflation. Political scientist Aaron Wildavsky tells us that Congress had frequently increased Social Security payments by taking a special vote each time an increase was considered. But today, he points out, Social Security, Food Stamp, and SSI program payments are automatically adjusted with the cost of living.[24] This practice is called *indexing*. Food stamp payments are adjusted twice a year and can be decreased as well as increased depending on whether the consumer price index rises or falls. Social Security payments are adjusted annually but cannot be decreased if the cost of living decreases. Wildavsky comments on the purpose of automatic cost of living increases:

> Such action was not intended to provide greater benefits to recipients but only to automatically assure them of constant purchasing power. The index makes changes non-discretionary.... Legislators may see such automatic increases as either favorable or unfavorable. Some may miss the almost yearly opportunity to show their constituents how much they have contributed to the nation's welfare. Others may be happy to continue constant benefits without being seen as wasteful spenders.[25]

Regardless of Congress's motivations, cost of living adjustments have meant rising social welfare costs.

Welfare Rights

The period of the 1960s, when blacks and other poor Americans showed their discontent with the welfare system, was called the "welfare rights movement." The poor expressed their dissatisfaction with a political system which had denied them the standard of living that other Americans were enjoying. The welfare rights movement was a stormy time in American domestic history, especially as major cities experienced a series of riots from 1964 to 1968. As the number of disturbances increased, so did the number of people applying for welfare. Also, a greater percentage of welfare applications were being approved than ever before. The welfare rights movement brought changes in the behavior and attitudes of welfare recipients.[26]

> The mood of applicants in welfare waiting rooms had changed. They were no longer as humble, as self-effacing, as pleading; they were more indignant, angrier, more demanding.[27]

The mood of welfare administrators and caseworkers had also changed. Many of the practices that had been part of lengthy background investigations ceased. The process of obtaining aid was speeded up; welfare agencies were not so quick to eliminate benefits when recipients did not comply with the rules.

> For all practical purposes, welfare operating procedures collapsed; regulations were simply ignored in order to process the hundreds of thousands of families who jammed the welfare waiting rooms.[28]

By 1968 the welfare rights movement was coming to a close. Riots were ceasing, but despite the demise of the welfare rights movement and the National Welfare Rights Organization, which had formed to improve the plight of the poor, a record number of people were being certified for welfare benefits. The rolls were continuing to grow.

The Aging of America

The growing number of elderly persons in the United States has put an increasing strain on the social welfare system. Today, those over age 65 comprise 11 percent of the population, as compared to 4 percent at the turn of the century. By the year 2000, the figure will be near 12 percent.[29] The elderly have greater health, financial, and other social welfare needs than the rest of the population. Advances in medicine and nutrition have helped Americans look foward to longer lives than ever before. But as people grow older they become increasingly vulnerable and are sometimes unable to meet their own needs. There is widespread agreement in the United States that the elderly deserve publicly supported care. The tripling of the size of the elderly population during this century has meant the need for greater planning to insure that older Americans receive proper treatment.

Increase in Single-Parent Families

The changing patterns of American family life are another factor which explains the increase in welfare expenditures. Divorce is rampant and the number of single-parent families, especially those headed by women, has grown considerably.

> In 1975, over 7 million families were female-headed families, double the number in 1950. Seven of ten have children, and one in four have children under 6 years of age. These percentages have increased considerably over the past 25 years when less than half were families with children. Female headed families represent 11 percent of all white families and 36 percent of all black families. Also, whereas in 1980, 39 percent of the family heads were divorced or separated, 6 years later, this percentage increased to 50 percent. Finally these 7 million families include over 10 million children.[30]

Female-headed households are much more likely to be poor than male-headed households. Women are less likely to hold jobs that pay well and to have the education and training to obtain satisfactory employment. While some of these trends are changing, the increase in poor, female-headed households has meant greater reliance on programs such as Aid to Families with Dependent Children (AFDC), Medicaid, and Food Stamps.

WHO PAYS FOR WELFARE PROGRAMS?: FEDERAL, STATE, AND LOCAL WELFARE SHARES

Who pays for welfare programs? Of course, citizens foot the bill through the taxes they pay. At the federal level, a special Social Security tax levied against an individual's income is used to finance the Social Security insurance program. Income taxes are another method of financing welfare programs. These taxes are channelled to the federal government's general revenue fund, which is used for many purposes, among them the financing of public assistance programs. The states also collect taxes in several ways. Most states levy an income tax like the federal government, although state income taxes are much less than federal income taxes. The sales tax is another mechanism used by states to generate revenues, a portion of which is used to provide social welfare services. At the local level, the property tax, principally used to fund education, is the major source of revenue. Local governments (cities, counties, and municipalities) provide the smallest share of welfare services.

But it has not always been the federal government that has paid the lion's share of welfare services. Before the Great Depression the trend was just the opposite. Local and state governments shouldered the major responsibility for welfare; the federal government was virtually uninvolved. Table 2–1 shows the social welfare expenditures of the federal and state/local governments since 1890. These figures illustrate the major role the federal government plays in financing social welfare programs today. While both federal and state/local welfare expenditures have increased, the federal government is clearly the largest welfare spender. In 1975 the federal government spent nearly $160 billion for welfare, three times as much as state/local government expenditures of $50 billion. Today, the federal government outspends the state and local governments by about four to one.

The federal government's major role in welfare also extends to social welfare policy-making. The federal government has gradually increased its role in setting eligibility requirements and payment levels for public assistance programs. However, President Reagan believes in returning to the states greater responsibility for determining public assistance services, payment levels, and eligibility requirements.

Table 2–1   Social Welfare Expenditures[a] by Source of Funds (millions of dollars) 1890–1980

	FEDERAL GOVERNMENT FUNDS	STATE AND LOCAL GOVERNMENT FUNDS
1890	$ 105	$ 203
1913	195	804
1930	777	785
1935	3,154	1,386
1940	3,368	2,864
1945	4,152	1,977
1950	10,384	6,450
1955	14,138	7,345
1960	24,089	10,579
1965	35,242	13,826
1970	71,464	23,582
1975	158,841	50,390
1980	280,000[b]	70,000[b]

[a]Social welfare includes social insurance, public assistance, health and medical, veterans, housing, and other social welfare programs.

[b]Estimates based on 1979 figures.

Sources: U.S. Bureau of the Census, *Historical Statistics of the United States, Colonial Times to 1970*, Series H 32-47, p. 341, Washington, D.C., 1975; and U.S. Bureau of the Census, *Statistical Abstract of the United States*, 1980, p. 330.

"REAGANOMICS" AND WELFARE

The economic ideas which have been labeled "Reagonomics," ideas which represent important political forces, are increasingly affecting social welfare policy in the 1980s. Whether or not one agrees with the ideas, it is essential to understand the Reagan administration's approach to welfare and the economy. Any brief description of "Reaganomics" risks oversimplification of many complex issues—inflation, economic growth, "supply side" economics, capital investment, and money supply. However, we can briefly describe some of the central ideas guiding the Reagan administration.

The "Misery Index"

An important component of "Reaganomics" is the belief that past Keynesian policies to reduce unemployment and hold down inflation have failed. (Keynesian economics is based on the notion that government can boost employment or cut inflation by manipulating the "demand side" of the economy—increasing government spending and expanding the money supply to boost employment, and doing just the opposite to hold down inflation.) According to Reagan, the most important cause of the nation's economic problems—unemployment, inflation, low productivity, and low investment—is the government itself. "The federal government, through taxes, spending, regulatory, and monetary policies, has sacrified long-term growth and price stability for ephemeral, short-term goals."[31]

According to Keynesian economic ideas, unemployment and inflation should not occur together. (Unemployment should reduce income, which in turn would force down prices.) But according to government figures, *both* unemployment and inflation remained high during the 1970s. Government efforts to reduce unemployment simply added to inflation; and government efforts to cut inflation simply added to unemployment. Reagan decided to combine the unemployment rate with the inflation rate and to call it the "misery index" (see Figure 2–2). In 1960 the misery index was 7.3, but by 1980 it had mushroomed to 17.2.

Taxes and the Inflation Ratchet

Because of the progressive rates of the federal personal income tax, the percentage of income claimed by the income tax increases with inflation. The federal personal income tax begins at 14 percent of the *first* 1,000 of *taxable* income. (Generally, the first $6,000 of income for a family of four is *non*taxable.) Tax rates increase to higher percentages for each $1,000 of additional income. A tax of 50 percent is levied on taxable income over $38,000. Prior to the Reagan-initiated taxcuts in 1981, the highest tax bracket of 70 percent was levied on taxable income over $200,000.

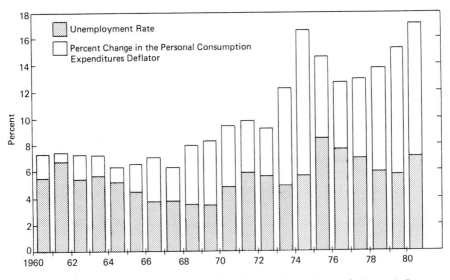

FIGURE 2–2 Unemployment rate plus inflation. (Office of the President, *A Program for Economic Recovery,* February 18, 1981. Washington, D.C.: Government Printing Office, 1981)

In the seventies, inflation pushed Americans into higher tax brackets even though their buying power remained the same. Goods simply cost more. This meant that Americans were paying an increasing amount of their incomes to the federal government as inflation pushed up their salaries, even though their salaries increases did not enable them to live a better life. These automatic tax increases caused by inflation were labeled "bracket creep."[32]

In 1981, the Reagan administration persuaded Congress to cut personal income taxes for all income groups by 25 percent over a three-year period. Moreover, Reagan persuaded Congress to "index" tax rates in the future to eliminate bracket creep. This means that if inflation carries taxpayers into higher tax brackets, their taxes will be adjusted, "indexed," so that the taxpayers will *not* carry a heavier tax burden.

"Supply Side" Economics

President Reagan has recommended a package of four sweeping policy directions designed to achieve "economic recovery."

1. Budget reform to cut the rate of growth in federal spending
2. Tax reductions of 25 percent over three years on personal income and additional tax reductions on business investment
3. Relief from federal regulations which cost industry large amounts of money for small increases in safety
4. Slower growth of the money supply, to be delivered with the cooperation of the Federal Reserve Board.

All of these policies are designed to provide incentives for Americans to work, save, and invest. Theoretically, the economy will grow more rapidly because Americans can keep more of what they earn. Inflation will be brought under control by producing more goods, rather than by limiting demand. Americans will be encouraged to save a greater proportion of their incomes, and businesses will be encouraged to build new plants and provide more jobs.

Critics of the new "supply side" economics argue that it is really a return to an old and discredited "trickle down" approach to the economy. Taxes and regulations on businesses and affluent Americans are reduced in the hope that they will reinvest their profits and expand job opportunities for the poor and working classes. In other words, incentives are provided for the wealthy in the hope that benefits will "trickle down" to the poor.

Tax Cuts

According to the new "Reaganomics," large tax cuts will not necessarily reduce government income or create large government deficits, at least in the long run. Taxes discourage work, productivity, investment and economic growth. Reduce taxes and the paradoxical result will be an *increase* in government revenue because more people will work harder and start businesses knowing they can keep a larger share of their earnings. Tax cuts will stimulate increased economic activity and, although tax rates are lower, this increased activity will eventually produce more government revenue.

Economist Arthur Laffer developed the diagram shown in Figure 2–3. If the government imposed no taxes (a zero tax rate), the government would receive no revenue (point A). Initially, government revenues rise with increases in the tax rate. However, when tax rates become too high (beyond point C), they discourage workers and businesses from producing and investing. When this discouragement occurs, the economy declines and government revenues fall. Indeed, if the government imposed a 100 percent tax rate and confiscated everything that workers or business produced, then everyone would quit working. Then government would receive *no* revenues (point B).

According to the "Laffer curve," modest increases in tax rates will result in increased government revenues, up to an optimum point (point C), after which further increases discourage work and investment. Laffer does not claim to know exactly what the optimum rate of taxation should be. But Laffer (and the Reagan administration) believe that the United States was in the "prohibitive range." Tax reductions, they believe, would actually increase government revenues. Even before Reagan won the presidency, Jack Kemp (Rep., N.Y.) and Senator William Roth (Rep., Del.) proposed drastic cuts in personal income taxes over three years. President Reagan committed himself to support the Kemp-Roth bill during the campaign.

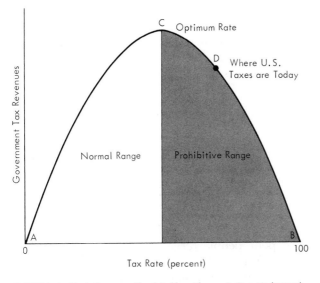

FIGURE 2–3 The Laffer curve. (Reprinted from Thomas R. Dye, *Understand-ing Public Policy,* 4th ed. Englewood Cliffs, N.J.: Prentice-Hall, 1981, p. 272.)

Although these cuts in taxes are expected to create temporary increases in budget deficits, the Reagan people hope that these cuts will eventually stimulate enough new economic activity to raise additional revenues and balance the budget.

The "Safety Net" Programs

The Reagan administration asserts that it will protect the "truly needy" by not making any significant cuts in basic income security pro-grams. These programs include

Social Security
Medicare
Unemployment Compensation
Veterans benefits
Supplemental Security Income
Head Start
Summer jobs for disadvantaged youth
Free school lunches and breakfasts

The Reagan administration refers to these programs as the "social safety net programs." Note, however, that Social Security, Medicare, and veterans benefits (which together account for most of the safety net spending) really affect the *aged* more than the poor. SSI affects the aged, blind, and disabled; and Headstart, summer jobs, and free school lunches and breakfasts mainly affect children.

Many core programs for the *poor* are not included in the "safety net" and are targeted for substantial budget savings. These include

Aid to Families with Dependent Children
Food Stamps
Medicaid
Housing assistance
CETA
Social services
Compensatory education
Legal services

The Reagan administration generally objects to overlapping programs—programs in which poor people receive more than one type of benefit. It also objects to programs which supplement the incomes of working families. Generally, the Reagan administration wishes to tighten eligibility requirements so that only those with little or no income receive benefits; it does not wish to supplement the income of families with low-income jobs.

Block Grants

The Reagan administration also wants to reduce federal spending for social programs through the use of block grants to the states. Block grants are federal payments to state or local governments for general functions, such as health, welfare, education, law enforcement, community development, and others. The money must be spent for the function specified in the block grant, but states or communities are free to decide specific uses for the money. The purpose of block grants is to reduce the power of "the Washington bureaucrats," to return decision-making to state and local officials, and to make federal money available for various purposes with "no strings attached." The Reagan administration considers *block* grants preferable to *categorical* grants, which are made by federal departments and agencies after reviewing specific applications of state or local governments on a project-by-project basis. The concept of block grants was developed as a reaction to centralization of power in the Washington bureaucracy. The first major block grants came in the field of law enforcement (the Crime Control and Safe Streets Act of 1968) and later in housing and urban affairs (the Housing and Community Development Act of 1974).

While the Reagan administration prefers to consolidate many social welfare programs into block grants to the states, the size of the block grant is often lower than the sum total of the social programs that are being consolidated. Moreover, by shifting decision-making about specific uses of federal social welfare dollars to the states, the Reagan administration is shifting decision-making to state political arenas where support for social welfare programs is not as great as in Washington. Indeed, many programs may lose funds or be killed altogether if they are lumped in with other programs in a block grant to the states.

THE "NEW FEDERALISM"

President Reagan has often expressed a desire to restructure federal-state relations—specifically, to turn over to the states many of the domestic programs of the national government. Initially, Reagan proposed a federal-state "swap" of these major social welfare programs: The federal portion of the AFDC program and the federal Food Stamp program would be given to the states and the states would turn over the Medicaid program to the federal government. (Chapter 6 describes the AFDC program; Chapter 8 describes the Food Stamp program; and Chapter 10 describes Medicaid.) It is argued that this swap would "end cumbersome administration," strengthen the states, and make these programs "more responsive to both the people they are meant to help and the people who pay for them."[33] It is also argued that the states would benefit financially from such a swap because the Medicaid costs which the federal government would assume are rising faster than AFDC and food stamp costs. Critics of the "New Federalism"—generally liberals and Democrats—are fearful that the states will not live up to their responsibilities to the poor. Many social welfare programs were launched by the federal government *because* the states failed to respond to the needs of the poor and of minorities. For the federal government to shift the responsibilities back to the states again would be viewed by many as a step backward in social welfare policy. Even if state governments were well-motivated to care for their poor, differences in the economic resources of the states would result in unequal treatment from state to state. In contrast, defenders of the "New Federalism" argue that reapportionment in the states, together with guarantees of minority voting rights, now insure that the states will be responsive to people's needs.

REAGAN'S WELFARE "CUTS"

Total federal spending for Social Security, welfare, and health is going *up* in the Reagan administration. The initial reports about "cuts" referred to the reductions which the Reagan White House made in the early Carter requests. It is true that Reagan will spend less than Carter *would* have spent. However, the Reagan budgets for Social Security, welfare, and health are higher than budgets in the Carter years.

The image of heavy budget cutting for welfare grew out of the reductions made by Reagan's Office of Management and Budget (OMB), and its director, David Stockman, in the requests made by the out-going Carter administration. Carter, for example, requested a total of $255 billion for Social Security and public assistance in 1982; Reagan reduced this request to $241 billion (a "savings" of $9 billion); but *both* the Reagan and Carter requests were well *above* the $232 billion spent in 1981. Carter, for example, requested a total of $75 billion for health, including Medicare and Medicaid, in 1982; Reagan reduced this request to $73 billion. But *both* the Reagan and Carter requests were well *above* the $66 billion spent in 1981. The press labeled Reagan's reductions in Carter's requests as "cuts," but the Reagan figures were increases over the previous year's budget.

Nonetheless, within these total dollar amounts, the Reagan administration has proposed various social welfare spending changes which may have profound consequences for the poor. Major changes initiated by the Reagan administration are outlined in Table 2–2. It is difficult to estimate the full impact of these changes on the poor. Critics of the Reagan administration charge that these changes will reduce or eliminate benefits to many millions of deserving poor and will contribute to hardship, deprivation, and hunger. The independent *Congressional Quarterly* says: "The overall effects of the cuts for individual poor people are difficult to predict accurately."[34]

THE POLITICS OF BUDGET AND TAX CUTTING

Republican Ronald Reagan won the presidency with 51 percent of the popular vote in 1980; Democrat Jimmy Carter received 41 percent of the vote and Independent John Anderson received 7 percent of the vote. Reagan's victory was portrayed as a "landslide" by the media, and spokespersons for the Reagan administration talked about a popular "mandate" to cut government spending, reduce taxes, and strengthen the military. Many presidents have found it difficult to transform their electoral victory into a mandate for policy change. However, Reagan was more successful than most modern presidents in convincing Congress that his "Program for Economic Recovery" ought to be enacted.

Reagan's political popularity (as judged by national opinion polls) was very high during the first year of his administration. His popularity soared after an assassination attempt and his courageous recovery. Unlike many presidents, Reagan was willing to use his personal popularity to advance his budget and tax cutting programs. Before Carter left office in January 1981, he submitted a $740 billion budget for the fiscal year 1982. In March, Reagan proposed a $695 billion budget for that same year. Reagan made

$45 billion in "cuts" from the Carter budget, all of them from domestic programs.

Reagan could rely on the Republican majority in the Senate to support his budget. However, in the House of Representatives the Democrats were in the majority. The Speaker of the House, Democratic Congressmen Thomas P. "Tip" O'Neill, confidently predicted that the House would restore moneys cut from social programs. But Reagan outsmarted O'Neill by appealing to Southern, Democratic, conservative representatives—the so-called "bollweevils" who Reagan invited to the White House to appeal to their conservative instincts. Reagan went on national television to make a plea for his budget and ask viewers to write their representatives in support of the president. The response was overwhelming: Thousands of calls, messages, and letters flooded into congressional offices. In the key vote on the budget, 62 House Democrats joined all 191 House Republicans to support the Reagan budget. Table 2–3 shows how Republicans and Democrats voted in response to President Reagan's budget and tax cuts.

Following his victory on the budget, Reagan introduced the largest tax cut in American history. Reagan proposed to reduce personal income tax rates from a scale of 16 to 70 percent to a scale of 14 to 50 percent. The greatest cuts came for upper-income groups. The tax cuts, amounting to a total of 25 percent, were spread out over three years. This tax cut was the core of the new "supply-side" economics: The cut was supposed to improve investment, create employment, and expand output.

Again, Reagan was able to count on support from a Republican-dominated Senate, but House Democrats tried to reduce the size of the tax cut and change its upper-income tilt. But Reagan emerged as the master in political persuasion. He lobbied individual members of Congress and made many special taxing and spending concessions to win votes. In the end, he persuaded 48 House Democrats to join the Republicans in winning a clear victory for his tax reduction program.

Later, David Stockman confided that he had serious doubts that the tax cut would expand the economy enough to cover the revenue loss to government. Stockman supported the budget cuts, but he believed the tax cuts would simply add to the government's deficits. Indeed Stockman even suspected that the real idea behind cutting taxes was to lower the top rate for those with the highest incomes from 70 to 50 percent. According to Stockman, the tax cut was only a "Trojan horse" used to disguise a "trickle down" economic program.[35]

It should be noted, however, that most major political figures in 1980 and 1981 (with the possible exception of Senator Edward M. Kennedy) supported budget and tax reductions. This is true of both Democrats and Republicans, liberals and conservatives. The only differences concerned how much to cut and how and where to cut. Most members of Congress felt a conservative "mood" in the nation for a reduction in government and taxation.

TABLE 2–2   Major Changes in Social Welfare Programs under Reagan Administration

PROGRAM	DESCRIPTION	CHANGE
Youth Conservation Corps	Youth employment and training	Eliminate program
Economic Development Administration	Regional planning for economic development	Eliminate program
Elementary & Secondary Education Act	Funds to school districts with pupils from low-income families	Consolidate with other educational grant programs
Basic Educational Opportunity Grants (Pell Grants)	Grants for college for low income students	Tighten eligibility to "truly needy" and require $750 self-help
CETA Public Service Jobs	Grants to state and local governments to promote employment	Eliminate program
CETA Job Training	Grants to state and local governments to train youth in jobs	Reduce and consolidate
Medicaid	Federal-state payments for medical care for poor	Place cap on federal contributions to state programs
Housing Assistance	Rent subsidies for low-income families; assistance to public housing projects	Reduce number of federally subsidized housing units
Food Stamps	Coupons for food purchases for low-income families	Tighten eligibility; end overlap with free school lunches
Supplemental feeding for Women, Infants, and Children (WIC)	Food packages provided to low-income mothers and children at "nutritional risk"	Tighten eligibility; limit benefits to persons with nutritional deficiencies
AFDC	Federal-state cash payments to low-income families with children	Tighten eligibility; require work; strengthen child support efforts
Social Services (Title XX of the Social Security Act)	Grants to states for day care, foster care, and family planning	Consolidate in block grant to the states
Legal services	Federal legal service corporation to provide legal assistance to poor in civil cases	Consolidate in block grant to the states
Community Services Administration	Grants to Community action agencies for social services	Consolidate in block grant to the states

TABLE 2–3   House Votes, Reagan Budget, and Tax Cuts, 1981

	BUDGET CUTS			TAX CUTS	
	Yes	No		Yes	No
Republicans	191	0		189	1
Democrats	62	182		48	196
Total	253	182		237	197

POLITICS AND THE WELFARE LOBBY

The poor are not represented in Washington in the same fashion as other groups in society.[36] The poor rarely write letters to members of Congress, and the poor are unlikely to make any significant campaign contributions. They are not usually found on a representative's home-state lecture circuit—service club lunches, civic meetings, memorials, and dedications. The poor seldom come to Washington to visit their representative's office. Indeed, the poor do not turn out at the polls to vote as often as the nonpoor.

To the extent that the poor are represented at all in Washington, they are represented by "proxies"—groups that are not poor themselves but claim to represent the poor. Many of these groups have organized and reorganized themselves under various names over the years—the National Welfare Rights Organization (dissolved in the mid-1970s), the Children's Defense Fund, the National Anti-Hunger Coalition, the Low Income Housing Coalition, the Food Research and Action Center.

Lobbyists for the poor can be divided roughly into three categories: (1) churches, civil rights groups, and liberal organizations, (2) organized labor, and (3) welfare program administrators and lawyers.

The churches (the National Conference of Catholic Bishops, the National Council of Churches, B'nai Brith, and others) often support programs for the poor out of a sense of moral obligation. Likewise, liberal activist groups (Common Cause, Americans for Democratic Action, and others) often support social programs out of an ideological commitment. Civil rights organizations (the National Urban League, the National Association for the Advancement of Colored People [NAACP], and others) support programs for the poor as a part of their general concern for the conditions affecting minorities.

Yet very often the success of lobbying efforts on behalf of the poor depends upon the addition of organized labor's considerable political power to the coalition of churches, civil rights groups, and liberal activists. Organized labor—for example, the AFL-CIO—does all of the things that the poor find difficult to do in politics—political organizing, campaign financing, letter writing, personal lobbying. Historically, organized labor has tended to support programs for the poor, even though union pay scales have moved a great distance from the poverty line. Labor *leaders* may be more likely to support social programs than the rank-and-file membership. Of course, the first concern of organized labor is labor legislation—labor relations, minimum wages, fair labor standards, and so on. But when labor leaders join others in support of social programs, the result is a strong political coalition.

Welfare program administrators and lawyers have a direct financial interest in supporting social welfare spending. These groups may take the lead in trying to organize the others into coalitions that support particular programs. Supporters of proposals to reduce spending for social programs complain: "Virtually all of the lobbying has come from people who are involved directly or indirectly in administering these programs."[37] The welfare bureaucracy is said to create a powerful "poverty lobby" which consists of "people doing well by the government's doing good."

Prominent among the organizations representing social program administrators and lawyers are the American Federation of State County and Municipal Employees (AFSCME), the Legal Services Corporation, and Community Services Administration. Affiliated with the AFL-CIO, AFSCME is a labor union which includes many public workers whose jobs are directly affected by cutbacks in social programs. As a labor union, it is funded primarily by the dues of its own members. But the Legal Service Corporation, whose 5,000 attorneys across the nation provide legal assistance to the poor, is itself funded by the federal government. Because the Legal Service Corporation has lobbied on its own behalf, its critics have charged that it is misusing its funds. The same charge has been leveled against the Community Services Administration, which is supposed to assist anti-poverty programs throughout the country and is not supposed to lobby Congress. However, there are very few government bureaucracies— from the Defense Department, to the National Aeronautics and Space Administration, to the Department of Agriculture—which do not, directly or indirectly, lobby Congress for their own programs.

The "welfare lobby" is strongest when its separate groups—churches, civil rights organizations, liberal groups, organized labor, and social welfare administrators—are unified and coordinated in their efforts.

SUMMARY

The roots of the American welfare system can be traced back to Elizabethan times. English poor laws stressed local government responsibility for welfare and emphasized distinguishing between the deserving and the nondeserving poor. Welfare in the United States today is not much different.

In the early days of the country there were no large governmental welfare programs. Welfare was provided by families, friends, private charities, and churches. But by the late nineteenth and early twentieth centuries, social problems were mounting. The Industrial Revolution had taken its toll on the country. Overcrowding in the cities led to a variety of social problems, including poverty. State governments began to enact programs for dependent children, the elderly, and disabled persons. When the Great Depression hit, state and local aid was no longer enough. In 1935 the federal government passed the Social Security Act as part of America's New Deal. But none of these social welfare programs eliminated poverty and suffering. In the 1960s President Johnson declared war on poverty by pouring millions of dollars into grass-roots social welfare programs. The Medicaid and Medicare programs and the Food Stamp program were also born in the sixties, but 25 million people remained poor. The welfare rights movement sprang up and died, and Americans witnessed a change in national budget priorities with welfare spending overtaking defense spending.

In the 1980s, America's welfare policies continue to be the focus of political conflict. President Reagan's administration has attempted to curb the growth of welfare spending, reduce some types of benefits, and consolidate many federal welfare programs. He has also introduced a number of other economic reforms. These reforms are based on certain economic theories about how the rate at which people are taxed affects their incentive to work. The president's program is intended to increase the incentive to work and slow inflation by reducing taxes and slowing down the growth of the money supply. Another important aspect of Reagan's proposal is to return to the states much of the decision-making power about how welfare dollars should be spent. While he has pledged to continue aid to the "truly needy" and to maintain a "social safety net," many critics of his program claim he is "balancing the budget on the backs of the poor and the aged." While the president is holding down welfare spending, defense spending is growing rapidly. Although the effects these changes in the welfare system will have on the poor may be difficult to predict accurately, critics maintain that they will be severe.

NOTES

1. See Ronald C. Federico, *The Social Welfare Institution: An Introduction*, 3rd ed. (Lexington, Mass.: D.C. Heath & Co., 1980), p. 42; and Blanche D. Coll, *Perspectives in Public Welfare: A History* (U.S. Department of Health, Education and Welfare, 1973), pp. 1–2 for an elaboration of the role of the church and feudal land holders in the provision of welfare benefits.
2. Coll, *Perspectives in Public Welfare*, p. 2.

3. Ibid., pp. 2–3.
4. Federico, *The Social Welfare Institution*, p. 104; Coll, *Perspectives in Public Welfare*, p. 4.
5. See Federico, *The Social Welfare Institution*, pp. 42–43 for further elaboration.
6. Ibid.
7. Philip Klein, *From Philanthropy to Social Welfare* (San Francisco: Jossey-Bass, 1968), p. 10, cited in Federico, *The Social Welfare Institution*, p. 53.
8. See Federico, *The Social Welfare Institution*, p. 53 and Coll, *Perspectives in Public Welfare*, pp. 5–6 for further elaboration on Elizabethan welfare.
9. Coll, *Perspectives in Public Welfare*, p. 20.
10. Ibid.
11. Ibid., p. 17.
12. Ibid.
13. Ibid.
14. Ibid., pp. 21–22.
15. Ibid., p. 27.
16. Ibid., p. 28.
17. Ibid., pp. 27–28.
18. This paragraph relies on Thomas R. Dye, *Understanding Public Policy*, 4th ed. (Englewood Cliffs, N.J.: Prentice Hall, 1981), pp. 116–17.
19. Paragraphs describing the Great Depression rely on Thomas R. Dye and L. Harmon Zeigler, *The Irony of Democracy*, 5th ed. (Monterey, Calif.: Duxbury Press, 1981), pp. 100–101.
20. Cited in Richard Hofstadter, *The American Political Tradition* (New York: Knopf, 1948), p. 316.
21. See Aaron Wildavsky, *Speaking Truth to Power: The Art and Craft of Policy Analysis* (Boston: Little, Brown, 1979), especially pp. 86–89 for further elaboration on this discussion of "the revolution no one noticed."
22. Robert D. Plotnick, "Social Welfare Expenditures: How Much Help for the Poor," *Policy Analysis* 5, No. 2(1979): 278.
23. Shapiro vs. Thompson, 394 U.S. 618 and see Frances Fox Piven and Richard A. Cloward, *Regulating the Poor: The Functions of Public Welfare* (New York: Random House, 1971) for an elaboration on residency requirements, especially pp. 306–8.
24. Wildavsky, *Speaking Truth to Power*, p. 98.
25. Ibid.
26. See Frances Fox Piven and Richard A. Cloward, *Poor People's Movements: Why They Succeed, How They Fail* (New York: Vintage Books, 1977).
27. Ibid., p. 275.
28. Ibid.
29. Robert M. Moroney, *Families, Social Services and Social Policy: The Issue of Shared Responsibility* (Washington, D.C.: U.S. Department of Health and Human Services, 1980), p. 58. SHHS Publication No. (ADM) 80-846.
30. Ibid., p. 43.
31. President of the United States, *A Program for Economic Recovery*, February 18, 1981 (Washington, D.C.: U.S. Government Printing Office, 1981).
32. Ibid., p. 6.
33. President Ronald Reagan, State of Union Address, January 26, 1982.
34. *Congressional Quarterly, Weekly Report*, April 18, 1981, p. 68.
35. William Greider, "The Education of David Stockman," *The Atlantic Monthly* (December 1981), pp. 27–54.
36. This discussion relies on "Special Treatment No Longer Given Advocates for the Poor," *Congressional Quarterly Weekly Report*, April 18, 1981, pp. 659–64.
37. Rep. Phil Gramm (D-Texas) quoted in ibid., p. 662.

3

Defining Poverty: Where to Begin?

DEFINING POVERTY

The very first obstacle to a rational approach to poverty in America lies in conflict over the definition of the problem. Defining poverty is a *political activity.* Proponents of increased governmental support for social welfare programs frequently make high estimates of the number and percentage of the population that is poor. They view the problem of poverty as a persistent one, even in a generally affluent society. They argue that many millions of Americans suffer from hunger, malnutrition, remedial illness, hopelessness, and despair. Their definition of the problem practically mandates the continuation and expansion of a wide variety of public welfare programs.

In contrast, others minimize the number of poor in America. They see poverty as diminishing over time. They view the poor in America today as considerably better off than the middle-class of fifty years ago and even wealthy by the standards of most societies in the world. They deny that anyone needs to suffer from hunger, malnutrition, or remedial illness, if they make use of the public services already available to them. They believe that there are many opportunities for upward mobility in America and that none should suffer from hopelessness or despair. This definition of the problem minimizes the need for public welfare programs and encourages policy-makers to reduce the number and size of these programs.

Political conflict over poverty, then, begins with contending definitions of the problem of poverty. In an attempt to influence policy-making, various political interests try to win acceptance for their own definitions of the problem. Political scientist E. E. Schattschneider explained:

> Political conflict is not like an intercollegiate debate in which the opponents agree in advance on a definition of the issues. As a matter of fact, *the definition of the alternatives is the supreme instrument of power;* the antagonists can rarely agree on what the issues are because power is involved in the definition.[1]

Indeed, "poverty" has only been a political issue for the last twenty years. Prior to the 1960s, the problems of the poor were almost always segmented into areas such as old age, disability, widows and orphans, unemployment, medical indigency, delinquency, slum housing, and illiteracy. According to one observer, it was not until the Kennedy and Johnson administrations that the nation began to see that these problems were tied together in a single "bedrock" problem—poverty:

> The measures enacted, and those proposed, were dealing separately with such problems as slum housing, juvenile delinquency, dependency, unemployment, illiteracy, but they were separately inadequate because they were striking only at surface aspects of what seemed to be some kind of bedrock problem, and it was the bedrock problem that had to be identified so that it could be attacked in a concerted, unified, and innovative way ... the bedrock problem, in a word was "poverty." Words and concepts determine programs; once a target was reduced to a single word, the timing became right for a unified program.[2]

But even political consensus that poverty is a problem does not necessarily mean that everyone defines poverty in the same fashion.

POVERTY AS DEPRIVATION

Poverty can be defined as *deprivation*—insufficiency in food, housing, clothing, medical care, and other items required to maintain a decent standard of living. This definition assumes that there is a standard of living below which individuals and families can be considered "deprived." This standard is admittedly arbitrary; no one knows for certain what level of material well-being is necessary to avoid deprivation.

Each year, the U.S. Social Security Administration estimates the cash income required for families to maintain minimum food, housing, clothing, and medical care needs. Families are classified by size, sex, and age of the family head and by farm or nonfarm residence. A *poverty line* in cash income is estimated for each classification of family, as well as for individuals living alone. (The poverty line is now officially called the *low income line,* but most commentators still use the original term *poverty.)* The dollar amounts rise each year to take into account the effects of inflation. For example, the poverty line in 1980 for an urban family of four was approximately $8,380, up from $3,968 in 1970 and $2,973 in 1959 (see Table 3–1). According to this definition, there are about 25 million poor people in the United States. This is approximately 12 percent of the population.

Even if we were to agree that poverty should be defined as deprivation, there would still be many problems in establishing an official poverty line based on money income as described above.

First of all, the Social Security Administration's definition of poverty includes only cash income and excludes "in-kind" (nonmonetary) benefits given to the poor. These benefits include free medical care, food stamps, free school lunches, and public housing. If these benefits were "costed out" (calculated as cash income), there would be *fewer* poor people in America than shown in official statistics. The official estimate of the proportion of poor in America, after costing out the benefits of all government programs, is 8.3 percent.[3] It should also be noted that many persons (poor and nonpoor) report their incomes at lower figures than they really are. This underreporting of income leads to overestimates of the number of poor. One study concludes that if "in-kind" benefits are considered *and* adjustments are made for underreporting, only 4.1 percent of the population is poor.[4]

There are still other problems in this definition of poverty. It does not take into account regional differences in the cost of living, climate, or styles of living. (It is unlikely that a family of four can live on $8,380 in New York City, even if it is possible to do so in Hattiesburg, Mississippi.) It does not account for family assets. (An older family that has paid off its mortgage does not usually devote as much income to housing as a family that rents.) It does not recognize differences in the status of families—for example, whether family members are students or retirees. Some of these people may not consider themselves "poor," although they are counted as poor in official government statistics. Finally, this definition does not recognize the special needs of families that may have incomes above the poverty line but have special problems or hardships that drain away income—chronic illnesses, large debts, alcohol or drug abuse problems, and others.

Despite these problems, some official definition of poverty is needed to administer government programs. As one observer commented:

> Although the existing poverty lines are abritrary both for statistical purposes and for operational purposes, some arbitrary lines are needed, and these serve well simply because they already exist as a convention. To reopen an argument as to whether they are "correct" seems a fruitless exercise.[5]

As so often happens, administrative efficiency, rather than the needs of the poor, turns out to be the underlying basis for an important policy decision—in this case, defining poverty.

TABLE 3–1   **Poverty Levels (Definitions of Poverty by Cash Income by Size of Family, Nonfarm[a])**

FAMILY		INCOME IN DOLLARS				
Size	Type	1959	1970	1977	1979	1980
1	Person					
	under 65	1,503	2,010	3,152	3,619	4,260
	65 and over	1,397	1,861	2,906	3,469	3,940
2	Persons					
	Head under 65	1,952	2,604	4,072	4,762	5,510
	Head 65 and over	1,761	2,348	3,666	4,362	4,950
3	Persons	2,324	3,099	4,833	5,624	6,540
4	Persons	2,973	3,968	6,191	7,381	8,380
5	Persons	3,506	4,680	7,320	8,690	9,920
6	Persons	3,944	5,260	8,261	9,843	11,180
7	Persons	4,849	6,468	10,216	12,077	13,860

[a]Poverty for farm families set at 85 percent of income of nonfarm families

Source. *Statistical Abstract of the United States, 1980,* p. 463.

WHO ARE THE POOR?

Poverty occurs in many kinds of families and many environmental settings. However, the incidence of poverty varies among groups in America (see Table 3–2).

More whites are poor than blacks. Of the 25 million poor people in the nation, by government definition, about 16 million are white and 8 million are black. However, the likelihood of blacks experiencing poverty is three times greater than it is for whites: *The percentage of the nation's black population falling below the poverty line is 29 percent compared to 9 percent for the white population.* In other words, whites outnumber blacks among the poor, but a much larger percentage of the nation's black population is poor. (This is because the total black population in the nation is only about 25 million or 11 percent of the total 226 million people.)

Many of the poor are children. Approximately 10 million children in the United States live in poverty. This is about 16 percent of the total population under 18. Later, we shall see that poverty affecting children may generate greater political concern than poverty affecting adults and that many social welfare programs are oriented toward children.

Over three million aged people live in poverty. This is about 14 percent of the total population 65 years of age or older. Only 8 percent of the working age population is poor. Again, as in the case with children, the aged poor generate greater political concern, and many social welfare programs are directed specifically at the aged.

Poverty occurs not only in large central cities, but in rural America as well. About 15 percent of the residents of central cities of metropolitan areas are poor, and about 14 percent of nonmetropolitan (rural) residents are poor. There is some poverty in the nation's suburbs, but proportionately this figure is low—7 percent. Suburban areas experience less poverty because the poor are unlikely to find low income housing there!

Approximately an equal number of male-headed and female-headed families are poor. However, female-headed families experience a much higher incidence of poverty: 35 percent of all female-headed families are poor compared to only 7 percent of all male-headed families. Families with both male and female adult members are much less likely to experience poverty than a family headed by a single woman.

How persistent is poverty? There are very few families who live all their lives in poverty. Researchers at the Survey Research Center, University of Michigan, tracked 5,000 American families for over ten years and found that only *3 percent* were persistently poor—that is, they were poor throughout this entire period. This is a much smaller figure than the 12 percent reported as poor at any one time. This means that people slip into and out of the poverty category over time. People can lose their jobs, retire, divorce or separate, or become ill, for example. Then later they may find new jobs, remarry, or get well, thus changing their financial condition.

Are the poor disappearing? Franklin D. Roosevelt said in his second inaugural address in 1937, "I see one-third of a nation ill-housed, ill-clad, ill-nourished." He was probably underestimating poverty; economic historians think that over 50 percent of the nation would have been classified as poor during the Great Depression. Since that time, the American political and economic system has succeeded in reducing the proportion of poor to less than 12 percent.

Figure 3–1 allows us to observe changes in the numbers and percentages of the poor since 1947. All of these figures account for the effects of inflation, so there is no question that poverty (as defined in official government statistics) has declined over the years. It should be noted, however, that in the last decade the number and percentage of the poor have not changed very much. The percentage of the population living below the official poverty line has remained between 11 and 12 percent. However, there has been continued expansion in government benefits, particularly "in-kind" benefits (Medicare, Medicaid, Food Stamps); the result has been a continuing decline in the number and percentage of poor after "adjusting" for these benefits.

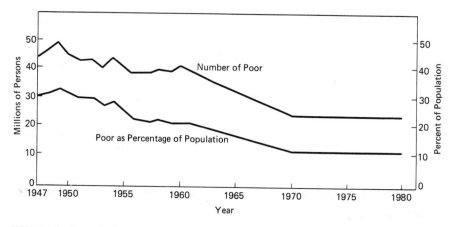

FIGURE 3–1 Poverty in the United States.

POVERTY AS INEQUALITY

Poverty can also be defined as *inequality in the distribution of income*. This definition is not tied to any *absolute* level of deprivation. Instead, it focuses on *relative deprivation*—some people perceive that they have less income or material possessions than most Americans, and they believe they are entitled to more. Even with a fairly substantial income, one may feel a sense of "relative deprivation" in a very affluent society where commercial advertising portrays the "average American" as having a high level of consumption and material well-being.

Today the poor in America are wealthy by the standards that have prevailed over most of history, and those that still prevail over large areas of

TABLE 3–2 Who Are the Poor?

POPULATION BY CATEGORIES, WITH INCOME BELOW POVERTY LEVEL

	Number (millions)	Percentage of category
Total	24.7	11.6
Whites	16.4	8.9
Blacks	8.3	29.0
Children under 18	10.0	16.0
Ages 22-64	9.2	8.3
65 Years and Over	3.2	14.1
Living in Central cities	9.2	14.4
Living in Suburbs	5.6	6.8
Living in Rural Areas	9.9	13.9

Source: *Statistical Abstract of the United States, 1980,* p. 465.

the world. Over half of the nation's poor families own automobiles, and nearly half own their own homes. Nearly 90 percent own television sets, and 90 percent own refrigerators.[6] Nonetheless, millions of American families are considered poor, by themselves and by others, because they have less income than most Americans. These people *feel* deprived—they perceive the gap between themselves and the average American family to be wide and they do not accept the gap as legitimate. Eliminating poverty when it is defined as relative deprivation really means achieving greater *equality* of income and material possessions.

> By the standards that have prevailed over most of history, and still prevail over large areas of the world, there are very few poor in the United States today. Nevertheless there are millions of American families who, both in their own eyes and in those of others, are poor. As our nation prospers, our judgment as to what constitutes poverty will inevitably change. When we talk about poverty in America, we are talking about families and individuals who have much less income than most of us. When we talk about reducing or eliminating poverty, we are really talking about changing the distribution of income.[7]

How can we measure poverty as inequality? Economists frequently measure the distribution of total personal income across various classes of families. For example, Table 3–3 divides all American families into five groups—from the lowest one-fifth in personal income to the highest one-fifth—and shows the percentage of total personal income received by each of these groups over three years. If perfect income equality existed, then each fifth of American families would receive 20 percent of all family personal income, and it would not even be possible to rank fifths from highest to lowest. But clearly personal income in America is distributed unequally.

The poorest one-fifth of American families receive only about 5 percent of all family personal income. This figure has remained relatively constant over the past thirty-five years. So, even though poverty defined by the government as a minimum subsistence level has declined during these years, poverty defined as the proportion of total personal income received by the bottom one-fifth of the population has remained constant. Several definitions of poverty give us different perspectives on the success of the American political and economic system in dealing with poverty.

The wealthy, defined in Table 3–3 as the highest one-fifth of Americans in personal income, received almost 49 percent of all family personal income in 1941; by 1980 this percentage had declined to 41.5. This was the only income group to lose income in relation to other income groups. The middle classes improved their relative income position. Another measure of the relative decline in the position of the wealthy was the decline in the percentage of income received by the top 5 percent in America. The top 5 percent received 24 percent of all family income in 1941, but less than 16 percent in 1980.

Not everyone in the lowest one-fifth suffers deprivation. Although the proportion of total personal income this group receives appears small (5.2 percent), some of the hardships of this lowest fifth are reduced by government services—benefits which are not counted as income. These "in-kind" benefits include Food Stamps, public housing, Medicare and Medicaid, school lunches, and similar programs. Indeed one economist estimates that if these benefits were counted, the "adjusted income distribution" of the lowest fifth would be raised to 12 percent.[8]

TABLE 3-3   The Distribution of Income in America (Percent Distribution of Family Personal Income, by Quintiles, and Top 5 Percent of Consumer Units, Selected Years)

QUINTILES	1929	1936	1941	1950	1960	1970	1980
Lowest	3.5%	4.1%	4.1%	4.5%	4.8%	5.4%	5.2%
Second	9.0	9.2	9.5	12.0	12.2	12.2	11.6
Third	13.8	14.1	15.3	17.4	17.8	17.6	17.5
Fourth	19.3	20.9	22.3	23.4	24.0	23.9	24.1
Highest	54.4	51.7	48.8	42.7	41.2	40.9	41.5
Total	100.0	100.0	100.0	100.0	100.0	100.0	100.0
Top 5 percent	30.0	26.5	24.0	17.3	15.9	15.6	15.6

Source: *Statistical Abstract of the United States, 1980,* p. 454.

WHY ARE THE POOR POOR?

Poverty is explained in many ways. We suspect that illness, old age, disability, lack of job skills, family instability, discrimination, unemployment, and general economic recessions all contribute to poverty. But how do these problems interact to create poverty?

Perhaps the most popular explanation among economists is the *human capital theory*. This theory explains income variations in a free market economy as a result of differences in productivity. The poor are poor because their economic productivity is low. They do not have the human capital—knowledge, skills, training, education—to sell to employers in a free market. As partial evidence for this theory, we can observe that poverty among families headed by a person with less than an eighth-grade education is 40 percent, while poverty among families headed by a person who completed high school is 7 percent.

Economists recognize that poverty may also result from inadequate demand, either in the economy as a whole or in a particular segment of the economy. A serious recession and widespread unemployment raise the proportion of the population living below the poverty line. Full employment and a healthy economy do not directly reduce poverty among persons who have no marketable skills, but nonetheless improve opportunities for marginal workers. Moreover, poverty can result from inadequate demand in a particular sector of the economy or in a particular region of the nation. For example, industrialization and technological development appear to have bypassed large segments of the Appalachian area. The closing of steel mills or auto plants in large eastern and midwestern cities can also force marginal workers into poverty.

Absence from the labor force is the largest single source of poverty. Over two-thirds of the poor are aged persons, children, or disabled people, who cannot reasonably be expected to find employment. No improvement in the general economy is likely to affect these people directly. They are outside of the labor market and are largely the responsibility of government rather than of the private economy.

Finally, we must consider poverty that is the direct effect of discrimination against blacks, other minorities, and women. It is true that *some* of the differences between black and white incomes are a product of educational differences between blacks and whites. However, *even if we control for education,* we can see that blacks with the same educational level as whites earn less. As shown in Table 3–4, white family income is substantially higher than black family income at every educational level. Blacks must finish high school to earn as much as whites with only an eighth-grade education. White families also earn more than Hispanic families at every educational level, although the income differences are not as large as those between whites and blacks.

TABLE 3–4   Black and White Incomes by Education Level

	White	Black	Hispanic
Education			
Elementary School:			
Less than 8 years	$ 9,179	$ 6,780	$ 9,167
8 years	11,040	8,617	10,805
High School:			
1–3 years	13,904	8,834	10,842
4 years	17,592	12,109	13,772
College:			
1–3 years	19,480	13,073	17,178
4 years	25,071	21,107	21,409

If human capital theory operated freely—without interference by discrimination—then we would expect very little difference between blacks and whites at the same educational levels. But, unfortunately, this is not the case.

When, in 1776, Thomas Jefferson wrote on behalf of the Second Continental Congress that "all men are created equal..," he was expressing the widespread dislike for hereditary aristocracy—lords and ladies, dukes and duchesses, and queens and kings. The Founding Fathers wrote their belief in equality of law into the U.S. Constitution. But their concern was *equality of opportunity,* not *absolute equality.* Indeed, the Founding Fathers referred to efforts to equalize income as "leveling," and they were strongly opposed to this notion. Jefferson wrote:

> To take from one, because it is thought his own industry and that of his fathers has acquired too much, in order to spare to others, who, or whose fathers have not, exercised equal industry and skill, is to violate arbitrarily the first principle of association, the guarantee to everyone the free exercise of his industry and the fruits acquired by it.[9]

Equality of opportunity requires that artificial obstacles to upward mobility be removed. Distinctions based on race, sex, ethnicity, birth, and region have no place in a free society. But this is not to say that all persons' incomes should be equalized. Andrew Jackson, one of the nation's first democrats, explained:

> Distinctions in every society will always exist under every just government. Equality of talents, education or wealth cannot be produced by human institutions. In the full enjoyment of the gifts of heaven and the fruits of superior industry, economy, and virtue, every man is entitled to protection by law; but when the laws undertake to add to these national distinctions, to grant titles, gratuities, and exclusive privileges, to make the rich richer ... then the humble members of society have a right to complain of the injustice of their government.[10]

How much equality can we afford? Utopian socialists have argued for a rule of distribution: "From each according to his ability, to each according to his needs." In other words, everyone produces whatever he or she can, and wealth and income are distributed according to the needs of the people. There is no monetary reward for hard work, or skills and talent, or education and training. Since everyone's needs are roughly the same, everyone will receive roughly the same income. Collective ownership replaces private property. If such a Utopian society ever existed, then near-perfect income equality would be achieved, with each fifth of the population receiving roughly 20 percent of the income.

But all societies—capitalist and socialist, democratic and authoritarian, traditional and modern—distribute wealth unequally. It is not likely that income differences will ever disappear. Societies reward hard work, skill, talent, education, training, risk taking, and ingenuity. Distributing income equally throughout society threatens the work ethic upon which our society is based. The only real question we must confront is *how much* inequality is necessary and desirable for a society. We may, or may not, believe that the current distribution of income (as shown on Table 3–3) is fair.

If the problem of poverty is defined as *inequality,* then it is not really capable of solution. Regardless of how well-off the poor may be in absolute standards of living, there will always be a lowest one-fifth of the population receiving something less than 20 percent of all income. We might reduce income inequalities, but *some* differences will remain, and even these differences might be posed as a "problem."

POVERTY AS CULTURE

Some argue that poverty is a "way of life" passed on from generation to generation in a self-perpetuating cycle. This *culture of poverty* involves not just a low income, but also attitudes of indifference, alienation, and apathy, along with lack of incentives and self-respect. These attitudes make it difficult for the poor to utilize the opportunities for upward mobility that may be available to them. Increasing the income of the poor may not affect joblessness, lack of incentives, lack of educational opportunities, unstable family life, or the high incidence of crime, delinquency, and other social problems among the poor.

There are sharp differences between scholars and policy-makers over the existence of a culture of poverty. The argument resembles the classic exchange between F. Scott Fitzgerald and Ernest Hemingway. When Fitzgerald observed, "The rich are different from you and me," Hemingway retorted, "Yes, they have more money." Observers who believe that they see a distinctive culture among the poor may say. "The poor are different from you and me." But opponents of the culture of poverty notion may reply, "Yes, they have less money." But are the poor undereducated, unskilled, poorly motivated, and "delinquent" because they are poor? Or are they poor because they are undereducated, unskilled, poorly motivated, and "delinquent"? The distinction is a serious one because it has important policy implications.

One especially controversial view of the culture of poverty is set forth by Harvard Professor Edward C. Banfield, who contends that poverty is really a product of "present-orientedness."[11] According to Banfield, individuals caught up in the culture of poverty are unable to plan for the future, to sacrifice immediate gratifications in favor of future ones, or to exercise the discipline that is required to get ahead. Banfield admits that some people experience poverty because of involuntary unemployment, prolonged illness, death of the breadwinner, or some other misfortune. But even with severe misfortune, he claims, this kind of poverty is not squalid, degrading, or self-perpetuating; it ends once the external cause of it no longer exists. According to Banfield, other people will be poor no matter what their "external" circumstances are. They live in a culture of poverty that continues for generations because they are psychologically unable to provide for the future. Improvements in their circumstances may affect their poverty only superficially. Even increased income is unlikely to change their way of life, for the additional money will be spent quickly on nonessential or frivolous items.

Opponents of the culture of poverty idea argue that this notion diverts attention from the conditions of poverty that *foster* family instability, present-orientedness, and other ways of life of the poor. The question is really whether the conditions of poverty create a culture of poverty or vice versa. Reformers are likely to focus on the conditions of poverty as the fundamental cause of the social pathologies that afflict the poor. They note that the idea of a culture of poverty can be applied only to groups who have lived in poverty for several generations. It is not relevant to those who have become poor during their lifetimes because of sickness, accident, or old age. The cultural explanation basically involves parental transmission of values and beliefs, which in turn determines behavior of future generations. In contrast, the situational explanation of poverty shows how social conditions and differences in financial resources operate directly to determine behavior. In this view, the conditions of poverty can be seen as affecting behavior not only directly, but also indirectly, through their impact upon succeeding generations. Perhaps the greatest danger in the idea of a culture of poverty is that poverty in this light can be seen as an unbreakable, puncture-proof cycle. This outlook may lead to a relaxation of efforts to ameliorate the conditions of poverty. In other words, a culture of poverty may become an excuse for inaction.

If one assumes that the poor are no different from other Americans, then one is led toward policies that emphasize opportunity for individuals as well as changes in their environment. If the poor are like other Americans, it is necessary only to provide them with the ordinary means to achieve—for example, job training programs, good schools, and counseling to make them aware of opportunities that are available to them. The intervention that is required to change their lives, therefore, is one of supplying a means to achieve a level of income that most Americans enjoy.

On the other hand, if one believes in the notion of a culture of poverty, it is necessary to devise a strategy to interrupt the transmission of lower-class cultural values from generation to generation. The strategy must try to prevent the socialization of young children into an environment of family instability, lack of motivation, crime and delinquency, and so forth. One rather drastic means to accomplish this would be simply to remove the children from lower-class homes at a very early age and to raise them in a controlled environment that transmits the values of the conventional culture rather than of the culture of poverty. Such a solution is not realistic. More acceptable solutions use special day-care centers and preschool programs to remedy cultural deprivation and disadvantage. Theoretically, these programs would bring about change in young children through "cultural enrichment."

The culture of poverty idea leads to another policy implication. If one believes that such a culture exists, then one must also conclude that little can be done to help people escape from poverty until there has been sufficient change in their life condition to permit them to take advantage of opportunity programs. According to this line of reasoning, one cannot change people without changing their environment; the poor cannot advance through schooling, or job training, or programs to develop better attitudes while they are still poor. The emphasis on "self-help"—education, information, job training, participation—is incomplete and misleading unless it is accompanied by a program aimed at directly altering the conditions of poverty. Hence, it is argued that a guaranteed minimum income is required to bring the poor up to a level where they will be able to take advantage of educational and training information, along with other opportunity programs.

POVERTY AS EXPLOITATION

Both Marxist and non-Marxist writers have defined poverty as a form of exploitation by the ruling class. Sociologist Herbert Gans contends that poverty serves many useful functions for the middle and upper classes in America.[12] Specifically, Gans lists thirteen reasons why a poverty class is maintained in the nation:

1. The poor are available to do society's "dirty work" such as "physically dirty or dangerous, temporary, dead-end and underpaid, undignified, and menial jobs"—the jobs that others will not do.
2. The poor perform work that helps those who are financially better off. For example, they do domestic work that allows others to pursue more rewarding activities.
3. Poverty creates jobs in a number of fields such as welfare and law enforcement.
4. The poor buy old, used, and defective merchandise that others do not want.
5. The poor are often punished and accused of wrong-doing as a means of upholding societal norms. For example, the poor are called lazy because society values hard-working, industrious people.
6. The poor allow the rest of society to live vicariously in a world of uninhibited sexual, drug-taking, and alcoholic behavior, because society believes that this is how poor people live.
7. The poor provide a source of cultural works such as art, literature, and music that the affluent would not otherwise have.
8. Poverty allows those in the middle and upper classes to maintain their higher status in society.
9. The poor allow others to improve their position in society by providing a market for legal (and illegal) business activities in the slums.

10. The poor provide a source of activities for the affluent who pursue charitable causes on behalf of the poor.

11. The poor bear the burden of societal growth as they did when their homes were destroyed in the name of urban renewal.

12. The poor serve political functions. For example, the poor are identified with the Democratic Party, which can count on their votes regardless of whether or not Democratic legislators are responsive to the needs of the poor.

13. Since the poor are considered lazy and unwilling to work, they are the target of social criticisms which shift criticism for maintaining poverty away from the more affluent.

Gans's implication is that poverty is maintained by ruling classes in order to make their own lives more pleasant. Poverty does not have to exist; it could be eliminated with the cooperation of the middle and upper classes. But it is unlikely that these classes will ever give up anything they believe they have earned through their own hard work, useful skills, or business enterprise. Most Americans believe that they are immune from financial disaster and poverty.

THE INVISIBLE POOR

In an influential book, *The Other America,* Michael Harrington argues that most Americans are blind to the poverty of many millions of poor people.[13] Harrington speaks of two nations within America. One is the nation of comfortable and affluent Americans. The other is a nation of the poor—those forced to suffer deprivation and humiliation because they are without access to adequate education, housing, employment, and health care. Most Americans are blind to poverty because the poor are invisible—invisible because they do not live or socialize or receive their education with the more affluent. Rural poverty is masked by a beautiful American countryside. Mass production of decent clothing also hides poverty. A poor person may be relatively well-dressed but unable to afford decent shelter or health care. The elderly poor are invisible because they do not venture far from home because of poor health, fear, and lack of somewhere to go. And finally, the poor are invisible because they have no political power; in fact, they are often the victims of political action.

Other authors have also written about the class-based nature of poverty. Influenced by the works of Harrington, two of these authors have called our society the "upside-down welfare state" because "the welfare state is a complicated system in which those who need help the most get the least, and those who need it least get the most."[14] They say that all Americans, rich or poor, benefit from government welfare programs. The poor receive government assistance through the Aid to Families with Dependent Children program, the Food Stamp program, and the Medicaid program. The middle class receives government assistance in the form of home mortgage loans and educational grants. The rich receive government assistance in the form of income tax deductions, government contracts, and subsidies to business and industry. The difference is that government assistance to the poor is called welfare, while government assistance to the rich is called good business. In the final analysis, the poor receive only a pittance of all government assistance. Most government assistance continues to go to the middle and upper classes.

Social scientists Frances Fox Piven and Richard A. Cloward also comment on the economic, political, and social utility that the upper classes see in maintaining poverty.[15] They claim that "the key to an understanding of relief-giving is in the functions it serves for the larger economic and political order, for relief is a secondary and supportive institution."[16] Piven and Cloward agree that many social welfare programs benefit the middle and upper classes more than the poor. They argue, especially with regard to Aid to Families with Dependent Children, that welfare has been used as a device to control the poor in order to maintain social stability. First, welfare programs are expanded in times of political unrest as a means of appeasing the poor. Second, welfare rules and regulations are used as a means of "forcing" the poor into the labor market during times of political stability, especially when there is a need to increase the number of people in the work force.

If poverty is defined as the exploitation of the poor by a ruling class, then it might be suggested that only a restructuring of society to eliminate classes would solve the problem of poverty. Marxists call for the revolutionary overthrow of capitalist society by workers and farmers, and the emergence of a new "classless" society. Presumably in such a society there would be no ruling class with an interest in exploiting the poor. Of course, in practice, communist societies have produced one-party governments that dominate and exploit nearly the entire population.

Nonetheless, these perspectives on poverty in America help us to understand that there are indeed class differences in views on poverty. If the upper classes do not deliberately exploit the poor, they sometimes express very paternalistic attitudes toward the poor. By paternalistic we mean that upper classes have little understanding of the lives of poor people, yet they believe they "know what's best" for the poor in social welfare policy. Moreover, the upper classes frequently engage in charitable activities and support liberal welfare programs to demonstrate their idealism and "do-goodism," whether the poor are actually helped or not.

SUMMARY

Defining *poverty* is a *political* activity, rather than a rational exercise. We have discussed four approaches to defining poverty—as deprivation, as inequality, as culture, and as exploitation. Society cannot agree on one "best" approach for defining poverty, and it cannot agree on solutions for alleviating poverty.

If we use the official government poverty line as our arbitrary yardstick there are about 25 million poor people in the United States, or about 12 percent of the population. However, if we count in-kind welfare benefits as well as cash benefits, the number of poor persons is lower. In the past decade, the number and percentage of poor persons have not declined. Poverty is most frequently found in black households and households headed by women and the elderly. Children also comprise a large number of the poor.

Poverty probably has many causes. Some people are poor because they lack the resources and opportunities of the nonpoor and some, such as the elderly, children, and the disabled, are not able to work. Discrimination is another source of poverty. Even with the same number of school years completed, blacks and some other minorities earn less than whites. Also, women earn less than men. Equality of opportunity remains a major obstacle to the elimination of poverty in the United States.

The way in which poverty is defined has important implications for strategies to alleviate the problem. Human service professionals have a commitment to increasing opportunities for poor persons as a means of reducing poverty. These professionals strive to maximize human potential whenever possible and believe the disadvantaged will make use of opportunities to overcome poverty. They reject the idea that many of the poor do not want to work and that they use their resources foolishly.

Finally, some writers view poverty as a form of exploitation by the ruling classes. The dominant classes in society maintain poverty in order to produce a source of cheap labor and to "use" the poor economically, socially, and politically. This definition of the problem magnifies class conflict and implies that only a radical restructuring of the social system can reduce poverty.

NOTES

1. E. E. Schattschneider, *The Semi-Sovereign People* (New York: Holt, Rinehart & Winston, 1961), p. 68.
2. James L. Sundquist, *Politics and Policy* (Washington, D.C.: Brookings Institution, 1968), pp. 111–12.
3. *Statistical Abstract of the United States, 1980,* p. 463.
4. Sheldon Danziger and Robert Haveman, "The Reagan Budget: A Sharp Break with the Past," *Challenge* 24 (May-June 1981): 5–13. The Congressional Budget Office estimates that if "in-kind" benefits are considered, the proportion of the U.S. population below the poverty level declines from 12 to 7 percent. *Congressional Quarterly Weekly Report* (January 22, 1977): 131.
5. Robert A. Levine, *The Poor Ye Need Not Have With You* (Cambridge, Mass.: M.I.T. Press, 1970), p. 19.
6. Herman P. Miller, "The Dimensions of Poverty," in *Poverty as a Public Issue,* Ben B. Seligman, ed. (New York: Free Press, 1965).

7. Victor R. Fuchs, "Redefining Poverty and Redistributing Income," *The Public Interest* (Summer 1967): 91.
8. Edgar K. Browning, "How Much More Equality Can We Afford," *The Public Interest* (Spring 1976): 90–110.
9. Cited in Richard Hofstadter, *The American Political Tradition* (New York: Knopf, 1948), p. 42.
10. Ibid., p. 45.
11. Edward C. Banfield, *The Unheavenly City* (Boston: Little, Brown, 1968).
12. Herbert J. Gans, "The Uses of Poverty: The Poor Pay All," *Social Policy 2*, no. 2 (July-August 1971), 20-24.
13. Michael Harrington, *The Other America: Poverty in the United States* (New York: Macmillan, 1962).
14. Thomas H. Walz and Gary Askerooth, *The Upside Down Welfare State* (Minneapolis: Elwood Printing, 1973), p. 5.
15. Frances Fox Piven and Richard A. Cloward, *Regulating the Poor: The Functions of Public Welfare* (New York: Random House, 1971).
16. Ibid., p. xiii.

4

Preventing Poverty: The Social Insurance Programs

PREVENTING POVERTY THROUGH COMPULSORY SAVINGS

Why not require people to insure themselves against poverty, in much the same fashion as people insure themselves against other tragedies such as deaths, accidents, and fires? The preventative strategy uses the *social insurance* concept. This involves compelling individuals to purchase insurance against the possibility of their own indigency, which might result from forces over which they had no control—loss of job, death of the family breadwinner, or physical disability. Social insurance is based on the same principles as private insurance—the sharing of risks and the setting aside of money for a "rainy day." Workers and employers pay "premiums" (Social Security taxes) which are held in trust by the government under each worker's name (and Social Security number). When age, death, disability, or unemployment prevents workers from continuing on the job, they or their dependents are paid out of the accumulated trust fund. Social insurance appears to offer a simple, rational approach for dealing with the causes of poverty.

It is important to distinguish between *social insurance* programs and *public assistance* programs. If (1) the beneficiaries of a government program are required to make contributions to it before claiming any of its benefits (or if employers must pay into the program on behalf of their workers), and if (2) the benefits are paid out as legal entitlements regardless of the beneficiaries' personal wealth, *then* the program is said to be financed on the social insurance principle. On the other hand, if (1) the program is financed out of general tax revenues and if (2) the recipients are required to show that they are poor in order to claim benefits, *then* the program is said to be financed on the *public assistance* principle.

Over the years, social insurance programs have been more politically popular than public assistance programs. Perhaps, people believe that social insurance is merely enforced savings and that eventually they will get back their own money (although we shall see that this is not entirely true). In other words, people feel entitled to Social Security because they have paid specific Social Security taxes. But public assistance recipients have never specifically "paid into" a public assistance fund. Their assistance checks come out of general tax funds. Moreover, while the vast majority of Americans expect to live to see some Social Security benefits returned to them, they do not expect to become public assistance recipients. Conservatives can support social insurance as a form of thrift; liberals can support it because it tends to redistribute income from workers to the aged, the sick, the disabled, the unemployed, and dependent children.

Government old age insurance, the first social insurance program, was introduced in Germany in 1889 by the conservative regime of Chancellor Otto von Bismark. The idea spread quickly and most European nations had old age insurance programs before the beginning of World War I in 1914. Private old age pension plans were begun in the United States by many railroads, utilities, and large manufacturers at the beginning of the twentieth century. The U.S. government began its own Federal Employees Retirement program in 1920. By 1931, seventeen states had adopted some form of compulsory old age insurance for all workers. During the Depression, a California physician, Francis E. Townsend, began a national crusade for old age pensions to be paid by the government out of taxes on banks. The "Townsend Movement" was perceived by government and business leaders as radical and unworkable, but the combination of economic depression and larger numbers of aged in the population helped to develop pressure for some type of old age insurance. Finally, in the presidential election of 1932, Franklin D. Roosevelt advocated a government insurance plan to protect both the unemployed and the aged. This campaign promise and party platform plank actually became law—the Social Security Act of 1935.

THE SOCIAL SECURITY ACT
OF 1935

Through the Social Security Act of 1935, the federal government undertook to establish the basic framework for social welfare policies at the federal, state, and local levels. As amended, this act now provides for (1) federal Old Age, Survivors, Disability, and Health Insurance (OASDHI), (2) unemployment compensation programs in the states, (3) federal public assistance to the aged, blind, and disabled under the Supplemental Security Income (SSI) program, (4) public assistance to families with dependent children under the Aid to Families with Dependent Children (AFDC) program, (5) federal health insurance for the aged (Medicare), and (6) federal-state assistance for the poor in paying medical costs (Medicaid). In this chapter we will examine OASDHI and unemployment compensation in detail. In Chapter 5 we will examine SSI; in Chapter 6 we will discuss AFDC; and in Chapter 10 we will examine Medicare and Medicaid.

The original Social Security program, as enacted in 1935, covered only retirement and survivor benefits for workers in about half of the labor force; many farm and domestic workers and self-employed persons were exempted, as were state and local government employees. This old age insurance was financed by employer-employee contributions of 1 percent each on a wage base of $3,000, or a maximum contribution by workers of $30 per year. It paid for retirement benefits at age 65 at a rate of about $22 per month for a single worker, or $36 per month for a married couple. Benefits were paid as a matter of right, regardless of income, as long as a worker was retired. Thus, retired workers were spared the humiliation often associated with public charity. Actually, no benefits were paid until 1940 in order to allow the trust fund to accumulate reserves. Economist Joseph A. Pechman writes of the original Social Security Act:

> The old age provisions in the Social Security Act were in part a first attempt to solve the long developing crisis of the aged and of economic security in general, in a reaction to the short-run crisis of the depression; and in part a compromise measure to blunt the political appeal of the enormously expensive and essentially unworkable Townsend Plan.[1]

One might attribute the Roosevelt administration's political success in gaining acceptance for the Social Security Act to several factors: (1) the decline of the extended family and the increasing inability of urban families to care for their aged members; (2) the economic insecurities generated by the Great Depression of the 1930s and the increasing fear of impoverishment even among the middle class; and (3) political movements on the left and right (the Townsend Plan, for example) which threatened the established order. One might add Roosevelt's skills as a national leader to these factors. Social Security was presented to the Congress as a *conservative* program which would eventually abolish the need for public assistance programs, in that individuals would be compelled to protect themselves against poverty.

The first major amendments to the original Social Security Act came in 1939 when Congress made survivors and dependents of insured workers eligible for benefits. In 1950 farmers and self-employed persons were added to the list of beneficiaries, bringing the total number of covered workers to over 90 percent of the work force. In 1956 disability insurance was approved for totally and permanently disabled workers. Later, workers were permitted to retire at age 62, rather than at 65, on the condition that they would accept 80 percent of the monthly benefit otherwise available at 65. In 1965 prepaid medical insurance, Medicare, was added to the program. And, in 1977, an automatic cost of living index was added to Social Security benefit payments.

OASDHI: THE NATION'S LARGEST SOCIAL PROGRAM

Today, OASDHI is the nation's largest social program.[2] It covers approximately nine out of ten workers. Both employees and employers must pay equal amounts toward the employee's OASDHI insurance. Upon retirement, an insured worker is entitled to monthly benefit payments based upon age at retirement and the amount earned during working years. Average monthly payments, however, are quite modest: The average monthly amount for a retired worker, aged 65, with a spouse, is less than $450. In addition to retirement benefits, survivor benefits are payable to the dependents of an insured worker. A lump sum benefit is also payable upon the death of an insured worker. Disability benefits are payable to an insured worker with a total and permanent disability. And *all* persons 65 years of age and over, whether or not they have ever paid into Social Security, are entitled to Medicare—hospital insurance which covers hospital and related services and voluntary supplemental medical insurance which covers a portion of physicians' services.

Social Security benefits are specifically exempted from federal income taxes. This is true regardless of any other income which a retired person may receive. Moreover, persons over 65 also receive a double personal exemption on their federal income taxes.

OASDHI is a completely federal program administered by the Social Security Administration in the Department of Health and Human Services. But it has an important indirect effect on federal, state, and local public assistance programs: By compelling people to insure themselves against the possibility of their own poverty, Social Security has reduced the welfare problems that government might otherwise face.

The growth of OASDHI in numbers of recipients (beneficiaries), average monthly benefits, and the percentage of the federal government total budget is shown in Table 4–1. Social Security taxes are the second largest source of income for the federal government; these tax revenues are exceeded only by the federal personal income tax.

What began as a very modest "insurance premium"—a maximum annual tax contribution of $30—is now a major cost for both employers and employees. Currently, Social Security taxes are scheduled to grow to 13.4 percent combined contribution of employees and employers. The maximum employee contribution has grown from $30 to $2,251, a 65-fold increase since the program was begun over 40 years ago (see Table 4–2).

TABLE 4–1   Social Security Growth

	1940	1950	1960	1965	1970	1975	1980
Numbers of beneficiaries (in thousands)	222	3,477	14,845	20,867	25,312	31,598	35,900
Average monthly benefit for retired workers (in dollars)	23	44	74	84	100	183	360
Social insurance taxes as a percent of all federal revenue	—	—	15.9	19.1	22.5	29.0	32.0
Medicare expenditures (in millions of dollars)	0	0	0	0	6,800	11,181	31,376

TABLE 4–2   Social Security Taxes

YEAR(s)	TAX RATE	MAXIMUM WAGES TAXABLE	MAXIMUM ANNUAL TAX
1937–1949	1.00%	$ 3,000	$ 30
1950	1.50	3,000	45
1955	2.00	4,200	84
1960	3.00	4,800	144
1966	4.20	6,600	277
1969	4.80	7,800	374
1973	5.85	10,800	632
1978	6.06	17,700	1,071
1980	6.13	25,900	1,588
1981	6.65	29,700	1,957
1982	6.70	30,000	2,010
1984	6.70	33,600	2,251

"THE BEST LAID PLANS...":
UNINTENDED CONSEQUENCES
OF SOCIAL SECURITY

The original strategy of the Social Security Act of 1935 was to create a trust fund with a reserve that would be built from the insurance premiums

(Social Security taxes) from working persons. This trust fund reserve would earn interest, and both the interest and principal would be used in later years to pay benefits. Benefits for insured persons would be in proportion to their contributions. General tax revenues would not be used at all. The Social Security system was intended to resemble private, self-financing insurance. But it has not turned out that way at all.

The Social Security system (OASDHI) is now financed on a "pay-as-you-go," rather than a reserve, system. This means the current income from Social Security taxes—over $200 billion per year—matches the outgo in Social Security benefits. Today's generation of workers is paying for the benefits of the last generation, and it is hoped that the next generation will pay for the benefits of today's generation of workers. Political pressure to raise benefit levels while keeping taxes relatively low has reduced the trust fund reserve to a very minor role in Social Security finance. Indeed, Social Security trust fund revenues are now lumped together with all other tax revenues in the federal government's budget.

The insurance trust fund notion was pushed aside in the very first years of the program, when Roosevelt's planners quickly realized that building the reserve was taking money out of the depressed economy and slowing recovery. The plan to build a large self-financing reserve was abandoned in 1939 under political pressure to pump more money into the economy. Over the years, Congress has come under political pressure to increase benefit levels to retirees, even though these retirees never paid enough money into their accounts to justify higher benefits. In 1977 Congress voted to allow benefits which automatically increase with inflation (measured by rises in the official Consumer Price Index). This is a very popular protection against inflation for older Americans, but the Social Security trust fund is unable to finance these regular increases. Moreover, benefits under Social Security are now no longer really proportionate to contributions; benefits are figured more generously for those whose wages were low than for those whose wages were high.

The only remaining aspect of an insurance program is that individuals must have paid into the system to receive its benefits (although even this requirement has been dropped for Medicare), and beneficiaries are not required to prove that they are needy. Most Americans view their Social Security benefits as a right.

There would be no real problem with pay-as-you-go financing for Social Security, *if* (1) today's workers and employers did not view the Social Security tax as overly burdensome; and (2) the number of aged persons supported by the working age population was not increasing. Unfortunately, however, there is reason to believe that current financing of Social Security is in need of reform, because Social Security taxes *are* increasingly being viewed as burdensome and because the ratio of beneficiaries to workers *is* growing rapidly.

To keep up with the increased benefits (which Congress has tied to the rate of inflation), the Social Security tax has risen very dramatically in two ways: First, the tax rate assessed against both employer and employee has been rising (6.7 percent each in 1982, or a 13.4 percent combined, contribution); second, the wages subject to taxation have risen to over $30,000. The Social Security tax is now the second largest source of federal revenue, and social insurance benefits are now the single largest expenditure of the federal government, even surpassing expenditures for national defense.

Up to now, almost everyone who has retired has received Social Security benefits which have greatly exceeded what they contributed in Social Security taxes over the years. This helps to explain the political popularity of the Social Security system among older citizens. But today's younger workers are not likely to ever get back as much as they will be required to pay into the program in the coming years. For example, if you are now 27, your contributions and those of your employer, from now until retirement at age 65, will total over $225,000, assuming that Congress does not raise Social Security taxes even higher! But if these same monies were set aside in a private account in your own name, and allowed to accumulate tax-free at even a low interest rate of 7.5 percent, you would wind up with a nest egg at age 65 of over $1 million.[3] Needless to say, Social Security benefits, even including survivors, disability, and health provisions, will never amount to $1 million for an individual. So today's young workers are indeed paying a price far in excess of anything they might hope to regain.

An even greater threat to the Social Security system is the increasing *dependency ratio.* This refers to the number of recipients as a percentage of the number of contributing workers. At present, each one hundred workers support about twenty-nine beneficiaries. But as the U.S. population grows older—because of lower birth rates and longer life spans (see Figure 4–1)—we can expect forty-four beneficiaries per one hundred workers after the year 2000. This will mean that every two workers must support one Social Security recipient—a very heavy burden that will place additional pressures on the system for financial support. If the Social Security system cannot finance these promised benefits, political pressures will mount to force Congress to use general tax revenues to keep the system from bankruptcy.

As a "regressive" tax, the Social Security tax takes a larger share of the income of middle and lower income workers than the affluent. This is because (1) the Social Security tax is levied only against wages and not against dividends, interest, rents, and other nonwage income sources, which are more frequently sources of income for the wealthy; and (2) the wage base which is taxed stops at about $30,000 and leaves all income in excess of this amount untaxed. This was not a serious factor when Social Security taxes amounted to very little, but today the size of Social Security

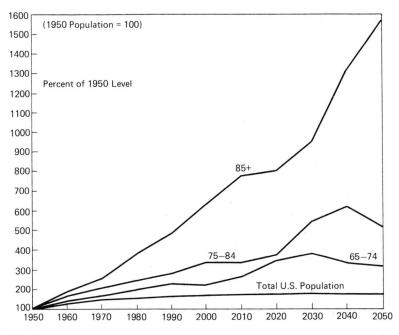

1600
1500
1400
1300
1200
1100
1000
900
800
700
600
500
400
300
200
100

(1950 Population = 100)

Percent of 1950 Level

85+

75–84

65–74

Total U.S. Population

1950 1960 1970 1980 1990 2000 2010 2020 2030 2040 2050

FIGURE 4–1 The graying of America. (U.S. Bureau of the Census)

revenues—nearly one-third of the federal government's income—has an important impact on the overall equity (fairness) of the revenue structure. Moreover, unlike the federal income tax, Social Security taxes make no allowance for family dependents or medical expenses. Finally, even though half of the full 13.4 percent Social Security tax is paid by the employee and half by the employer, most economists agree that the full burden of these taxes falls on the workers. This is because employers must consider the Social Security tax as a cost of hiring a worker, and the worker's "take home" pay is reduced by the amounts paid into the Social Security trust fund by both the employer and the employee.

THE POLITICS AND THE FUTURE OF SOCIAL SECURITY

The political obstacles to Social Security reform are awesome.[4] The 36 million people receiving Social Security benefits are the largest block of recipients of *any* government program. They are especially sensitive to any talk of "reform" which suggests any reduction in their benefits. Mostly elderly, these persons vote more regularly than *any* other age category. They want to keep the Social Security program financially sound, but they do not want to give up any benefits, including annual cost-of-living increases.

Many reforms have been proposed for the Social Security system in order to insure its continued solvency:

1. Congress has responded to immediate shortfalls in revenues by increasing the Social Security tax and increasing the taxable wage base. In 1979 the tax rate was moved up in annual steps from 5.85 percent to 6.70 percent and the taxable base increased from $17,700 to over $30,000. This was the largest peacetime tax increase ever passed by Congress.

2. Congress may eventually be forced to contribute to Social Security from general tax revenues. The first movement in this direction came with Medicare in 1965 when Congress agreed to pay part of the cost through general tax revenues and part through Social Security taxes.

3. Congress could allow persons over 65 to continue working without losing their Social Security benefits. Their wages would be subject to Social Security taxes and at least part of their benefits would be recovered.

4. Congress could reduce or eliminate the automatic cost of living increases for Social Security recipients.

5. Congress could gradually increase the age at which individuals can retire and receive Social Security benefits. If the retirement age were gradually moved from sixty-five to sixty-six to sixty-seven years of age, recipient payments would be delayed and the system could be financed on roughly the same basis as it is today. It is also argued that vitality and life span have increased dramatically since the beginning of the system forty-five years ago and that a higher retirement age would better reflect the original intention of the system.

6. Congress could reduce the benefits of persons retiring early at age sixty-two to 30 or 50 percent of regular benefits instead of the 80 percent currently allowed.

Liberals sometimes argue that Social Security benefits should be paid out of general tax revenues whenever the trust fund becomes empty. Alternately, they suggest that wealthier retirees should be denied Social Security benefits. But these proposals threaten the image of an "insurance" program. The political popularity of Social Security, and the willingness of American workers to pay such a large amount into Social Security taxes, is based in part on the idea that "contributions" and benefits are linked. Workers believe that they are saving for their *own* retirement or disability or death. Workers can see the "earmarked" portion of the federal payroll deductions that go into Social Security. They believe that they are building protection for themselves and their families. If the Social Security program were turned into a welfare program, it would surely lose its political support. If it became "just another welfare program," then benefits could be cut because workers would no longer feel they had a personal stake in the program.

The Reagan administration has been especially careful about Social Security. Although Social Security is the largest single category of federal spending, and President Reagan is committed to reducing federal spending and balancing the budget, he has nonetheless tried not to offend the nation's 36 million Social Security recipients. Reagan has pledged that no one *currently* receiving Social Security benefits will suffer any reductions because of his proposals. By implication, however, this pledge indicates that benefits to *future* retirees might be reduced. The most common suggestion is to reduce the benefit levels to future retirees who choose the early—age 62—retirement option.[5]

The Reagan administration initially placed Social Security and Medicare (OASDHI) among its "safety net" programs—programs which would not be significantly affected by efforts to reduce federal spending. Indeed, even the expensive, automatic, annual cost-of-living adjustment was retianed by the Reagan administration. Nonetheless, there is real concern in the White House and on Capitol Hill that the Social Security trust fund will be emptied in a few years—that is to say, a concern that Social Security taxes will not be able to cover Social Security benefits.[6] At the same time, there is real concern—especially among the aged—that the Reagan budget-knife will eventually cut into the programs for the elderly. Indeed, threats to the politically popular Social Security system—or even misunderstandings about efforts to guarantee its future stability—may turn out to be the "Achilles' heel" of the Reagan administration.

UNEMPLOYMENT
COMPENSATION

A second major insurance program—unemployment compensation—was included in the original Social Security Act of 1935. Again, the underlying rationale was to compel employers to contribute to trust funds which would be held for the employees in the event of job loss. The federal government requires employers to pay into *state* unemployment insurance programs that meet federal standards. These programs are administered by the states. The federal standards are flexible, and the states have considerable freedom in shaping their own unemployment programs. In all cases unemployed workers must report in person and show that they are willing and able to work in order to receive unemployment benefits. In practice, this means that unemployed workers must register with the U.S. Employment Service (usually located in the same building as the state unemployment compensation office) as a condition of receiving unemployment compensation. States cannot deny workers benefits for refusing to work as strikebreakers or refusing to work for rates lower than "prevailing" rates.

But basic decisions concerning the amount of benefits, eligibility, and length of time that benefits can be paid are largely left to the states. However, in all states, unemployment compensation is temporary (usually thirty-nine weeks maximum). Unemployment compensation is not a protection against long-term or "hard-core" unemployment.

Each state maintains an unemployment compensation trust fund of its own, financed from taxes on employers ranging from 1 percent to 4 percent of their total payroll. The federal government also maintains an unemployment compensation trust fund to bail out any state trust fund that becomes exhausted. Average state payments to the unemployed range from lows of $70 per week to highs of over $100 per week.

WHAT IS UNEMPLOYMENT
AND WHO IS UNEMPLOYED?

When unemployment compensation insurance was first adopted in 1935, the loss of one's job was an economic catastrophe. The alternative to work could be starvation. Most families depended on the support of one worker—usually the father. If he lost his job, the family's income was immediately reduced to zero. But today almost three-fifths of American families benefit from the earnings of more than one worker. Unemployment is still serious, but a second income provides a buffer against economic catastrophe. A combination of (1) short-term help from unemployment insurance, (2) food stamps, and (3) welfare and other forms of public assistance for the long-term unemployed, reduce the real "cost" of becoming unemployed. The cost of unemployment can be viewed as the difference between income from unemployment insurance and other public assistance programs and the wages of a potential job. These changes have had an important effect on the motivations and expectations of the unemployed. A jobless person need not jump at the first available job that comes along, regardless of salary or working conditions. He or she may now decide to pass up, at least for a while, low-paying or undesirable jobs in the hope of finding better-paying, more satisfying employment.

The unemployment rate is a monthly estimate by the U.S. Department of Labor of the percentage of the work force that is out of work and actively seeking jobs. Each year the total work force grows as the population increases. This means that the total number of jobs must grow each year just to keep pace with population growth. An overall unemployment rate of 7 percent has become quite common. This is far below the 20 percent to 30 percent unemployment rate estimated during the Depression of the 1930s, but somewhat above the 3 percent to 4 percent lows achieved during the 1950s.

Clearly there is some unavoidable minimum unemployment. In a large, free economy, hundreds of thousands of people move and change jobs and temporarily find themselves unemployed. This "frictional" unemployment is estimated to be about half of the total unemployment during normal (nonrecession) periods. Others find themselves unemployed because of poor job skills, poor health, low mental capacities, or geographic locations far from work places. These "structurally" unemployed are estimated to be less than 20 percent of the total unemployed.

But there are many other people who may become discouraged and who may quit looking for work. These persons are not counted in the work force and are not counted among the officially unemployed because they are not actively looking for work.

Women and blacks and teenagers suffer from substantially higher unemployment rates than adult white males. In good times or bad, the black unemployment rate is nearly double the white unemployment rate. Unemployment rates for women are slightly higher than unemployment rates for men. But the teenage (16 to 19 years old) unemployment rate is usually three times higher than the adult male rate. The highest unemployment rate of all is for black teenagers; a 40 percent unemployment rate for this group is not uncommon.

How much unemployment is enough? There is an old saying: "When your neighbor is unemployed, it's a recession. When you are unemployed, it's a depression." It has been argued that unemployment among women and teenagers, in families where others are working, is not as urgent a problem as unemployment among adult family breadwinners. Others reject this notion, contending that at least one-third of working women support families and that many other women work because of low family income. It is also argued that jobs for teenagers produce long-term social benefits— teens learn work habits and the importance of holding a steady job in later life.

The Labor Department is frequently criticized for excluding "discouraged workers" from its unemployment statistics. A related criticism is that the Labor Department counts part-time workers as employed; yet many part-time workers would prefer full-time work. Many of the poor in America are never counted as unemployed because they have given up even trying to find a job. On the other hand, in order to qualify for public assistance, such as food stamps, able-bodied individuals must sign up with their local state employment office. Some argue that this drives unemployment figures up, because some of these individuals may not really intend to seek employment.[7]

ILLUSTRATION: UNFILLED JOBS AND UNEMPLOYED WORKERS

In 1980 the *Wall Street Journal* reported that a Burger Chef manager in Detroit had spent several months trying to fill 40 cook and counter jobs starting at $3.10 an hour.[1] "I've gone everywhere looking," she said. Metropolitan Detroit's unemployment rate hit 12.5 percent in September 1980, but "nobody here wants work," she complained. Yet, when the Social Security

Administration in Baltimore advertised 75 unskilled clerical and warehouse jobs at an annual wage of $7,960 to $11,565, there was a mad dash to apply. "At 5:30 A.M. one Monday, 14,000 anxious job-seekers—most of them black and some of them women carrying infants—began to line up for employment applications for these 75 jobs."

These stories raise the question: Why do mundane jobs, offering low wages and low status, go unfilled in some high unemployment areas but get snapped up elsewhere? In some communities, thousands of skilled workers laid off from good jobs are getting by comfortably on jobless benefits; they will not stoop to doing menial work. But, in other places many of the jobless do not have such comfortable financial cushions and cannot afford to be so choosy.

The mismatching of job opportunities with people out of work worsens the unemployment rate. In September 1980, when 7.8 million Americans were out of work, the U.S. Department of Labor reported more than 430,000 job openings at state employment offices. While some employers were seeking highly skilled workers such as aerospace engineers, two-thirds of the job openings called for unskilled workers at salaries less than $9,000 a year. Among the unfilled jobs were those for janitors, dishwashers, laborers, maids, and security guards.

Is there some way that the unemployed can be better matched with available jobs? The alternatives suggested are politically controversial. Some economists urge reductions in generous unemployment benefits given to many jobless auto and steel industry workers; with high benefits, idle workers have little incentive to look for work. But others believe that unemployment benefits protect individuals against swallowing their pride and reducing their standard of living by being forced to go to work at jobs below their skill and pay levels.

Service, domestic, and seasonal jobs are referred to as "the secondary labor market." Job seekers usually do not stay at these jobs long because such jobs are short on security, benefits, and opportunity for advancement. They are not very appealing to the average experienced auto worker, even when unemployment strikes. This worker may have earned $10.75 an hour at his job. When he is laid off he can collect 90 percent of his take-home pay for a year from state unemployment insurance and employer-financed supplemental benefits.

To illustrate, the *Wall Street Journal* also reported the case of a 24-year-old Flint, Michigan, autoworker. When General Motors laid him off as a spark-plug division plant inspector in November 1979, he collected between $165 and $253 a week tax free. His take-home pay had been $260 a week. He spent last spring and summer fishing, hiking, and kayaking in northern Michigan. "'Being laid off and making that much income spoils you a bit,' concedes the worker, who didn't hunt for work after returning to Flint because he expected to be recalled soon."

In California and Oregon, out-of-work loggers and fishermen do not receive as extensive jobless benefits as auto workers do. Even so, most refused to become farm laborers and pick lily bulbs for $3.25 an hour. In part it is a matter of status. "White men used to working with heavy equipment have 'measurable, significant prejudice against physical work in the fields,' says an official of a privately owned company that was left short handed even after filling most field jobs with Mexican immigrants." The company official also complained that the same men "who don't come rushing out here to work...sign petitions to get rid of the illegal Chicanos."

What is unemployment? The U.S. Department of Labor defines the unemployment level as everyone 16 years old or over who does not have a job and is looking for work.[2] Each month a large scientific sample of the entire population is asked "Do you have a job?" If the answer is "No," then a second question is asked: "Are you looking for a job?" If the answer is yes, the individual is considered a member of the labor force and unemployed. In 1980 there were approximately 100 million people in the work force, about 92 million had jobs and 8 million (or 8 percent) said they were "looking for work."

How accurate are unemployment figures? Many economists believe these figures greatly overestimate hardship. Over one-quarter of the unemployed are teenagers who say they are "looking for work" but are seeking only part time, temporary work. Many workers are moving from job to job and seeking the right positions for themselves. Economists call this "frictional unemployment." Other unemployed persons have only recently entered the labor market. Less than half of the unemployed actually lost their jobs. On the other hand, unemployment figures do not count "discouraged workers" who do not say they are "looking for work" because they have given up hope of finding a job. Discouraged workers might add 1 percent to the official unemployment rate.

The unemployed are *not* a large mass of people who are unable to find any work. The average duration of unemployment is 12 to 16 weeks. Less than one out of five unemployed are out of work for as long as six months.

[1] Information and quotations rely on *Wall Street Journal*, December 5, 1980, p. 1, for quotations.
[2] See George Leland Bach, *Economics: An Introduction to Analysis and Policy* (Englewood Cliffs, N.J.: Prentice-Hall, 1980), chap. 8.

Source: *Wall Street Journal*, December 5, 1980, p. 1.

SUMMARY

One strategy for preventing poverty in the United States is through social insurance programs. The purpose of social insurance is to help workers insure themselves and their dependents against poverty which may result from advanced age, death, disability, and unemployment. The major social insurance program is known as the Social Security program. It is financed through premiums paid by both workers and employers and is administered by the federal government.

Social insurance programs differ from public assistance programs. Social insurance programs require that beneficiaries make contributions to the program; contributors are entitled to benefits regardless of their wealth. Public assistance recipients must prove that they are poor before they receive benefits, and benefits are paid from general tax revenues rather than through recipients' contributions.

The Social Security Act of 1935 was the first major piece of federal welfare legislation. This act has been amended many times; today it includes a number of social welfare programs. The social insurance programs it includes are Old Age, Survivors, Disability and Health Insurance, Unemployment Compensation, and Medicare. The public assistance programs it embraces are Aid to Families with Dependent Children, Supplemental Security Income, and Medicaid.

There have been some unintended consequences of the Social Security program. The original intention was that the contributions would build up in a reserve fund so that the program would be self-financing, but today the program is financed on a "pay-as-you-go" basis. The original reserve fund plan was abandoned because of (1) the desire to pump money back into the economy rather than holding it in trust; (2) pressure on Congress to raise benefits; and (3) the growing proportion of older Americans. To keep up with the growth in the program, the amount employers and employees are required to pay has increased. The Social Security tax is now the second largest source of federal revenues and the single largest federal government expenditure.

The Social Security system is in trouble. Today's young workers cannot expect to claim what they will contribute to the system over their lifetimes. The Social Security tax has also been criticized because it is regressive. Only wages are taxed, and wages in excess of $30,000 are not taxed at all. Poorer Americans, therefore, pay a higher percentage of their total wages in Social Security taxes. In addition, other sources of income such as interest and dividends, which the rich, not the poor, are likely to have, are not considered in computing the Social Security tax.

Social policy analysts have proposed several alternatives for rescuing the Social Security program: continue to increase the taxable wage base, provide funds from the general revenue fund, allow people to work *and* collect Social Security benefits which would force them to pay taxes on their earnings, reduce or eliminate increases in benefits, or raise the retirement age.

President Reagan included Social Security in his "social safety net." The political strength of 36 million Social Security recipients makes major reductions unlikely. Proposals to reduce benefits to retirees have been unpopular among citizens in general, and among both Democrats and Republicans.

Unemployment Compensation is another large insurance program. While national unemployment rates have fluctuated at around 7 percent, unemployment among blacks, women, and teenagers is much higher. Minority youth have been hit hardest by unemployment. Unemployment would be reduced if unemployed workers were better matched with available jobs.

NOTES

1. Joseph A. Pechman, Henry J. Aaron, and Michael K. Taussig, *Social Security: Perspectives for Reform* (Washington, D.C.: Brookings Institution, 1968).
2. For further discussion of provisions under the Social Security Act, see Robert M. Ball, *Social Security Today and Tomorrow* (New York: Columbia University Press, 1978).
3. William G. Flanagan, "Social Security–Don't Count On It," *Forbes* 126, no. 12 (December 8, 1980), 161–62.
4. For discussions about what may be ahead for the Social Security programs, see Alice H. Munnell, *The Future of Social Security* (Washington, D.C.: Brookings Institution, 1977); and Bruno Stein, *Social Security and Provisions in Transition* (New York: Free Press, 1980).
5. Office of Management and Budget, *A Program for Economic Recovery*, February 18, 1981 (Washington, D.C.: Government Printing Office, 1981), p. 17.
6. Also see Sar A. Levitan, *Programs in Aid of the Poor for the 1980's*, 4th ed. (Baltimore: Johns Hopkins University Press, 1980) for additional discussions of the future of social welfare.
7. Kenneth W. Clarkson and Roger E. Meiners, "Government Statistics as a Guide to Economic Policy: Food Stamps and the Spurious Increase in the Unemployment Rates," *Policy Review* 1, No. 1 (Summer 1977): 27–51.

5

Helping
the "Deserving Poor":
Aged, Blind,
and Disabled

The aged, blind, and disabled are among the groups considered to be the "deserving poor"—those whom society has moral and ethical obligations to assist. Two major types of programs are available to these persons: (1) Public assistance programs serve the poor aged, blind, and disabled in cases where the individual's condition is not likely to improve and other means of support are not available; and (2) social service programs assist those who can benefit from a wide range of rehabilitative services.[1] In addition to these programs, recent legislation for the disabled is aimed at reducing discrimination in employment and education and at providing greater access to public facilities.

EARLY AID FOR THE DESERVING POOR

Most states had programs to assist the elderly poor before the Social Security Act of 1935 was passed. Massachusetts was among the first states to appoint a commission to study the problems of the elderly.[2] In 1914 Arizona passed a law establishing a pension program for the aged.[3] The territory of Alaska passed a law entitling elderly persons to pensions in 1915.[4] By the time the federal government adopted the Social Security Act, thirty states already had their own old age assistance programs.[5] Eligibility requirements for state old age programs were very stringent. In order to qualify, recipients generally had to be at least sixty-five years old, be citizens of the United States, and meet residency requirements in the location where they applied for benefits. In cases where relatives were capable of supporting an elderly family member, benefits were often denied. Often those elderly who did participate had to sign all of their assets over to the state in the event of their death.[6]

Old age was not the only disabling condition which concerned Americans. The blind were also considered "deserving." In fact, terms of residence and other entrance requirements were often more lenient in the state pension laws for the blind than they were for the elderly. By 1935, twenty-seven states had pension programs for the blind.[7] Other types of diseases, injuries, and handicaps were also considered disabling, but early in the 1900s policies to assist persons disabled because of conditions other than old age and blindness varied considerably from state to state,[8] and some states had no programs at all.

When the Social Security Act of 1935 was passed, its most far-reaching provision was the Social Security insurance program which provided financial payments to retired workers. However, the Social Security Act also included public assistance programs for some special target groups. Following the precedent established by many states, the programs included were Aid to Dependent Children (ADC), Old Age Assistance (OAA), and Aid to the Blind (AB). In 1950 the Social Security Act was amended to include the Aid to the Permanently and Totally Disabled (APTD) program. OAA, AB, and APTD were called the adult categorical assistance programs. Although the programs were authorized by the federal government, each state could decide whether or not it wanted to participate in any or all of the programs. All states eventually adopted the OAA and AB programs, but several states chose not to participate in the APTD program. The federal government shared costs with the states and set minimum requirements for participation in the programs. Elderly persons had to be at least sixty-five years old to receive federal aid. Blind and disabled persons had to be at least eighteen years old. The states were primarily responsible for administering the programs and retained a great deal of discretion in determining eligiblity requirements. Residency requirements and income limitations were determined by the states as were the amount of payments. The states also determined the definitions of disability and blindness.

State administration of the OAA, AB, and APTD programs had serious ramifications for some beneficiaries. An individual who moved to another state was often denied benefits until residency was reestablished. Benefits also varied drastically and were often meager. In the OAA program in 1964, the state of West Virginia paid an average monthly benefit of $50, while Wisconsin paid an average benefit of $111.[9] The differences in benefits far outweighed the differences in the cost of living from state to state. Beneficiaries from poorer states often received less because their states had less money to operate the program.

SSI: "FEDERALIZING" THE AGED, BLIND, AND DISABLED PROGRAMS

When President Nixon took office in 1972 he wanted to clean up the "welfare mess." Nixon's welfare reform was to provide a minimum income to poor Americans that would replace the AFDC, OAA, AB, and APTD programs and bring an end to the uneven treatment of welfare recipients from state to state. His *guaranteed annual income* proposal, known as the Family Assistance Plan (FAP), was the target of controversy in Congress. Liberals believed that the reforms were too stingy. Conservatives believed that the reforms provided too much in welfare benefits and would reduce the incentive to work. Daniel P. Moynihan, advisor to President Nixon, supporter of the FAP, and author of *The Politics of a Guaranteed Annual Income*, tells us that most of the controversy focused on the reform of the AFDC program.[10] AFDC was never reformed, but in the midst of the controversy, the OAA, AB, and APTD programs underwent substantial revisions which went almost unnoticed.[11]

In 1972 Congress made major changes in OAA, AB, and APTD by federalizing these programs under a new program called Supplemental Security Income (SSI). "Federalizing" meant that Congress took the programs out of the hands of state governments. The state governments would no longer determine eligibility requirements or the amounts of payments, nor would they directly administer the programs. These changes represented the most sweeping reform of the adult categorical assistance programs since APTD was added in 1950. SSI replaced the OAA, AB, and APTD programs by establishing a minimum income for recipients and by standardizing eligibility requirements in all states. Regardless of where a beneficiary lives, eligibility requirements and minimum payment levels are now the same; however, a number of states supplement the minimum payment to recipients. The SSI program is administered by the Social Security Administration. Once a person qualifies for benefits, a monthly check is mailed directly to the recipient, in the same way a retired person receives a Social Security check.

THE COSTS OF SSI

Since 1972, when the OAA, AB, and APTD programs were federalized, costs have generally continued to rise, even after accounting for inflation (see Table 5–1). In 1940 the costs of OAA were $473 million. By 1960, OAA costs had quadrupled to almost $2 billion. In 1980, under SSI, costs amounted to more than $2.7 billion. The AB program has not been as expensive a program because of the smaller number of blind recipients. In 1940 the program cost $22 million to operate; today it costs $190 million. The most dramatic growth in expenditures has been for disabled recipients. Costs rose from $259 million in 1960 to more than $5 billion in 1980.

Payments to recipients have also increased although they remain quite modest. And once we consider the high rate of inflation, especially in recent years, payments may leave recipients with little more purchasing power than they had before the enactment of SSI. An elderly recipient now receives an average of $128 per month. This is lower than payments to the blind and disabled: The blind receive the highest payments, averaging $213 monthly, and disabled recipients receive an average of $198 monthly (see Table 5–2).

TABLE 5–1   The Costs of the Adult Public Assistance Programs for Selected Years (Millions of Dollars)

YEAR	AGED	BLIND	DISABLED
1940	473	22	—[a]
1950	1,485	53	8
1960	1,922	83	259
1970	1,862	98	1,000
1980	2,734	190	5,014

[a]Program did not begin until 1950.

Sources: *Historical Statistics of the United States, Colonial Times to 1970,* U.S. Department of Commerce, Bureau of the Census, 1975, p. 356 and *Statistical Abstract of the United States, 1981,* p. 343.

TABLE 5–2   Average Monthly Payments for the Adult Public Assistance Programs for Selected Years (in Dollars)

YEAR	AGED	BLIND	DISABLED
1940	19.30	26.10	—[a]
1950	43.05	25.35	44.10
1960	58.90	46.00	56.15
1970	77.65	104.00	97.65
1980	128.00	213.00	198.00

[a]Program did not begin until 1950.

Sources: *Historical Statistics of the United States, Colonial Times to 1970,* U.S. Department of Commerce, Bureau of the Census, 1975, p. 356, and *Statistical Abstract of the United States, 1981,* p. 343.

WHO RECEIVES SSI?

Over the years the number of elderly and blind SSI recipients has decreased, especially when compared with the rate of growth in the general population. However, the number of disabled beneficiaries has increased rapidly (see Table 5–3). In 1950 about 2.8 million people received Old Age Assistance. Today there are fewer than 2 million recipients. The declining number of recipients can be primarily attributed to the increasing number of persons who have become eligible for Social Security insurance benefits. Aged SSI recipients are generally older than the average elderly in the United States; they often reside in rural or small towns and have few financial assets; many suffer from physical illnesses or psychological problems; they are predominantly women who live with a spouse or other relatives who care for them.[12] When SSI was enacted, it was anticipated that many more elderly would become eligible for assistance. Low participation may be because of the stigma associated with being a welfare recipient. Others do not apply, believing they do not qualify.[13]

Since 1960, the number of blind recipients has dropped from a high of more than 100,000 to about 78,000. The decrease can be attributed to advances in the prevention and treatment of blindness and to the growing numbers of blind persons who are self-supporting; about one-fourth of blind persons in the United States receive aid.[14]

Most of the growth in SSI has been because of the number of permanently and totally disabled recipients. The number of recipients has grown from nearly 370,000 in 1960 to over 2 million today. Half of all permanently and totally disabled recipients are 55 to 64 years old; many have multiple physical illnesses; their most frequent medical problem is heart disease.[15]

TABLE 5–3   Numbers of Recipients of the Adult Public Assistance Programs for Selected Years (in Thousands)

YEAR	AGED	BLIND	DISABLED
1940	2,070	73	—[a]
1950	2,786	97	69
1960	2,305	107	369
1970	2,082	81	935
1980	1,808	78	2,256

[a]Program did not begin until 1950.

Sources: *Historical Statistics of the United States, Colonial Times to 1970,* U.S. Department of Commerce, Bureau of the Census, 1975, p. 356; and *Statistical Abstract of the United States, 1981,* p. 343.

DEFINING DISABILITY

Since considerable attention is devoted to the elderly in Chapters 4 (Social Security) and 7 (Social Services), most of this chapter is devoted to an analysis of social policies and services for the disabled. Most Americans agree that the "disabled" are among the "deserving" poor. However, defining *disability* is not an easy task. There are many types of disabilities and handicaps. Amputations, arthritis, blindness, bone problems, brain injuries, burns, cancer, cerebral palsy, cleft lip and palate, deafness, diabetes, disfigurement, emotional disturbances, epilepsy, heart disease, mental retardation, mongolism, multiple sclerosis, muscular atrophy, muteness, paralysis, respiratory disorders, stroke, and stuttering are just some.[16] In addition to classifying these problems as disabilities or handicaps, one might classify them in terms of degree of impairment.[17] For instance, a person may be legally blind but still have some sight. Some persons are so severely handicapped that they can perform few of life's day to day functions, yet other disabled persons are able to function quite well in society. *Disabilities* have traditionally been defined as *health-related problems that prevent the individual from working*.[18] A broader definition might include not only employment limitations, but also limitations on all roles and tasks a person usually performs in society, especially if these limitations exist for long periods of time.[19]

The U.S. government, which supports a large number of programs for the handicapped and disabled, has developed a definition of disability. This definition is used to determine which individuals are eligible to participate in federally funded programs for the disabled.

A handicapped person is anyone with any type of physical or mental disability that substantially impairs or restricts one or more such major life activities as walking, seeing, hearing, speaking, working, or learning. Handicapping conditions include but are not limited to:

Cancer	Muscular dystrophy
Cerebral palsy	Orthopedic, speech, or
Deafness or hearing	visual impairment
impairment	Such perceptual handicaps as
Diabetes	Dyslexia
Emotional illness	Minimal brain dysfunction
Epilepsy	Developmental aphasia
Heart Disease	
Mental Retardation	
Multiple Sclerosis	

The U.S. Attorney General has ruled that alcoholism and drug addiction are physical or mental impairments that are handicapping conditions if they limit one or more of life's major activities.[20]

There are several ways that residents of the United States learn about programs that can provide financial and social services to them. Public service announcements on the radio and television reach many people, even those who are unable to read. Friends and family often know of programs that can assist a needy person or family. The federal government also publishes many pamphlets that describe social welfare programs. In Figure 5–1 we have reproduced a pamphlet "SSI for the Aged, Blind, and Disabled in Florida" which briefly explains the program, who qualifies, potential benefits, and the documentation needed to apply.

SSI for the aged, blind, and disabled in Florida

SSI for the aged, blind, and disabled in Florida

People in financial need who are 65 or older or needy people of any age who are blind or disabled (including children) may be eligible for monthly cash payments from the Federal Government. The payments are called supplemental security income (SSI). Eligible people get checks from the Federal Government every month. In some cases Florida provides additional money to supplement the Federal payment. This additional monthly payment is sent to eligible people in special living arrangements in a separate check from the State.

People may be eligible for payments if they have little or no regular cash income and don't own much in the way of assets that can be turned into cash.

To qualify for SSI payments because of blindness, a person must have central visual acuity of 20/200 or less in the better eye with the use of a corrective lens, or visual field restriction of 20 degrees or less.

SSI payments for disability may be made if an individual is unable to engage in substantial gainful activity because of a physical or mental impairment which can be expected to result in death or which has lasted (or is expected to last) for 12 months or longer.

The basic Federal payment can be as much as $208.20 a month to an eligible individual, or $312.30 a month to an eligible couple. Federal payments will go up automatically in the future to keep up with increases in the cost of living.

Maximum monthly payment amounts for eligible people in special living arrangements are shown in the table below. The amounts shown include both Federal and State money. Not all eligible people receive checks in these amounts. Payments may be smaller if they have other income.

Living Arrangements	Total maximum payment
Adult foster care	
Eligible Individual	$254.00
Eligible Couple	$508.00
Room and board with personal care	
Eligible Individual	$254.00
Eligible Couple	$508.00

Payment amounts shown for couples apply only if the living arrangement is the same for both husband and wife.

SSI recipients in public or private institutions receiving Medicaid payments covering more than 50 percent of the cost of care are not entitled to a full SSI payment. They may be eligible, however, for a reduced payment of up to $25 to cover personal expenses.

Things you own

If you are single (or married but not living with your spouse), you can have assets—things you own—worth up to $1,500 and still get payments. The amount for a couple is $2,250. This includes savings accounts, stocks, bonds, jewelry, and other valuables.

Not everything owned counts as an asset. A home doesn't count. And the Federal Government does not ask for

2

3

FIGURE 5–1

liens on the homes of people who get SSI.

Your personal effects or household goods don't count as assets if their total equity value is $2,000 or less. If the total equity value exceeds $2,000, the excess counts. The equity value is what you can sell the item for, less the amount of any legal debt against it.

Insurance policies are not counted either if their total face value on any one person is $1,500 or less. If the total face value is more than $1,500, only the cash surrender value counts.

If you own one car, only the portion of the current market value which exceeds $4,500 may be counted as an asset. The value of one car isn't counted at all if it is used by the household for transportation to a job or to a place for regular treatment of a specific medical problem, or if it is modified for use by a handicapped person. If you own any other cars, the equity value of each is counted. Also, the value of any car you own may not be counted if it is used for self-support, under certain conditions.

Income you have
You can have some money coming in and still get SSI. The first $20 a month in income generally won't affect the payment.

In addition, if you work, the first $65 in earnings in a month won't count against the payment, and only half of any additional earnings will be deducted from the monthly payment.

Apart from earnings, any other income above the first $20 a month generally will reduce the payment amount. This includes social security checks,

veterans compensation, worker's compensation, pensions, annuities, gifts, and other income.

Also, if you live in someone else's household—your son's or daughter's home, for example—your payment may be reduced.

Not social security
Even though the Social Security Administration runs the program, supplemental security income is not the same as social security. Money for SSI payments comes from general funds of the U.S. Treasury. Social security benefits are paid from contributions of workers, employers, and self-employed people. There are no limits on the amount of money or property you can have and still get your social security benefits. Social security funds are not used to make SSI payments.

You can get social security and supplemental security income, too, if you are eligible for both.

Medicaid
If you receive SSI payments, you get medical assistance (Medicaid) automatically. You don't need to apply separately for Medicaid. If you are not eligible for SSI payments, you may still be eligible for Medicaid. If you are in a nursing facility or State institution, it's necessary to apply with your local Health and Rehabilitative Service (HRS) office.

Social services
Social services will be provided by the HRS. People can get information about these services at their local social security office or local HRS office.

How to apply
If you believe you may be eligible for SSI payments, you may apply at any social security office. When you apply you should bring along:

▶ Proof of age, unless you are already receiving social security checks.
▶ Your latest tax bill or assessment notice if you own real property other than your home.
▶ Names of any persons who help with your support and the amount of money provided.
▶ Bank books, stock certificates, and bonds.
▶ Motor vehicle registration.
▶ Proof of pensions and annuities.
▶ A copy of your most recent tax return if you are presently self-employed.
▶ If blind or disabled, a list of medical sources (doctors, hospitals, or clinics) where you have received treatment.

You have the right to appeal if you disagree with the decision on your application.

If you want more information about the SSI program, call any social security office.

U.S. Department of
Health, Education, and Welfare
Social Security Administration
HEW Publication No. (SSA) 79-11184
November 1979
☆ U.S. GOVERNMENT PRINTING OFFICE 1979: 620-329/137

4   5

FIGURE 5–1 (continued)

REHABILITATIVE SERVICES FOR THE DISABLED

Financial assistance through SSI is an important resource for elderly, handicapped, and disabled persons who are unable to work or who earn so little that they cannot maintain an adequate standard of living. However, handicapped and disabled persons often need more than financial assistance. Even the most severely and profoundly retarded person can benefit from programs of physical stimulation. For those with less severe disabilities, physical therapy or artificial limbs may be important in order to interact in society. Others need special educational programs and learning devices. Still others require vocational education and reeducation.

The Vocational Rehabilitation Program

One of the first training programs to assist the disabled was developed in Massachusetts in 1916.[21] Then, in 1920, Congress passed the Vocational Rehabilitation Act to assist vocationally disabled civilians and disabled veterans returning from World War I by providing funds through a federal-state matching formula. The federal and state governments shared program costs on a fifty-fifty basis. The appeal of vocational rehabilitation is that it is less costly to rehabilitate people to work than to provide them with public assistance payments.

Today the federal government provides the majority of funding for the Vocational Rehabilitation (VR) program. Each state operates its own program according to federal guidelines and also supplements federal funding of the program. An individual who applies for VR services is evaluated by a doctor and/or other experts to determine whether a disability exists. Only those who have a reasonable chance of becoming employed or reemployed qualify for services. For women at home, the criteria is that they have the potential to perform independent living skills.[22] Each person who qualifies for assistance is assigned a VR counselor who develops an individualized plan for the disabled client; the plan may include medical services, training, guidance, and placement services.

The concept of the individualized rehabilitation plan sounds like a rational way to optimize services to the disabled. However, in actuality, some clients may not receive all the services they need. For example, the emphasis of the vocational rehabilitation program changes from time to time. Some of the target populations have been the mentally ill, the mentally retarded, the culturally disadvantaged, and the severely handicapped.[23]

When available funds cannot be stretched to meet the needs of all eligible participants, clients' needs must be prioritized. In addition, because each state administers its own program, persons with the same or similar disabilities may receive different types and amounts of services depending on the state in which they live.

About one million persons are referred to state Vocational Rehabilitation programs each year.[24] Of those referred for services, about half actually become clients of Vocational Rehabilitation programs. Federal and state governments spend about one billion dollars for the program each year, and approximately 65 percent of all clients are rehabilitated. The most common disabling conditions of recipients are mental illness, orthopedic impairment, and mental retardation. Clients who are rehabilitated are likely to assume semiskilled and unskilled jobs, service jobs, clerical jobs, and sales jobs. A number of clients also assume professional, technical, and managerial positions. Others are able to function as homemakers.

Creaming

In its early days critics charged the Vocational Rehabilitation program with a practice called *creaming*. Creaming means accepting into the program those candidates who are most likely to become rehabilitated. While the goal of the program is rehabilitation, it is easier for some disabled persons to be rehabilitated than others. Most of the program's early clients were young white males whose disabilities were neither chronic nor severe.[25]

Many capable, handicapped persons face a variety of barriers in everyday life. These barriers prevent us from developing a rational approach to assisting persons with handicaps. In the following examples, we see how prejudice, fear, ignorance, and administrative policies can limit full participation for the 36 million handicapped in the United States.

First grader Chris Powers was the only youngster left behind when his class went to the zoo. He was the only one asked to step aside when the class picture was taken. He was also the only pupil forbidden to eat with his classmates in the school cafeteria. In each instance, the principal felt that the emotional outbursts Chris is subject to would upset other children. Chris is an autistic child.

When George C. Jackson, a psychologist and professor at Howard University in Washington, D.C., was recuperating from surgery, the hospital staff insisted that he stay in his room rather than walk down the hall to visit with other patients in the solarium. The operation had nothing to do with the restriction. Dr. Jackson is blind. "They thought I might fall over something in the hallway," he recalls, "but they never offered to guide me through that hallway obstacle course a time or two."

Thomas Maske, disabled as a teenager by polio, knows most of the world's airline routes by heart, as his job with an agricultural supply firm in Wheeling, Illinois, requires almost constant foreign travel. Nonetheless, some airlines, citing safety factors, have refused to accept Mr. Maske as a passenger unless he flies with a companion. Other airlines have stored—and sometimes damaged—his wheelchair in aircraft luggage compartments after refusing his request to store it in the passenger cabin. Mr. Maske has threatened to go to court on both counts. He now flies alone and carries a special Federal Aviation Administration permit for passenger cabin storage of his wheelchair.

Barbara A. Hoffman, a clinical psychologist with a successful private practice in Houston, Texas, works primarily with brain-damaged children but is seldom invited to share her expertise with other psychologists at professional meetings. She has cerebral palsy. Conference planners assume, falsely, that she also has a speech impairment, a condition often associated with the disease. "I have learned not to waste my time showing my genuine interest in community projects," Dr. Hoffman says, "because the doors are closed to handicapped persons."

John Lancaster, a 1967 Notre Dame graduate, went to Viet Nam as a Marine Corps second lieutenant. Wounded in action, he came home paralyzed from the waist down. Despite his disability, he returned to college and earned a law degree. Looking back, he says that was the easy part. Finding a job was harder.

"I looked pretty good on paper," Mr. Lancaster says, "but when I showed up for an interview in a wheelchair, that was usually the end of it. I applied to more than 40 companies and government agencies before I finally landed a job."

Today Mr. Lancaster is director of Barrier-Free Design for Paralyzed Veterans of America.

Source: "It's a New Day for Disabled People," HEW Task Force on Public Awareness and the Disabled, *American Education,* December 1977, unpaginated.

In 1938 the federal [vocational rehabilitation] office captured the policy that lay behind the selection of the vocational rehabilitation case load when it told the states that eligibility does not necessarily imply feasibility. Anyone over 18 was technically eligible for rehabilitation, but such factors as advanced age, extreme disability, bad attitude of mind, or low social status limited feasibility.[26]

Although this attitude has changed since the early days of the program, the fact remains that VR is not an entitlement program. Funds are limited. Not everyone who needs assistance can be served, and for those who are served, counselors may not be able to procure all the funds and services the client needs.

Deinstitutionalizing

One of the first responses of modern society to the severely physically and emotionally handicapped was "indoor" relief—the "warehousing" of these persons in large institutions. Over the years, conditions in institutions became more humane, but until recently these large facilities were the primary means of assisting those considered too severely handicapped to remain at home and in the community. The advancement of educational techniques, physical therapies, and medical technologies has also made it possible for these persons to live more independently. But, while it seems logical from both humanistic and cost savings perspectives, the deinstitutionalization of the handicapped has met with serious problems.

Consider these ten *barriers* which handicapped people face in the community:

The existence of large residential facilities which provide minimal care at low cost without emphasis on rehabilitation.

Lack of access to buildings; other architectural barriers.

Lack of public transportation facilities.

Negative attitudes among professional persons who do not believe that handicapped persons can function at a normal level.

Negative attitudes of the general public.

Community rejection of people with problems.

Negative attitudes of professional people toward an establishment they believe is unconcerned.

Negative attitudes by employers.

The professionals and the public do not always understand each other's language making it difficult to arrive at solutions.

Lack of manpower and resources to change the community.[27]

Many of these barriers are attitudinal. Social welfare policies can help to change the behavior of the public toward handicapped persons, but attitudes are much more difficult to change.

Children with Handicaps

There are nearly ten million children in the United States under age twenty-two who need special services because of one or more physical or mental handicaps. Over $7 billion is spent annually on a myriad of programs to assist these children.[28] One study revealed five major problems in providing services to handicapped children.

1. *Inequity:* Handicapped children are treated differently from state to state. In some states, children are provided more services and more adequate services than in other states.
2. *Gaps in Services:* In some cities and states, certain types of services are not available to children. Eligibility requirements vary from location to location. Prevention services are the most seriously lacking type of service. Responsibility for providing a service may rest with more than one agency.
3. *Insufficient Information:* There is a lack of information concerning the number of children in need. There is also a lack of information on the effectiveness of services provided to children.
4. *Inadequate Control:* There is no comprehensive national social service policy or service delivery system for handicapped children. Parents and children must often search for the right services.
5. *Insufficient Resources:* Under current expenditure levels, some children are not served or they are underserved.[29]

Handicapped adults and children face barriers that result from one of the most troublesome features of the social welfare system—welfare in the United States is really not a system composed of an organized, coordinated set of interrelated policies and programs. The lack of a true welfare system makes rational planning difficult.

Mainstreaming

Another struggle faced by handicapped and disabled children and their families is called *mainstreaming*. Through mainstreaming handicapped and disabled children are placed and taught in regular public school programs whenever possible rather than in separate schools or in separate classrooms. A result of the Education for All Handicapped Children Act of 1975, mainstreaming, like all the social policies and programs we have discussed, is not without its conflicts.

Some people hail mainstreaming as a sensible and effective way to insure that physically and mentally handicapped children are afforded the opportunity to learn and to interact with other children. In this way they are not made to feel more different than need be and "normal" children learn much about the similarities they share with these "special" children.

Children who are mainstreamed may attend some special classes, and their teachers in regular classrooms are assisted in developing educational programs to meet the needs of their handicapped pupils.

However, there are some concerns about mainstreaming. First, there is the possibility that appropriate educational plans will not be made for these students and that they will be left in regular classrooms without special assistance because of lack of time and resources. Others believe that the regular classroom teacher is already overburdened. Teachers who want to be helpful may have large classes and heavy workloads which prevent individualized instruction.

A Bill of Rights for the Handicapped

Strides have been made in better integrating handicapped and disabled persons into society. In many cases these strides have been made through the persistent political efforts of the handicapped and their families. Title V of the Rehabilitation Act of 1973 is an example of these accomplishments. All programs and facilities, such as schools and hospitals, receiving federal funds must comply with these rules:

1. Federal agencies must have affirmative action programs to hire and promote qualified handicapped persons.
2. The Architectural and Transportation Barriers Compliance Board is charged with enforcing a 1968 law requiring that all buildings constructed in whole or in part with federal funds—as well as buildings owned or leased by federal agencies—have ramps, elevators, or other barrier-free access for persons who are blind, deaf, in wheelchairs, or otherwise disabled.
3. All business firms, universities, foundations, and other institutions holding contracts with the U.S. government must have affirmative action programs to hire and promote qualified handicapped persons.
4. Discrimination against qualified disabled persons—employees, students, and receivers of health care and other services—in all public and private institutions receiving federal assistance is prohibited.[30]

But, although restaurants, stores, and other establishments may choose to provide easy access for the handicapped, this so-called "Bill of Rights for the Handicapped" does little to encourage private sector participation. Suitable living environments are also difficult to find. For the wheelchair-bound, many apartment complexes and housing developments are not equipped with extrawide doorways or appliances that can be easily reached. Even if the individual can afford to make such changes in an apartment, permission must be granted by the owner. Many of the points contained in this bill of rights are still goals to be achieved. Negative attitudes and prejudices, while sometimes blatant, are often subtle and difficult to overcome.[31] The rewards of providing for the integration of handicapped persons may not be apparent; and so, people do not bother.

Access for the Handicapped

In the last few years almost everyone in the United States has become familiar with the blue and white symbol of the person in the wheelchair shown in Figure 5–2. In a parking lot it means that certain parking spots are reserved for handicapped drivers. On a building door it means that handicapped persons can move about in the building independently. On a bathroom door it means that stalls are equipped with hand rails and raised toilets so that handicapped persons can use the facilities more easily.

Several steps have been taken to promote access for handicapped persons. In 1968 the Architectural Barriers Act adopted specifications aimed at making buildings accessible and safe for the blind, the deaf, the wheelchair bound, as well as those with other handicaps. Making buildings accessible for the handicapped sounds like an expensive proposition, but one writer argues that the cost to the builder is only "one-tenth of one percent of the total cost of a new building."[32] The results of the legislation are far from adequate. Most buildings fall short of meeting the standards for restrooms, parking lots, doors, and warning signals.

GENERAL ASSISTANCE: THE STATE AND COMMUNITY RESPONSE TO WELFARE

Most major social policies and programs today are totally or partially the responsibility of the federal government. But there are some social welfare programs which are developed, administered, and financed by state and local governments, independent of the federal government. The term used to describe state and local financial aid to the poor is *General Assistance.*

General Assistance programs are administered differently from state to state, and even from one locality to another. The types and amounts of services vary, as well as the types of recipients served. In some states, the state government is entirely responsible for administering General Assistance. The state determines the policies and procedures for General Assistance, and state workers accept applications and provide assistance to recipients. However, in other states, the state sets policy and determines eligibility requirements, but General Assistance is administered through local governments—usually cites or counties. In still other states, the state

FIGURE 5–2 International Symbol of Access for the Handicapped

government has no involvement in General Assistance. Local governments are free to establish General Assistance programs if they desire. If not, there may be no General Assistance available in a community.

Why is General Assistance needed when there are a number of federally mandated and funded programs designed to assist persons who are aged, blind, disabled, and dependent? General Assistance exists because the United States uses a fragmented approach to social welfare needs. *Some poor people do not meet the criteria for any of the major federal or federal-state welfare programs.* They may not be aged, or blind, or disabled, and they may have no dependent children. They may need immediate assistance and are unable to wait for federal benefits which may take thirty days or more to begin. In other words, to qualify for most welfare programs, simply being "needy" is not always enough.

While most Americans have heard of the AFDC, Food Stamp, and Medicaid programs, General Assistance is not as well-known. In some places it is referred to as "county aid" or "county welfare." Some programs provide cash assistance. Others rely on in-kind assistance. Some programs use a combination of the two. In some areas the bulk of aid is for medical costs.

General Assistance may provide help to persons who receive public assistance payments from federal or federal-state welfare programs because their payments are low and may be inadequate to cover an emergency. But in about half of the states, SSI and AFDC recipients are not eligible for General Assistance. Others receive General Assistance because of advanced age, disability, unemployment, or as a supplement to very low wages.[33] Those who receive General Assistance are usually in dire circumstances. In communities which provide General Assistance, aid is often available on a short-term basis only.

The former Department of Health, Education and Welfare, now called the Department of Health and Human Services, has compiled a state-by-state description of General Assistance programs. We reproduce two plans here to show the variety in programs.

TABLE 5–4   General Assistance Programs

YEAR	TOTAL EXPENDITURES IN MILLIONS OF DOLLARS	AVERAGE MONTHLY PAYMENTS	BENEFICIARIES IN THOUSANDS
1940	1,433	41	1,239
1950	295	47	413
1960	322	72	431
1970	618	112	547
1980	1,445	162	796

Sources: U.S. Bureau of the Census, *Statistical Abstract of the United States, 1943,* p. 192; *1965,* p. 306; *1980,* pp. 304, 354, *1981,* p. 343.

ITEM	CHARACTERISTIC
	A. General Description
1. Type of program	General Assistance (General Relief) is administered by the 99 counties. Criteria of eligibility, amount of aid given, and duration of aid vary among the counties and may not be consistent within a county. In about one-fourth of the counties the responsibility is given to an "Overseer of the Poor."
2. Most common uses	Generally provided on a short-term basis. Need pending categorical public assistance,* emergency needs for food, shelter, utility payments, medical and transportation, and, in many counties, to meet need for prescription drugs.
	B. Conditions of Eligibility
3. Definition	Applicants are considered on an individual basis. Aid is not limited to unemployables; however, employable persons are urged or required to register for employment.
4. Residence	Must reside in county for one year to gain legal settlement. General Assistance usually provided without regard to settlement; however, the county may bill the county in which applicant has legal settlement. Migrants and transients are given emergency assistance or referred to other available resources.
5. Citizenship	No requirement.
6. Employment and employability	Most counties will assist a family with an employed or employable person when the employed person is temporarily disabled or there is some other emergency basis.
7. Property limitations	Some counties follow AFDC-SSI guidelines. Some are less restrictive where the need is a medical one.
8. Lien and limitations	County may recover amount expended (1) from legally responsible relatives, (2) from

---

*The General Assistance program may make emergency or short-term payments to an individual or family that is applying for AFDC or SSI but whose application is pending approval.

| | the person himself within two years after he becomes able to repay such amounts, or (3) from estate of the person by filing claim as provided in statute. |
| 9. Other | About half the counties have no other conditions. Others will not assist an SSI or AFDC recipient, but most will assist a person eligible for, but not receiving, AFDC or SSI. Some will provide assistance in an emergency to AFDC or SSI recipients. |

C. Standards of Assistance and Payment

10. Standards of assistance	Varies a great deal. Some counties use the AFDC-SSI standards as guidelines, but each county is free to vary the assistance given.
11. Limitations on payment	Usually given on a temporary basis; limitations on amount and duration vary among the counties.
12. Method of providing assistance	*Maintenance Items:* Usually a vendor payment. Some counties give cash assistance. *Medical care:* Vendor payments. Often hospital care at University of Iowa hospitals. General Assistance medical care is not covered under the State Medicaid program.

D. Administration

13. State agency	No state agency responsibility for general assistance.
14. Local agency	County Boards of Supervisors in one-fourth of the counties place the responsibility with an "Overseer of the Poor." In three-fourths of the counties, the responsibility is delegated to the local office of the Department of Social Services.
15. Financing	General Assistance is paid out of county funds in the same manner as other county disbursements.

CHARACTERISTICS OF GENERAL ASSISTANCE—ARIZONA

ITEM	CHARACTERISTIC

A. General Description

| 1. Type of program | General Assistance is administered by the Arizona Department of Economic Security throughout the six districts; in effect uniformly in all districts but not on Indian reservations. Two programs (1) General |

Assistance and (2) "Emergency Relief." (Characteristics of these two programs in subsequent entries are identified by these numbers.) The same agencies administer the federal-state public assistance programs.

2. Most common uses

(1) Response to any kind of need of an eligible individual. (2) Emergency situations pending receipt of categorical assistance,* short-term assistance to meet temporary need, transportation of nonresidents to place of legal residence, purchase of food stamps on emergency basis.

B. Conditions of Eligibility

3. Definition

(1) General Assistance covers "either permanently or temporarily disabled, totally or partially"; couples, and nonfamily individuals. (2) "Emergency Relief" covers dire emergency needs for employable persons or families.

4. Residence

(1) If a person is present in the state and intends to remain, he or she is a resident. (2) *Nonresidents:* may be aided in emergency situations only, pending return to place of legal residence. *Transients or migratory labor:* aided only in emergency situations.

5. Citizenship

(1) must be a citizen of United States, a resident in United States for 15 years, or a legally admitted alien. (2) Not applicable to emergency situations.

6. Employment and employability

No requirements.

7. Property limitations

(1) Limitations on property holdings generally the same as for AFDC.

8. Lien and recovery

No lien provision. Recovery made only when there is fraud or ineligibility.

9. Other

None.

C. Standards of Assistance and Payments

10. Standards of assistance

Same as for AFDC

11. Limitations on payment

(1) The assistance grant will be equal to the standard budgetary need amount multi-

---

*General Assistance is provided to persons who have applied for AFDC or SSI and are waiting for payments to begin.

	plied by the percentage of need factor for which funds are available (80%), less income.
	(2) The payment is limited to $100 for one adult plus $25 for each additional individual. No emergency assistance for more than three months in any twelve-month period may be issued.
12. Method of providing assistance	*Maintenance items:* (1) Monetary payment to recipient, by warrant each month. (2) Monetary payment to meet "emergency needs ... within the limits specified above." *Medical care:* None
	D. Administration
13. State agency	Arizona Department of Economic Security through its local county offices has administrative responsibility.
14. Local agency	District offices of the Department of Economic Security (6). Does not cover persons living on Indian reservations.

Source: *Characteristics of General Assistance in the United States,* 1978 edition, Department of HEW, Social Security Administration, Office of Family Assistance, HEW Publication No. (SSA) 78-21239.

When Congress passed the Social Security Act in 1935, General Assistance expenditures decreased sharply from almost $1.5 million in 1935 to about $450,000 in 1936. Since then the amount states and communities have spent for General Assistance has fluctuated, but more recently there has been considerable growth in expenditures for General Assistance. Today expenditures are nearly $1.5 billion (see Table 5–4). In 1950 the average monthly payment per recipient was $47. In 1970 it was $112 per recipient. Today, the nearly 800,000 beneficiaries receive an average of $162 a month.

POLITICS, WELFARE, AND AMERICAN FEDERALISM

American federalism—the constitutional division of power between the national government and the states—affects the administration and financing of social welfare programs. The major public assistance programs in the United States (AFDC, SSI, Medicaid, Food Stamps, and General Assistance) are administered and funded in several different ways. AFDC and Medicaid are joint ventures of the federal government and the states which share in funding the programs, but the states play the primary role in determining eligibility requirements and payment levels. The Food Stamp and SSI programs are to a great extent controlled by the federal government. The federal government pays for minimum benefits and establishes basic eligibility requirements. The states may supplement basic SSI payment levels, and many do. SSI checks are mailed directly to recipients through the Social Security Administration in Washington. Food Stamps are generally distributed through state and local welfare offices. General Assistance is the only major public assistance program which is funded and administered solely by state and/or local governments with no federal participation. Most social service programs are joint federal and state responsibilities.

Is there a best structure for administering and funding welfare programs? In recent years the trend has been toward "federalizing" or centralizing welfare programs. The most notable example of the federalizing of welfare programs has been the establishment of the SSI program to replace the OAA, AB, and APTD programs in 1972. Federalizing welfare programs gives the advantage of reducing disparity from state to state or locality to locality in payments made to beneficiaries. Federal programs set minimum floors for payments and make eligibility criteria uniform. Proponents of greater centralization of welfare programs believe that reducing disparities in both eligibility requirements and payments to beneficiaries is especially useful in assisting people from the poorer states that are unable to make adequate payments. States that desire to pay greater benefits to recipients are always free to supplement the federal government's minimum payments. Centralization also results in a more comprehensive and uniform approach to policy-making in the United States, which may be better than fifty states or many local governments operating under different policies and programs.

The federalization of welfare programs is not a universally accepted method of providing welfare benefits in the United States. The SSI and Food Stamp programs are more uniformly administered than the AFDC, Medicaid, and General Assistance programs, but at present there is little likelihood that all programs will be uniformly administered since proposals for a guaranteed annual income for all Americans or poor Americans have failed to gain approval.

President Reagan believes that a *block grant* system of providing many welfare services is more useful than federalizing welfare programs. Under block grant proposals, the federal government would allocate sums of money to each state for broad purposes such as health, mental health, and other categories of social welfare services. Each state would then determine which specific types of services to provide under each of the broad program categories. The president and other proponents of block grants believe that states and communities know the needs of their citizens better than the federal government. Block grant proposals are based on the assumption that social welfare needs vary from locality to locality. Proponents advocate greater state and local participation in determining and meeting social welfare needs. They believe states can also get assistance more quickly and directly to beneficiaries.

Opponents fear that the use of block grants will multiply the political conflicts over social welfare, since each state will have to make many individual determinations about which programs to fund. Opponents also believe that national coordination in providing social welfare services to recipients will be lost if the block grant method is used to fund social welfare programs.

What is the best alternative for getting aid to recipients? Should all welfare programs be federalized? Should some, like cash assistance programs, be federalized, while other social services like foster care for children, adoption, and adult protective services, be the responsibility of state governments? Is equalizing payments and making eligibility requirements uniform more important than allowing states to determine what programs best meet their own needs? Can a rational approach to social welfare policy and planning assist us in making these choices, or will the types of social service programs and the methods of administering them be left to the political process? The constraints on a rational approach to social welfare policy have led to a multitude of different programs administered in a variety of ways.

SUMMARY

Two major types of assistance are available to the aged, blind, and disabled: public assistance and rehabilitative services. The major cash assistance program for these groups is the Supplemental Security Income (SSI) program. In 1972 Congress passed legislation that federalized the adult categorical assistance programs—Old Age Assistance, Aid to the Blind, and Aid to the Permanently and Totally Disabled under the SSI program. SSI has been one of the major innovations in providing welfare benefits to Americans since the original Social Security Act became law in 1935. Under SSI states no longer administer the adult categorical programs. The federal government now sets minimum payment levels and eligibility requirements for beneficiaries. These changes helped to reduce inequitable treatment of recipients from state to state. SSI was the only portion of President Nixon's welfare reform package that Congress passed.

One of the largest social service programs for the disabled is the Vocational Rehabilitation (VR) program. VR is a limited program because not everyone who is disabled is entitled to assistance. The primary criterion for participation is the individual's potential for returning to work. In the case of a homemaker, there must be potential to return to caring for the home. The VR program has been accused of creaming—taking on the clients who are most easy to rehabilitate while the more severely disabled may have to do without services.

Individuals with physical and mental handicaps face a number of obstacles in achieving independence. Some of the more severely handicapped are housed in large institutions with little chance for realizing their maximum potential. In other cases community rejection, lack of transportation, and lack of access to buildings and other facilities prevent the disabled from interacting in society. Laws designed to eliminate structural and architectural barriers from buildings have been unsuccessful in removing many obstacles faced by the handicapped.

Handicapped children face as many problems as handicapped adults. Mainstreaming, an attempt to include handicapped children in as many regular school activities as possible, has met with resistance. Opponents believe that mainstreaming sounds like a good idea, but in practice handicapped children may not receive the attention they deserve. Proponents of mainstreaming believe that children are more likely to achieve their maximum potential if they are not made to feel different from other children by being isolated all day in special classrooms.

Title V of the Vocational Rehabilitation Act of 1973 prevents programs and agencies that receive federal funds from discriminating against the handicapped in terms of access, employment, and education. It is referred to as a "bill of rights for the handicapped."

Another program which helps the poor, aged, disabled, dependent children, and the unemployed is called General Assistance. General Assistance programs are solely funded and administered by state and local governments. There is no federal involvement in these programs. Administration of General Assistance varies from state to state and from community to community. Eligibility criteria and payment levels also differ considerably. In some cases, General Assistance is used as unemployment relief and as a means for assisting those who do not qualify for other welfare programs. In many cases it is used to help the indigent with medical expenses. Aid may be limited to emergency situations and is usually short-term. Some communities have no General Assistance program at all.

It can be argued that all welfare programs should be federalized so that poor persons are guaranteed a minimum standard of living and level of social services regardless of where they live. Federalizing all welfare programs would help to eliminate inequitable treatment of the poor. Proposals to do this have run up against opposition from those who believe that minimum payments would still fall short of what poor Americans need to live adequately, from those who believe that federalizing all welfare programs would be too costly, and from those who believe that decisions about social welfare are best left to state and local governments.

NOTES

1. Garry D. Brewer and James S. Kakalik, *Handicapped Children: Strategies for Improving Services* (New York: McGraw-Hill, 1979) for a discussion of available sources.
2. John G. Turnbull, C. Arthur Williams, Jr., and Earl F. Cheit, *Economic and Social Security* (New York: Ronald Press, 1967), p. 83.
3. Ibid.
4. Robert J. Myers, *Social Security* (Bryn Mawr, Pa.: McCahan Foundation, 1975), p. 400.
5. Ibid.
6. Ibid., pp. 400–401.
7. Ibid., p. 401
8. Ibid.
9. U.S., Department of Commerce, *Statistical Abstract of the United States, 1965* (Washington, D.C.: Bureau of the Census, 1965), p. 309.
10. Daniel P. Moynihan, *The Politics of a Guaranteed Income* (New York: Random House, 1973).
11. *Future of Social Programs* (Washington, D.C.: Congressional Quarterly, 1973), p. 15.
12. Charles A. Schottland, *The Social Security Program in the United States* (New York: Appleton-Century-Crofts, 1963), pp. 104–105.
13. John A. Menefee, Bea Edwards, and Sylvester A. Schieber, "Analysis of Nonparticipation in the SSI Program," *Social Security Bulletin* 44, no. 6 (June 1981): 3–21.
14. Paul A. Brinker, *Economic Insecurity and Society Security*(New York: Appleton-Century-Crofts, 1968), p. 103.
15. Schottland, *Social Security Program*, p. 111.
16. This list was taken from Jane Mullins and Suzanne Wolfe, *Special People Behind the Eight-Ball: An Annotated Bibliography of Literature Classified by Handicapping Conditions* (Johnstown, Pa.: Mafex Associates, 1975).
17. Saad Z. Nagi, "The Concept and Measurement of Disability" in Edward D. Berkowitz, ed., *Disability Policies and Government Programs* (New York: Holt Rinehart & Winston, 1979), p. 2, and Shirley Cohen, *Special People: A Brighter Future for Everyone with Physical, Mental, and Emotional Disabilities* (Englewood Cliffs, N.J.: Prentice-Hall, 1977), p. 8.
18. Monroe Berkowitz, William G. Johnson, and Edward H. Murphy, *Public Policy Toward Disability* (New York: Holt, Rinehart & Winston, 1976), p. 7.
19. Nagi, *Concept and Measurement of Disability*, p. 3.
20. "It's a New Day for Disabled People," HEW Task Force on Public Awareness and the Disabled, taken from *American Education* (December 1977).
21. Edward D. Berkowitz, "The American Disability System in Historical Perspective" in Berkowitz, ed., *Disability Policies and Government Programs*, p. 43.
22. Berkowitz, Johnson, and Murphy, *Public Policy Toward Disability*, p. 34.
23. Ibid.
24. Information in this paragraph comes from *Statistical Abstract of the United States, 1979*, p. 346.
25. Berkowitz, *Disability Policies and Government Programs*, p. 45.
26. Ibid. Cites FBVE, "Administration of the Vocational Rehabilitation Program," Bulletin 113, revised under imprint of the U. S. Department of Interior, Office of Education (Washington, D.C.: Government Printing Office, 1938).
27. Roberta Nelson, *Creating Community Acceptance for Handicapped People* (Springfield, Ill.: Charles C Thomas, 1978), pp. 12–22.
28. Brewer and Kakalik, *Handicapped Children*, pp. 3, 5.
29. Ibid., pp. 15–19.
30. "It's A New Day for Disabled People."
31. Ibid.
32. Cohen, *Special People*, p. 132.
33. For a discussion of the uses of General Assistance, see Duncan M. MacIntyre, *Public Assistance: Too Much or Too Little?* (Ithaca, N.Y.: New York State School of Industrial and Labor Relations, Cornell University, 1964), p. 51.

6

Assisting Poor Families: Aid to Families with Dependent Children

Aid to Families with Dependent Children (AFDC) is one of the most controversial of the public assistance programs. The purpose of AFDC is to provide cash assistance to poor families so that children can continue to be cared for in their own homes. If there is any segment of society for whom people have compassion, it is for children who are completely dependent on others to meet their needs. Why, then, has the AFDC program been a political tug of war? The struggle has little to do with the millions of dependent children served by the program. As we will see, political controversy has focused on the *adult* beneficiaries of the program.

THE DEVELOPMENT OF AFDC

Mother's Aid

A dependent child, in terms of public assistance programs, is one whose parents or guardians lack the financial assistance to provide for the child's care. The states began formalizing laws to assist such children in the early twentieth century, with local governments often providing the financing. These laws were established to assist children whose fathers were deceased; sometimes assistance was also provided to children whose fathers were disabled or absent through divorce or desertion. These early programs were called *mother's aid* or *mother's pensions.*

ADC

The federal government stepped in to share responsibility for dependent children in 1935 when the Aid to Dependent Children (ADC) program was included as part of the original Social Security Act. At first the ADC program was conceived of as a short-term device to assist financially needy children. It was intended that the program would diminish and eventually become *outmoded* as more and more families came to qualify for assistance under insurance programs of the Social Security Act.[1] "The program began," as Daniel P. Moynihan puts it, "as one whose typical beneficiary was a West Virginia mother whose husband had been killed in a mine accident."[2] But the emphasis of the early ADC program was not on providing aid for the wives of deceased workers; it was on providing assistance to mothers on behalf of their *children.*

Keeping the Family Together

From 1935 until 1950 the ADC program grew slowly. There were some changes made in the program, but they did not arouse much public notice. The needs of the adults in ADC families were eventually considered when in 1950 adult heads of families were also made eligible for ADC assistance. Other improvements were made in the program. Medical services, paid in part by the federal government, were made available to recipients. In 1958 a formula was developed so that states with lower per capita incomes received more financial assistance for their ADC programs than wealthier states.

But other parts of the program were becoming sore spots. One of the most stinging accusations leveled against the ADC program was that it contributed to the desertion of fathers from families. While the argument has been difficult to prove empirically,[3] we can see how the concern arose. Under the ADC program, families in which an able-bodied father was residing were not eligible for benefits. In many cases unemployed fathers qualified for other types of assistance—unemployment compensation, disability insurance, or Aid to the Permanently and Totally Disabled. But it was also possible that the father did *not* qualify for any of these programs or had exhausted his benefits. In other words, some fathers fell through the cracks. The unemployed, able-bodied father who could not find work did not qualify for ADC and could not support his family. However, if the father deserted the home, the family became eligible for ADC assistance. It is not known how many fathers did this. Fathers (or mothers) may be absent for many reasons. They may be in institutions, or separated from their spouses because of incompatibility or other reasons. But regardless of the reason for absenteeism, when a father was at home and unemployed, the family could not receive ADC.

As a result, two changes were made in the ADC program. In 1961 a new program component called the ADC-Unemployed Parent (UP) program was enacted. This made it possible for a child to receive aid because of his or her parent's unemployment. In 1962 the name of the program was changed to Aid to Families with Dependent Children (AFDC) to emphasize the *family* unit. A second adult was considered eligible for aid in states with AFDC-UP programs and also in cases where one of the child's parents was incapacitated.

In 1967 the AFDC-UP program was changed to the AFDC-Unemployed Father (UF) program, but in 1979 the Supreme Court ruled that it was unconstitutional to provide benefits to unemployed fathers but not to unemployed mothers. The name of the program was changed back to the AFDC-UP program.

Since the AFDC-UP and UF programs were never made mandatory, states have been free to accept or reject them. Even today, only about half of the states have an AFDC-UP program. Eligibility requirements are very strict, and the number of fathers who receive aid remains very small.

A recent review of studies of state AFDC-UP programs did not show that these programs were associated with increased marital stability. In fact, evidence pointed in the opposite direction.[4] However, studies of AFDC payments show that "while there is some support for high AFDC payment levels being a marriage destabilizer, there is very little support for its being a powerful destabilizer."[5] The relationship of the AFDC program to family stability remains a troublesome issue.

Man in the House Rules

The number of able-bodied fathers who might receive welfare assistance is one area of public concern over the morality of welfare recipients. The work ethic is firmly entrenched in American culture. According to this ethic, no one who is capable of self-support should be entitled to public benefits.

This concern about the morality of welfare recipients was reflected in "man in the house rules." It was clear that only in extreme circumstances, and only in certain states, could able-bodied fathers be present while the family collected AFDC benefits. And before 1962 no able-bodied father could be present. These rules about fathers also carried over into welfare mothers' relationships with other men. The thought of welfare mothers allowing able-bodied men to reside with them presented a threat to those who wanted to insure that ADC payments went to the "right" people. The

AFDC check was intended for the *children* and *mother,* and, in some cases, the children's *father.* It was considered immoral and *illegal* for the mother to allow anyone else to benefit from the welfare check. "Midnight raids" — home visits to welfare mothers late at night—were sometimes conducted to insure that no able-bodied males resided in AFDC households. An able-bodied adult male who resided with the family was considered responsible for its financial support. Today, midnight raids are considered unethical by most professional standards.

Making Parents Pay

In 1968 the Supreme Court determined that man in the house rules could not be used as a method for "flatly denying" children public assistance. The emphasis today has shifted to methods of making children's *legal* fathers and mothers support their dependents. In 1974 federal law was amended for the purpose of enforcing child support obligations owed by absent parents to their chilren by locating absent parents, establishing paternity, and obtaining child support. Concerns regarding these measures arose because of the rising number of children dependent on AFDC who are born to parents not legally married. The Office of Child Support Enforcement in the Department of Health and Human Services is responsible for this program.[6] Enforcing child support obligations is a difficult task. Few absent parents of children receiving AFDC contribute to their children's support. Despite any moral obligation parents have to support their young children, child support enforcement programs may cost more than they collect from parents.

WHO RECEIVES AFDC?

There are many misconceptions about the beneficiaries of AFDC. Here are some facts about AFDC families.[7]

1. Almost 79 percent of all AFDC families are headed by one parent, usually the mother. Only about 7 percent are headed by two parents. The remaining 14 percent of child recipients do not live with either parent but live with guardians or foster parents.
2. Contrary to common belief, AFDC families are usually small, and the trend is toward even smaller families. The average AFDC family has 2 children. Almost 68 percent of all AFDC families have one or two children, while only 8 percent have five or more children.
3. The children in most AFDC families have fathers who do not live with the family and provide limited financial support, if any. Almost 34 percent of AFDC children have parents who are not married to each other.
4. Most (93 percent) AFDC children live with their mothers. Only 13 percent live with their fathers. Few AFDC children live with both parents. In many cases (41 percent) the father cannot be located, but only 2 percent of the mothers cannot be located.

5. Fourteen percent of all AFDC mothers are working full or part time. The primary reason that AFDC mothers are not working is that they remain at home to care for their small children. Many fathers (39 percent) receiving AFDC are unable to work because of mental or physical disability.

6. Most AFDC parents who have worked or are working are employed in blue collar and service jobs, rather than in professional jobs.

7. Young families are more likely to receive AFDC than older families. Most mothers (51 percent) are under age thirty and 8 percent are teenagers. Fathers tend to be older.

8. Thirty-five percent of AFDC children are five years of age or younger. This fact accounts for the large number of AFDC mothers who remain at home in order to care for their children.

9. Most AFDC families live in rented housing. Fifteen percent of all families rent public housing and 64 percent rent private housing. Only 10 percent own or are buying their own homes.

10. AFDC families move often. Forty-five percent have lived at their current address one year or less and 2 percent for two to five years. Only 12 percent have been at the same address six years or more.

11. Not all AFDC families receive food stamps, even though they are automatically eligible to participate in the Food Stamp program. Seventy-four percent of the recipients receive food stamps.

12. AFDC families are more likely to live in urban rather than rural areas. Fifty-six percent of all families live in central cities.

13. Similar numbers of black and white families receive AFDC. Whites comprise 41 percent of all recipients; blacks comprise 43 percent. An additional 12 percent are Hispanic. One percent are Native Americans.

In addition, it is important to note that the majority of these families are not on AFDC caseloads year after year. Receiving AFDC tends to be a short-term phenomenon. The Department of Health and Human Services reports that 25 percent of cases are closed within a six-month period and almost one-third within the first year. Half are closed within two years and three-fifths within three years.[8]

AFDC AND WORK

Historically, Americans have been unwilling to provide money and services to those who are able to work. This feeling is evident in the AFDC program. There have been two major approaches to encouraging adult AFDC recipients to work: (1) rehabilitating the poor for work, and (2) job training and assistance in securing jobs.

Rehabilitation for Work

In 1962 social service amendments were added to the AFDC and other public assistance programs as a means of "rehabilitating" the poor. The rehabilitation approach was designed to reduce poverty by treating

personal and social problems which stood in the way of financial independence.[9] Services included counseling, vocational training, child management training, family planning services, and legal services. States found a
bonus in providing social services to clients. Offering social services meant
that states received additional federal funds. For every dollar spent by the
states, the federal government matched it with three dollars. States were
criticized for claiming federal funds for many of the services they were
already providing to clients.[10] To insure the success of the social service
amendments, worker caseloads were to be small—no more than sixty
clients—but it was difficult to find enough qualified social workers to
provide services.[11] What had sounded good in theory could often not be put
into practice.

Job Training and WIN

By 1967 enthusiasm for the rehabilitation approach to helping welfare
clients began to fade. The approach had not been a booming success;
welfare rolls continued to climb. A new approach was needed and the
chosen approach was tougher; the theme of the 1967 amendments was
work, and both "carrot" and "stick" measures were employed to achieve this
purpose.[12] The "stick" included work requirements for unemployed fathers
on AFDC, as well as for mothers and some teenagers. The "carrot" was the
Work Incentive Now (WIN) program, established by Congress to train
recipients for work and to help them locate employment. The federal
government threatened to deny federal matching funds to states that paid
benefits to those able-bodied recipients who refused to work or receive job
training.

Other measures were also taken to encourage recipients to work.
According to the "thirty plus one-third rule," welfare payments were not
reduced for the first $30 of earned income and one-third of all additional
income was disregarded in determining eligibility until the limit on
earnings was reached. Day care services were provided for WIN participants, but in some cases shortages of licensed day care facilities prohibited
placements for children while their mothers worked or trained for jobs.
And the cost of working—clothes, transportation, and child care—often
outweighed what the mothers earned.

Nonetheless, the AFDC rolls continued to climb. In other words,
strategies aimed at encouraging welfare recipients to work did not produce
the results that rational planners had intended. Perhaps the failure of these
approaches had much to do with the fact that AFDC recipients may not
have earned enough in marginal, low-income, or minimum wage jobs to
make work a rational alternative for them after deducting child care,
transportation, and other work-related expenses. Short-term training programs generally do not enable recipients to substantially increase their
earning capacities. Moreover, some recipients have disabilities or handicaps—mental, physical, or both—that do not allow them to work or to earn

enough to support themselves. Some welfare recipients are forced to survive on a combination of "a little work and a little welfare."

Separating Payments and Services

When social services were first introduced as a means of helping welfare recipients overcome obstacles to financial independence, the AFDC caseworker was responsible for seeing that the family got its benefit check and its social services. In fact, AFDC mothers may have feared that if they did not accept social services offered or urged by the caseworker, benefits might be terminated.

In 1967 Congress chose to separate the provision of social services to AFDC recipients from the issuance of benefit checks. A payments worker was responsible for matters related to the distribution of the welfare check, while another worker was responsible for obtaining social services for recipients. This approach was based on the recognition that not all poor families are necessarily in need of social services, since poverty may be attributable to a variety of causes. The 1967 amendment was also aimed at eliminating some AFDC families feelings that they must accept social services from the AFDC caseworker in order to receive their financial benefits. Families who wished to receive social services were still entitled and encouraged to do so.

GROWTH OF THE AFDC PROGRAM

The growth of welfare programs is generally observed in three measures: the number of program recipients, the total costs of the program, and the benefits received by each recipient. During the 1960s and 1970s, the number of AFDC families rose sharply. The total costs of the program also grew rapidly, even after controlling for inflation. But we cannot say the same about the payments to AFDC families; average payments have not kept pace with the cost of living.

Increase in Number of Recipients

ADC was originally designed as a short-term program to help dependent children whose deceased or disabled fathers were ineligible for Social Security insurance benefits. As more fathers became eligible for Social Security benefits, the need for the AFDC program was supposed to diminish. However, it did not turn out that way. Today AFDC is fast approaching its fiftieth birthday. During its fifty years the number of families receiving AFDC has grown dramatically (see Figure 6–1). For example, in the ten-year period between 1968 and 1978, the number of families receiving AFDC doubled. Consider the number of individuals

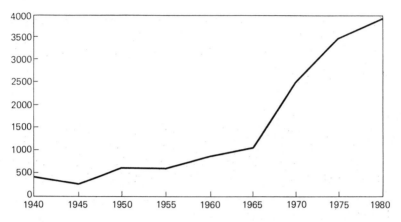

Figure 6-1 Aid to Families with Dependent Children program, number of recipient families in thousands, 1940-1980. (U.S. Department of Commerce, *Historical Statistics of the United States, Colonial Times to 1970*. Washington, D.C.: U.S. Bureau of the Census, 1975, p. 356; and *Statistical Abstract of the United States, 1977*, p. 345; *1981*, p. 343.)

receiving AFDC as a percentage of the total U.S. population. In 1950, the group amounted to 1.5 percent; by 1970, the porportion had reached 4.7 percent; but it has not exceeded 5.3 percent since that time. Today over 3.8 million families are supported in whole or in part through AFDC payments. The large number of families dependent on AFDC is directly related to the increase in the number of children who do not receive financial support from their fathers.

Increasing Costs

AFDC costs grew incrementally during the first thirty years of the program, but since the late 1960s program costs have escalated rapidly. In 1940 the total cost of the program was $133 million; by 1960 costs had risen to $750 million; and by 1980 the figure was nearly $12.5 billion. Even after controlling for inflation, the costs of the program have spiraled. Increases in costs, beginning in the 1960s, have been a consequence of the large numbers of new families who joined the rolls during that time. "The welfare rights movement," a period of increased awareness of the needs and demands of the poor, is closely related to this growth. Even if AFDC rolls remain relatively stable in the next few years, the costs of the program will remain high, unless tighter eligibility requirements or dramatic alternatives to the program are considered.

The Decrease in Average Monthly Payments

Rising costs in the AFDC program might lead us to believe that payments to AFDC families have also increased, but this is not actually the case. In 1963 the average AFDC family received $122; by 1978 this payment had more than doubled to $250. But, after controlling for inflation, we see that AFDC recipients in 1978 had no more purchasing power than they did in 1963. More people have access to the AFDC program today than ever before, but public assistance payments to AFDC families have not really changed much in the last twenty years.

VARIATIONS IN AFDC PROGRAMS

A great deal of diversity exists from state to state in AFDC programs. Notice that the range of payments is quite large (see Figure 6–2). New York has one of the highest AFDC payment levels—an average of $370 per month for a family. Mississippi is lowest at $84. In other words, a recipient family in New York is likely to receive almost four and one-half times more than a recipient family in Mississippi. Even taking into consideration differences in the cost of living between the two states, the difference in payments is still pronounced. Each state determines its payment levels in a seemingly rational manner. The costs of food, shelter, and other necessities are calculated depending on family size. The figure obtained is called the *standard of need,* but a number of states pay recipients less than the minimum standard of need, and the standard might stay the same for several years before adjustments are made. In addition, cost of living increases are not automatic in the AFDC program; state legislatures must vote to increase payments.

Eligibility requirements also differ considerably from state to state. To illustrate this point, we can compare the AFDC programs of Massachusetts and Mississippi.[13] Massachusetts can provide emergency assistance to eligible recipients under the AFDC program, while Mississippi does not offer this provision. In Massachusetts, children, if they are attending school, can receive AFDC until their twenty-first birthday; but, in Mississippi, a child is eligible only until age eighteen. In Massachusetts, poor pregnant women are eligible for assistance; but they are not eligible in Mississippi. Massachusetts has an AFDC-UP program, but Mississippi does not. Recipients in Massachusetts are able to own more property than are recipients in Mississippi; for example, a recipient family may own a home of any value in Massachusetts, but in Mississippi the family may not own a home assessed at more than $5,000. In both states a family may own an automobile; in Massachusetts the value is not specified, but in Mississippi the automobile may not be worth more than $1,500. Massachusetts allows the family to reserve money for college education for children; Mississippi does not permit this practice. Standards of assistance also vary. Mississippi is a much poorer state than Massachusetts, but poor people in Mississippi are forced to survive on much less because of their place of residence.

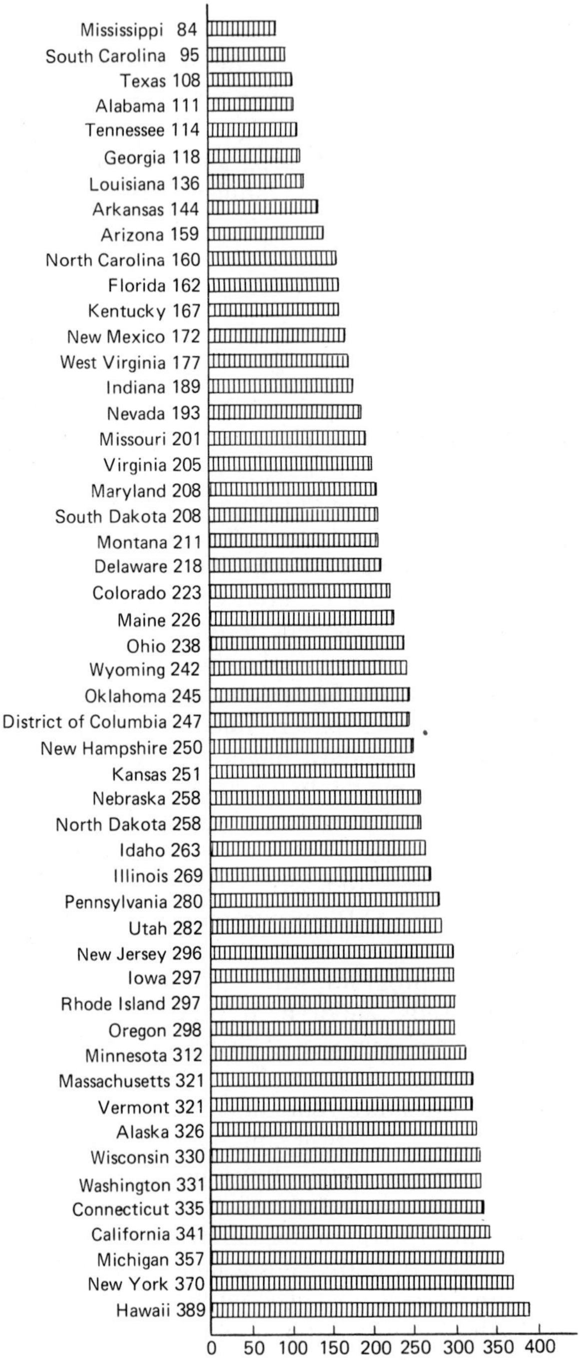

State	Value
Mississippi	84
South Carolina	95
Texas	108
Alabama	111
Tennessee	114
Georgia	118
Louisiana	136
Arkansas	144
Arizona	159
North Carolina	160
Florida	162
Kentucky	167
New Mexico	172
West Virginia	177
Indiana	189
Nevada	193
Missouri	201
Virginia	205
Maryland	208
South Dakota	208
Montana	211
Delaware	218
Colorado	223
Maine	226
Ohio	238
Wyoming	242
Oklahoma	245
District of Columbia	247
New Hampshire	250
Kansas	251
Nebraska	258
North Dakota	258
Idaho	263
Illinois	269
Pennsylvania	280
Utah	282
New Jersey	296
Iowa	297
Rhode Island	297
Oregon	298
Minnesota	312
Massachusetts	321
Vermont	321
Alaska	326
Wisconsin	330
Washington	331
Connecticut	335
California	341
Michigan	357
New York	370
Hawaii	389

0   50   100 150 200 250 300 350 400

Figure   6-2   Aid to Families with Dependent Children program, average monthly payment by state in dollars.   *(Statistical Abstract of the United States, 1980*, p. 356.)

110

Most Americans have never seen an AFDC application nor will they ever know what it is like to apply for public assistance. Application procedures and forms have been simplified over the years to make it easier to apply. In addition, because AFDC recipients are also eligible for Medicaid and food stamps, some states use a combined application form for the three programs. Florida's combined application form, a twelve-page application, is reproduced as an example of what it is like to apply for welfare.

Applying for welfare is a cumbersome and sometimes uncomfortable process. After providing basic information—name, social security number, and address—the applicant is informed of the rights of AFDC recipients. Applicants are assured that they will not be discriminated against because of race, color, sex, age, handicaps, religion, national origin, or political belief. They are also told that they will be informed of whether or not they are eligible for assistance within 30 days, and that they may request assistance in completing the application form.

There are also a number of responsibilities of AFDC recipients. Recipients must notify the public assistance office of any changes in income, employment, assets, family composition, and living arrangements. They must register for the Work Incentive Program unless exempt from work requirements. In addition, a controversial responsibility of applicants is that they cooperate in establishing paternity and obtaining child support unless there are reasons which do not make this feasible. Providing incomplete or false information on the application may be punishable by fine, imprisonment, or both.

Information must be provided about each child for whom aid is requested, including the reason why the child is considered to be "deprived." Detailed information must also be provided about where the family resides and the amount and type of its living expenses. An individual's assets are also carefully considered since there are limitations which vary from state to state on the amount of assets an individual can possess while remaining eligible for AFDC. Sources of income must also be specified as must information about the work of those 14 years of age or older for whom assistance is requested.

Applying for public assistance requires more than filling out an application form. It also requires evidence of expenses and income through rent and utility receipts, pay statements, and other documentation. The applicant must also agree to an investigation: The application states that the public assistance office has the right to "contact anyone necessary to determine the assistance group's eligibility for public assistance." A review of the application procedure makes it easier to see that applying for welfare can be a disconcerting process.

Applicants' expectations may also make a difference in the eligibility process. Qualified applicants may not be aware that it may be several weeks before payments begin. Applicants may be upset or angry when they are not able to receive on-the-spot payments or when they are deemed ineligible. Other factors also enter into the application process. The applicant may not come prepared with the proper documentation. The atmosphere of the waiting room and the treatment of applicants by the receptionist and the

AFDC eligibility worker are also important considerations in the conduct of eligibility interviews. AFDC applicants are generally under stressful conditions when they come in to apply. Eligibility workers also find their jobs stressful as evidenced by their high turn-over rates. Making the eligibility process better for both clients and workers is a challenge to those concerned about improving the welfare system.

WELFARE POLITICS:
"REGULATING" THE POOR

Social scientists Frances Fox Piven and Richard A. Cloward suggest that welfare programs may be used to "regulate the poor."[14] Many people believe that welfare policy has become increasingly generous since the 1930s. Piven and Cloward take exception to this thesis. They believe that welfare policies follow a cycle fluctuating from more liberal to more conservative depending on the political climate of the country. In times of political unrest, welfare policies are relaxed to include more beneficiaries in order to prevent rioting and other forms of civil disorder. In times of political stability, policies are developed that enforce work requirements and restrict eligibility to keep people off the "dole."

Consider the AFDC program. The original Aid to Dependent Children program was part of the New Deal legislation. The New Deal was a response to political unrest caused by the Great Depression of the 1930s, when unemployment and poverty were rampant. Americans in the thirties were increasingly unable to pay the rent or feed and clothe themselves. During the 1940s and 1950s, however, the country experienced a period of political stability in which work requirements for AFDC recipients were stressed. Monthly welfare payments were kept below the amount earned at the most menial jobs. Recipients were often not informed of all the benefits to which they were entitled. The value of applicants' possessions was often overestimated, resulting in lower payments or ineligibility. Such practices restricted the number of beneficiaries.

But during the 1960s the country was again threatened with civil unrest by minorities, especially blacks. They displayed their resentments toward a society which kept them in a subservient status. The result was the Great Society programs of the Kennedy and Johnson administrations. Eligibility requirements for welfare programs were relaxed, and many new programs were added, most notably the Food Stamp, Medicaid, and Medicare programs. This "welfare rights movement" brought about changes in the attitude of welfare recipients. They no longer meekly approached the welfare office. Welfare was no longer conceived of as a "favor." Recipients demanded what they considered to be rightfully theirs. Welfare administrators and payment workers treated welfare clients with

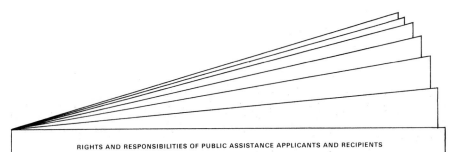

RIGHTS AND RESPONSIBILITIES OF PUBLIC ASSISTANCE APPLICANTS AND RECIPIENTS

A. I KNOW PUBLIC ASSISTANCE RECIPIENTS (APPLICANTS) HAVE THE RIGHT TO:

● Apply for public assistance and food stamps, and have a determination of eligibility made without discrimination because of race, color, sex, age, handicap, religion, national origin, or political belief.

● Have a decision made on eligibility within 30 days from the date of application.

● Receive the amount of benefits for which they are eligible, have action taken on application or change in benefits promptly, and be notified of such action.

● Receive Medicaid benefits for the persons who are determined to be eligible under the AFDC Program

● Have eligible members of the assistance group referred for family planning services at no cost.

● Be informed of other available services of the Department of Health and Rehabilitative Services.

● Accept the Department's standard allowance for work related expenses and verified work related child care costs or assume total responsibility for providing written documentation or staisfactory verification of actual work related expenses and/or work related child care costs.

● Be referred to the Work Incentive Program (WIN) which is designed to help people receiving AFDC become self supporting through employment.

● Get help from the Payments Worker in filling out eligibility forms or getting information needed to determine eligibility if the applicant/recipient is too disabled, ill, etc. to do so, and cannot find other help.

● Request a hearing before a State Hearings Officer when a claim for assistance is denied or is not acted upon with reasonable promptness, or when the recipient does not agree with the level of benefits. A hearing may be requested either orally or in writing. The case may be presented at the hearing by the recipient (applicant) or by any person chosen by the recipient (applicant), such as a relative, a friend, legal counsel or other spokesman.

B. THE DEPARTMENT OF HEALTH AND REHABILITATIVE SERVICES AND/OR DIVISION OF PUBLIC ASSISTANCE FRAUD HAVE THE RIGHT TO:

● File a seventh place claim against my estate after my death for the total amount of public assistance (not reimbursed) paid to me by the State of Florida after August 31, 1967.

● Contact anyone necessary to determine the assistance group's eligibility for public assistance.

● Use the Income Verification System to check on the amount of income.

C. I KNOW PUBLIC ASSISTANCE RECIPIENTS (APPLICANTS) HAVE THE RESPONSIBILITY TO:

● Provide the Department of Health and Rehabilitative Services with proof of any information needed to determine eligibility for assistance.

● Provide the Department with Social Security numbers of all persons in the assistance group. This is a condition of eligibility for AFDC and is required by section 402(a)(25) of the Social Security Act. The Department will use these Social Security numbers only in the administration of the assistance programs.

● Notify the Department of any changes in the assistance group's situation IMMEDIATELY, BUT NO LATER THAN TEN DAYS. Changes in income, employment status, assets (resources), family composition or living arrangements must be reported. Failure to report such changes can result in the receipt of benefits which may have to be repaid to the Department.

● Register and participate in the Work Incentive Program (WIN) unless determined exempt from this requirement. As a food stamp recipient, it may be necessary to register for work even though exempt from WIN.

● Cooperate in establishing paternity and obtaining support for the children, unless good cause can be shown not to do so.

● Use the AFDC check to the best advantage of the children in the assistance group. Florida law provides that a person who misuses money intended for the support of a child can be fined, sent to jail, or both.

● Repay the Department for any assistance received for which they are not eligible.

D. I KNOW THAT BY ACCEPTING PUBLIC ASSISTANCE I AM ASSIGNING TO THE STATE MY RIGHTS TO ANY CHILD SUPPORT PAYMENTS RECEIVED FOR THE CHILDREN IN THE AFDC GRANT.

E. I UNDERSTAND THAT THE INFORMATION GIVEN BY ME IN THIS APPLICATION WILL ALSO BE USED TO DETERMINE MY ELIGIBILITY TO THE FOOD STAMP PROGRAM, IF I AM APPLYING FOR AFDC AND FOOD STAMPS. I UNDERSTAND I AM SUBJECT TO THE CRIMINAL PENALTIES OF EITHER PROGRAM FOR GIVING FALSE STATEMENTS.

F. I UNDERSTAND THAT INFORMATION WHICH THE DEPARTMENT HAS ABOUT ME WILL BE TREATED CONFIDENTIALLY IN ACCORDANCE WITH FEDERAL AND STATE LAW.

DO NOT SIGN THE STATEMENT BELOW UNTIL YOUR WORKER ASKS YOU TO DO SO. THIS STATEMENT MUST BE SIGNED IN THE PRESENCE OF THE WORKER.

The worker has discussed all my rights and responsibilities with me, has answered my questions and given me a copy of HRS-SES Form 2611, Rights and Responsiblities. I understand that if I do not give complete, honest information and do not let the Department staff know when changes happen, that I may be prosecuted for fraud and be fined, sent to jail, or both.

Your signature_____, Date _____, Worker's signature _____

| FOR OFFICE USE | Did applicant/recipient appear to understand explanations of rights and responsibilities? | Yes ☐ | No ☐ If no, explain: |

SERVICE REFERRALS:
Family Planning ☐ Yes ☐ No

Other Services ☐ Yes ☐ No

2

Figure 6-3 Part of AFDC application.

greater respect and were more lenient in interpreting and administering welfare policies.

If Piven and Cloward's thesis about the expansion and contraction of welfare programs is correct, we would expect the next phase of the welfare cycle to be one of restrictive policies and contraction of welfare programs. Indeed, the Reagan administration is placing greater emphasis on "work-fare" —performing work for the government in exchange for welfare payments and tightening eligibility requirements as a means of controlling the growth of the welfare rolls.

Like other presidential administrations, the Reagan team is com-mitted "to determine welfare needs more accurately, improve program administration, reduce fraud and abuse, and decrease federal and state costs."[15] As policy goals, similar announcements have been made in the past; but as a practical matter, the AFDC program is not an area where major savings are likely to be made.

Despite the administration's rhetoric, specific program changes initi-ated by the Reagan team will probably not result in any substantial reduction in AFDC payments or recipients. These changes include (1) counting the income of stepparents as a source in determining a child's eligibility; (2) limiting deductible child care costs and other work-related expenses; (3) requiring states to determine eligibility based on previous actual income; (4) improving the states' efforts at child support enforce-ment; and (5) allowing the federal Internal Revenue Service (the nation's chief tax collecting agency) to intercept federal income tax returns to collect child support.[16]

DO WELFARE RECIPIENTS REALLY WANT TO WORK?

Some people argue that many welfare recipients could work if they "really wanted to." However, many welfare recipients are not capable of regular, full-time employment. The largest group of welfare recipients is children. The mothers of these children also comprise a considerable portion of those who receive benefits. Many of these women do not work because they must care for their very young children; some are too ill, physically or mentally, to hold jobs; and many also lack the skills to earn a wage which is adequate to support their children. Recipients of other welfare programs such as the SSI program are too old or too disabled to hold jobs in today's labor market.

Several researchers have concluded that welfare benefits, such as a guaranteed income, do *not* reduce the incentive to work,[17] but others, including some economists, do not view the problem in the same way. For example, earning even a small amount of money may result in the termination of Medicaid payments. Take the case of a near-poor working family with a chronically ill child that receives Medicaid benefits. Once the family reaches its limit of earnings, its Medicaid benefits are completely stopped. The family is forced to decide whether to continue working and face catastrophic medical bills *or* "go on welfare" so medical benefits will be provided to their child. There is little tapering off of benefits as earnings increase.

Economist Martin Anderson believes that these practices have created a "poverty wall" in America.[18] The poverty wall is the disincentive to work created by the structure of the welfare system in the United States. Anderson believes the way to tear down the poverty wall is to adopt a welfare plan that would provide *only* for the needy and would include clearly defined *work requirements*.

WELFARE REFORM

There is widespread agreement that the welfare system in the United States is in urgent need of reform, but there is little agreement on how reform should take place.

Most proposals for major welfare reform center around the concept of a guaranteed annual income or a negative income tax. Examples of these proposals are Milton Freidman's negative income tax plan and President Nixon's Family Assistance Plan. Negative income tax and guaranteed annual income plans are based on the premise that welfare reform has not worked. The current welfare system could be replaced by a negative income tax which would guarantee everyone a minimum income and encourage recipients to work by allowing them to keep a portion of their earnings without severe reductions in benefits.

Each negative income tax or guaranteed annual income plan has its own set of procedures and requirements, but let us consider one example of how such a plan might work. Let us say that the guaranteed annual income for a family of four is set at $4,000 with an earnings deduction of 50 percent. A family with no income would receive $4,000. A family with $2,000 in earnings would receive a payment of $3,000 for a total income of $5,000. A family earning $6,000 would receive a payment of $1,000 for a total income of $7,000, while a family earning $8,000, the break even point, would receive no payment. The program is a logical extension of the income tax system already in place in the United States. Everyone would file an income tax statement as they do today. Many citizens would pay taxes, but those at the lower end of the income scale would receive payments or negative income taxes. Checks would be mailed through the U.S. Treasury Department as income tax refunds are mailed today. Since welfare applications, means tests, and other eligibility procedures would be eliminated, much of the welfare bureaucracy could be reduced.

But the United States has no practical experience with a guaranteed income or negative income tax. There is a possibility that near-poor persons would qualify for benefits and prefer accepting the guarantee. This threat to the work ethic is probably the greatest fear working against implementing such a proposal in the United States. Planners would need to estimate how many persons might qualify for payments at various levels. The plan would then be debated. A decision on payment levels, however, may not be based on what seems to be a fair standard of living, but how much decision-makers believe the country can afford to make in guaranteed annual income payments.

In 1970 President Nixon proposed the Family Assistance Plan (FAP). The FAP, an example of a guaranteed income, was designed to address many of the problems of the welfare system: disincentives to work, discouragement of family life, inequities among the states, and discrimination against the working poor. "However, the FAP failed in Congress because of the combined opposition of those who felt it was too much welfare and those who felt it was not enough."[19] The problem of welfare reform is one example of how a rational approach to meeting the basic needs of Americans has failed. Americans have not been able to agree on who is poor, who should receive assistance, or what methods should be used to alleviate poverty. Until we agree on these questions, rational planning cannot take place. The policy process remains a series of political struggles over "who gets what, when, and how."

SUMMARY

Perhaps the most controversial of all the welfare programs is Aid to Families with Dependent Children. Most of the criticism is directed toward the adult beneficiaries of the program, who, some believe, are capable of "making it on their own." The first programs to assist dependent children were state mother's aid programs. The federal government became involved as part of the 1935 Social Security Act. Midnight raids and man in the house rules were used to insure that mothers were not "harboring" men who could support their children, but Supreme Court action has discouraged these practices.

Many Americans have an incorrect picture of the average AFDC family. AFDC families are usually small; most have only one or two children. There are about as many white AFDC recipients as black recipients, although blacks are overrepresented among the total. The majority of AFDC families stay on the program less than three years.

Various approaches have been used to get adult AFDC recipients to work. Rehabilitating AFDC recipients so that they could overcome personal problems which prevented them from being self-supporting was one method. Another method was job training and job development. But many adult AFDC recipients are the mothers of small children, day care is expensive, and these mothers may earn so little from what employment they can find that work programs may cost more than they are worth financially.

Frances Fox Piven and Richard A. Cloward offer a political explanation of welfare programs in the United States. They believe that welfare programs both expand and contract. The government expands welfare programs during times when the poor threaten to revolt because of their oppressed living conditions, and it contracts welfare benefits through the enforcement of work norms during periods of political stability. Piven and Cloward call these practices "regulating the poor."

AFDC caseloads and costs rose dramatically during the 1960s, the period called the "welfare rights movement." Much of the growth was because of the increase in single-parent families, which are headed mostly by women. After controlling for inflation, however, the average AFDC payment per family has not really grown since the sixties. Caseloads have also remained stable in the past few years and are not expected to grow much. Since AFDC is a joint federal-state program, payments and eligibility requirements vary considerably from state to state.

The question of whether or not welfare recipients "really want to work" has been the subject of much debate. Conservative economists believe that the current welfare system destroys the incentive to work; others disagree. Disagreement over questions like the incentive to work have helped to bog down AFDC reform. Every president has taken his turn at welfare reform. In 1969 President Nixon proposed the Family Assistance Plan to guarantee all poor families a minimum income. The plan failed because liberals thought it was too little welfare and conservatives thought it was too much welfare. President Reagan also wishes to reform AFDC, but his proposals are not likely to result in major program changes. Current efforts focus on enforcing support payments from absent parents. Such measures are expensive and may not yield great returns. Another recent reform is to limit the thirty-plus-one-third rule to a four-month period.

NOTES

1. Laurence E. Lynn, Jr., "A Decade of Policy Developments in the Income-Maintenance System," in Robert H. Haveman (ed.), *A Decade of Federal Antipoverty Programs: Achievements, Failures and Lessons* (New York: Academic Press, 1977), p. 60; and Martin Rein, *Social Policy: Issues of Choice and Change* (New York: Random House, 1970), p. 311.
2. Lynn, "Decade of Policy Developments," p. 73.
3. Gilbert Y. Steiner, *The State of Welfare* (Washington, D.C.: Brookings Institution, 1971), p. 81.
4. John Bishop, *Jobs, Cash Transfers, and Marital Instability: A Review of the Evidence* (Madison, Wisc.: Institute for Research on Poverty, University of Wisconsin, Madison). Written testimony to the Welfare Reform Subcommittee of the Committees on Agriculture, Education and Labor, and Ways and Means, of the U.S. House of Representatives, October 14, 1977, p. 9.

5. Ibid., p. 8.
6. *Paternity Determination: Techniques and Procedures to Establish the Paternity of Children Born Out of Wedlock.* Department of HEW, Office of Child Support Enforcement, April 30, 1977.
7. *Aid to Families with Dependent Children: A Chartbook.* U.S. Department of HEW, Social Security Administration, Office of Policy, Office of Research and Statistics, HEW Publication No. (SSA) 79-11721, 1979.
8. *Welfare Myths vs Facts.* Department of HEW, Social and Rehabilitation Service, Washington, D.C. (SRS) 71-127.
9. Steiner, *State of Welfare*, p. 36 and Lynn, "A Decade of Policy Developments," pp. 62–63.
10. Donald Brieland, Leila B. Costin, Charles R. Atherton, and contributors, *Contemporary Social Work: An Introduction to Social Work and Social Welfare* (New York: McGraw-Hill, 1975), p. 100; Steiner, *State of Welfare*, p. 37.
11. Steiner, *State of Welfare*, p. 37.
12. Lynn, "Decade of Policy Developments," p. 74.
13. U.S. Dept. of Health and Human Services, *Characteristics of State Plans for Aid to Families with Dependent Children Under the Social Security Act, Title IVA,* Characteristics Series Data as of September 1979, pp. 89–92 and 101–103, SSA Pub. No. 80-21235.
14. Frances Fox Piven and Richard A. Cloward, *Regulating the Poor: The Functions of Public Welfare* (New York: Random House, 1971).
15. Office of Management and Budget, *A Program for Economic Recovery,* February 18, 1981 (Washington, D.C.: Government Printing Office, 1981), pp. 1–11.
16. Ibid., pp. 1–12.
17. U.S. Office of Economic Opportunity, "Preliminary Results of the New Jersey Graduated Work Incentive Experiment," February 18, 1970 and *Final Report of the New Jersey Graduated Work Incentive Experiment,* David Kershaw and Jerelyn Fair, eds., Madison: University of Wisconsin, Institute for Research on Poverty, 1974.
18. The statement of Professor Martin Anderson of the Hoover Institution at Stanford University in *How to Think About Welfare Reform for the 1980s.* Hearings before the Committee on Public Assistance of the Committee on Finance, United States Senate, 96th Congress, 2nd session, February 6 and 7, 1980.
19. Thomas R. Dye, *Understanding Public Policy,* 3rd ed. (Englewood Cliffs, N.J.: Prentice-Hall, 1978), p. 131.

7

Providing
Social Services: Helping
the Mentally Ill, Children,
and the Elderly

DEFINING SOCIAL SERVICES

Social welfare programs are often equated with programs for the poor. But there are some social services that people may need regardless of their income and social status. Developing a list of all the social services provided in the United States is a major task, but such a list would include:

1. Day care and similar child development and child programs (Head Start, family day care, group care for infants or for 3-to-5-year olds in centers, after school care, and so on)
2. Homemaker, home help, and chore services
3. Personal and family guidance and counseling, including marital counseling
4. Child welfare activities such as foster home care, adoption, and protective services for neglected or abused children
5. Assessments for courts, schools, or camps of parental relationships (are parents neglectful? with which member of a separated couple should a child reside?) or of a child's personality and capacities (is he capable of adjusting to a normal group?)
6. Big Brother, Big Sister, and related volunteer helping and guidance efforts
7. Family planning services (advice, counseling, referral)

8. Community centers for the aged, for youth, for families
9. "Meals on wheels," nutrition, senior citizen programs, transportation, and special protective programs for the aged
10. A diversity of such group programs as therapeutic group work with adolescents, organization of tenants in a housing project, organization of the parents of retarded children
11. Home management counseling and educational activity, as well as home improvement services
12. Rural welfare programs and special programs for migrant laborers
13. Special programs to counsel potential migrants or immigrants and help them cope with new surroundings
14. Assistance to residents of poverty areas or members of underprivileged population groups, so that they may come together with mutual aid activity
15. Information, advice, referral, complaint, and advocacy services of many kinds
16. Institutional programs for the neglected, dependent, disturbed, or frail (state training schools, homes for the aged, adult homes, residential treatment for children, and so on)
17. Counseling, therapeutic, rehabilitation and education services for drug addicts and alcoholics
18. Social services in schools, hospitals, clinics, churches, industrial establishments, and other settings[1]

At some time in our lives many of us are likely to make use of some of the social services in this list.

WHO PROVIDES SOCIAL SERVICES?

Social services are provided by four types of organizations: (1) public agencies; (2) private not-for-profit corporations; (3) private profit-making corporations; and (4) self-help groups. Social services like day care are provided by several types of agencies. Other services, like child and adult protective services, are provided by public agencies, since these agencies have the legal right to intervene in cases where a child or adult might be the victim of neglect or abuse.

Public agencies are established by law and are operated by federal, state, or local governments. The Department of Health and Human Services is the major federal agency responsible for providing social services. Each state has a department which administers most of its social welfare programs, and some counties and cities also operate welfare agencies.

Private not-for-profit agencies, also called voluntary agencies, are governed by boards of directors or boards of trustees that are legally responsible for the agencies. These agencies may receive funds from donations, client fees, or government payments, such as grants or contracts.

Private not-for-profit agencies provide a multitude of services, such as day care for children, mental health services, and nursing home care. Many of these agencies, such as community mental health centers, charge fees to clients on a sliding scale, based on the clients' abilities to pay for the services. Other not-for-profit agencies do not charge their clients. Socialization activities at senior citizen centers are often provided at no cost. Some not-for-profit corporations act as policy advocates for their clientele by lobbying policy-makers and making them aware of their clients' needs. They may also educate the public about their clients' problems. The National Association of Retarded Citizens and its local affiliates, the Children's Home Society, and the National Council on Alcoholism are private not-for-profit agencies.

Private profit-making organizations are also called proprietary agencies. They also provide services like child care, nursing home care, and mental health care, but private profit-making agencies charge their clients for services at the current market rate. Government agencies often purchase services from private agencies when they do not directly provide these services for their clients. For example, specialized medical services to disabled individuals are often purchased by the government from physicians engaged in private medical practices.

Self-help groups also provide social services but generally do not rely on governmental funding at all. The structure of self-help groups is less formal than other social service agencies. Alcoholics Anonymous is a self-help group which assists persons with drinking problems. The only requirement for membership is the desire to stop drinking. The group relies only on its members for support and does not accept outside contributions. Other self-help groups are Narcotics Anonymous, Gamblers Anonymous, and Parents Anonymous.

THE DEVELOPMENT OF SOCIAL SERVICES IN THE UNITED STATES

Before the 1900s, social services were historically provided by family members, neighbors, church groups, private charitable organizations, and local governments. State governments did not become involved in social welfare services until early in this century, when they began providing financial assistance and commodity foods to the destitute. The federal government did not become directly involved in financial and food programs until 1935. Other social welfare services remained largely outside the range of government activities until 1956 when the Social Security Administration encouraged Congress to amend the Social Security Act to provide social services to families on relief.[2]

The rationale for federal funding of social services was to rehabilitate the poor, help them overcome their personal problems, and thereby reduce their dependence on welfare. To carry out this plan, the federal government gave the states three dollars for every one dollar the states spent on social services. But this approach did not reduce poverty. Views on the causes of poverty have since changed. Today, just because one is poor does not necessarily mean one is in need of rehabilitation. In 1967 Congress officially recognized this position by separating welfare payments from social service provisions. Although welfare recipients are no longer expected to receive social services along with their checks, those services continue to be used by many clients.

Another development in the growth of social services has been the recognition that those who are not poor can also benefit from social services. The growth of public and private social service agencies which assist middle- and upper-class families, in addition to poor families, is an indication that mental health, family counseling, child guidance, and other types of social services can be useful to many Americans.

TITLE XX AND SOCIAL SERVICES

The federal government's willingness to subsidize social services was a boon to the states that were willing to increase the amount of social services available to clients. But the costs of social services were rising so fast (from $282 million in 1967 to $1.7 billion in 1973)[3] that Congress decided to take action to curb spending. In 1976 Title XX was added to the Social Security Act to place a ceiling on expenditures and to insure that the majority of federally funded social services go to the poor. Title XX legislation requires that states submit annual plans for providing social services. The five goals of Title XX are:

1. Achieving or maintaining economic self-support to prevent, reduce, or eliminate dependency;
2. Achieving or maintaining self-sufficiency, including reduction or prevention of dependency;
3. Preventing or remedying neglect, abuse, or exploitation of children and adults unable to protect their own interests; or preserving, or reuniting families;
4. Preventing or reducing inappropriate institutional care by providing for community-based care, home-based care, and other forms of less intensive care; and
5. Securing referral or admission for institutional care when other forms of care are not appropriate, or providing services to individuals in institutions.[4]

The mentally ill, abused children, and the elderly are examples of social service beneficiaries who have gained increasing attention since the 1960s. We have chosen to explore policy as it relates to these groups at greater length.

SOCIAL SERVICES
FOR THE MENTALLY ILL

The first obstacle to rationalism in providing mental health services is a lack of consensus about how to define mental health problems. There is no single definition of mental illness.

Defining Mental Illness

Psychiatrists, mental health workers, and the general public disagree about the definition of mental illness.[5] Mental health and mental illness may be thought of as two ends of a continuum. At one extreme are people who behave in an acceptable manner in the community. At the other extreme are psychotic persons who are unable to cope with reality and cannot function within the community. Depression is one common mental health problem that can range from mild and temporary to depression so severe that an individual may become suicidal.

Everyone experiences emotional stress at some time in his or her life. For most, professional care is not needed, but today more emphasis is being placed on preventing mental health problems. Mental health professionals are as likely to see family members adjusting to a divorce or the loss of a loved one as they are to see the severely depressed, suicidal, or schizophrenic.

Most people needing assistance seek mental health treatment voluntarily, but some persons with severe mental health problems may not recognize their need for treatment. In these cases, state and local policies stipulate the conditions under which an individual may be judged mentally ill and in need of treatment. Involuntary admission to a mental health hospital is generally reserved for persons whom psychiatrists believe are dangerous to themselves or others, and who may not perceive the need for treatment.

Estimating Mental Health Problems

Although we cannot specifically define mental health or mental illness, estimates have been made of the numbers of persons who experience mental health and related problems, such as alcohol and drug abuse. The federal government's Alcohol, Drug Abuse, and Mental Health Administration (ADAMHA) reports that:

> Recent surveys have shown that 15 and possibly 20 percent of American citizens need some form of mental health care in the course of a given year. There are today nearly 10 million adults with alcohol problems in the United States, plus an estimated 3.3 million youths having trouble related to alcohol abuse.

Drug problems among youth continue to grow, with 10.3 percent of high school seniors reporting daily use of marijuana in 1979. PCP and cocaine use were on a steady rise.[6]

Only a small percentage of persons with mental health, alcohol, and drug problems receive assistance for these problems. The ADAMHA reports that about one million people per year receive alcoholism treatment services in special programs for alcoholics. In addition, the general health care sector assists another one-half million persons with alcohol-related problems. Approximately 700,000 persons participate in Alcoholics Anonymous.[7] Yet these figures fall very short of the thirteen million adults and youths estimated to be directly harmed by alcohol problems. About one-half million persons receive drug abuse services annually.[8] Mental health services are provided each year to about seven million individuals.[9] While the number of persons who receive treatment for drug abuse and mental health problems grows each year, many who are in the need of treatment remain outside of the service delivery system.

Discovering Mental Illness

The mentally ill were once thought to be possessed by the devil and were hidden away from public view, but by the nineteenth century treatment of the mentally ill began to take different forms. Phillipe Pinel, a French physician, introduced "moral treatment" for the mentally ill. Moral treatment consisted of treating the mentally ill with kindness and consideration, providing the opportunity for discussion of personal problems, and encouraging an active orientation to life.[10] Surely, this approach to treating mental illness made good sense, but it was not the kind of treatment offered to most mentally ill persons.[11] For those who could not afford moral treatment, institutionalized treatment or incarceration was the general method of providing mental health care. Dorothea Dix, a social reformer during the mid-1800s, sought to improve the plight of severely mistreated mental patients. Dix succeeded in improving conditions within institutions for mental health patients, but with the increasing numbers of persons being labeled mentally ill in the nineteenth century, institutions grew larger and larger and less capable of helping the mentally ill.

The Industrial Revolution intensified a number of social problems, including mental illness.[12] People came to the cities seeking jobs and wealth and instead found overcrowding, joblessness, and misery. Those migrating to the cities were often without support of family and friends, and coping with urban problems was difficult. Immigrants from other countries also flocked to the cities. Those who did not acculturate or assimilate quickly into American society were often labeled as deviant or mentally ill.[13] City dwellers, overwhelmed with problems, had little tolerance for what they considered deviation from normal behavior.[14] This increased the number of persons sent to mental health institutions.

Apart from state institutions, there was little in the way of social policies and public programs for the mentally ill. After Dix's efforts to reform mental institutions, Clifford Beers was responsible for introducing the "Mental Hygiene Movement" in the early twentieth century. Beers knew well the dehumanizing conditions of mental institutions; he himself had been a patient. Beer's efforts to expose the inhumane conditions of the institutions, like Dix's, resulted in better care, but the custodial and institutional philosophies of mental health treatment continued.[15]

During World War II, a large number of young men were needed for military service. Part of the screening procedure for new recruits was a psychiatric examination. The number of young men rejected as unfit for military service or later discharged for psychiatric reasons was alarming. While the accuracy and methods of these psychiatric screening procedures have been criticized, the identification of so many young men with mental health problems brought about renewed concern for mental health.[16] This concern was reflected in the Mental Health Act of 1946. The act established the National Institute of Mental Health (NIMH), with its focus on training, education, and research.

In the 1950s another important development occurred in mental health treatment—the discovery of improved psychotherapeutic drugs. These drugs reduced many of the *symptoms* of mental health patients. This allowed hospital staffs to eliminate many restrictions placed on patients and made patients more acceptable to the community.[17]

But the use of drug therapy has been criticized, not only because of the potential side effects of drugs, but also because drugs may be used to replace other forms of treatment. Consider, for example, the complaint of "radical therapists":

> Radical therapists—and others not so radical—ask a question we cannot ignore. Isn't the drug revolution an excuse for therapy on the cheap, for leaving therapy of the severely ill to social workers and paraprofessionals, for substituting a chemical reaction for the skilled deep human contact that alone can heal? Isn't it still another way of shortchanging the poor—since all studies show that the upper socio-economic groups are far more likely to get intensive psychotherapy, while the lower socio-economic groups get mostly somatic treatments?
>
> Fortunately, treatments are not necessarily second-rate because the poor get them—in spite of what radical therapists maintain. And unfortunately, deep human contact, though it may help a patient feel and act better, rarely heals severe mental illness—anymore than it heals severe physical illness. (On the rare occasions when it does, we have a word for it—a miracle.) Nor is it true that more drug treatment means less psychotherapy—rather, it's the reverse.[18]

The use of drug therapies has been widely debated. What *is* evident is that the advent of psychotherapeutic drugs has deemphasized the need for hospitalization for many patients.

Psychotherapeutic drugs laid some of the groundwork for the passage of the Community Mental Health Act in 1963. As part of an emerging community mental health movement, the act emphasized more federal involvement in community-based care, as well as coordination between community services with hospitals, improved services to the chronically mentally ill, a reduction in state hospital treatment, an increase in community treatment, education and prevention services, and greater utilization of paraprofessional staff.

The Community Mental Health Center

The Community Mental Health Act of 1963 provided funds for the establishment and staffing of community mental health centers (CMHCs) throughout the nation. Today there are over 781 CMHCs in the United States. Figure 7–1 shows the number of CMHCs in each state. Funding for CMHCs has come primarily from the federal government, with some state and local support, as well as from fees paid by clients. Persons with very low incomes may pay little or no fee. As federal grants to community mental health centers terminate, states and communities are being forced to replace funds or reduce staff and services.

The Community Mental Health Act originally mandated that federally funded CMHCs provide five "essential services." These services are (1) inpatient care, (2) outpatient care, (3) emergency care, (4) partial hospitalization, and (5) consultation and education. Inpatient care is usually provided within a psychiatric hospital or in a psychiatric unit of a general hospital within the community. Generally this care is short-term. If long-term care is needed, the patient may be transferred to a state mental health hospital or, if the patient can afford private care, to a private hospital outside the CMHC system.

Outpatient care covers a wide range of services. Among these services are individual therapy or counseling, group therapy, family therapy, and alcohol and drug abuse services. Among the personnel who provide care are psychiatrists, nurses, psychologists, social workers, counselors, rehabilitation specialists, and paraprofessionals. Which staff member provides the service depends upon the needs of the client.

"Emergency services," also known as "crisis services," are provided on a twenty-four-hour basis. They may include the use of telephone hot lines and outreach services to clients who cannot reach a mental health facility in time of emergency. Crisis services are often involved in responding to persons who are contemplating or who have attempted suicide, or who are experiencing other acute emotional problems.

"Partial hospitalization" is the name generally given to supervised activities and mental health services that the client receives during part of the day. One type of partial hospitalization service provides a structured environment for mental health clients during the day, with the clients' spending evenings at home. Partial hospitalization services help clients who are attempting to reintegrate themselves back into the community, perhaps following a psychiatric hospitalization.

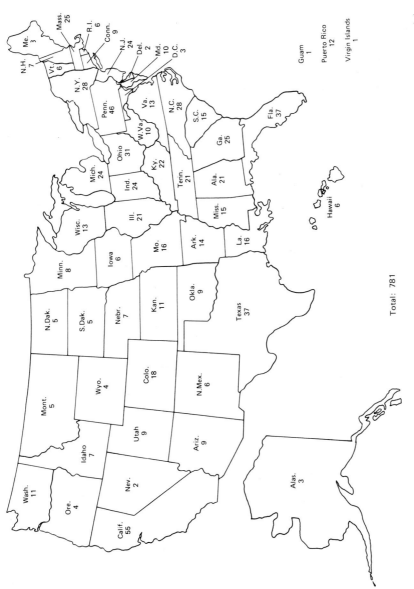

Figure 7-1 Community mental health centers, 1980, number in state. (U.S. Department of Health and Human Services, *Report of the Administrator, Alcohol, Drug Abuse, and Mental Health Administration, 1980.* Washington, D.C.: Public Health Service, 1981. DHHS Publication No. (ADM) 81-1165.

The fifth essential service is consultation and education (C&E), which also may be thought of as "prevention services." C&E services are provided to many groups throughout the community: medical professionals, courts, law enforcement agencies, schools, civic groups, religious groups, social service agencies, and the elderly and other citizens who want to learn about mental health and mental illness. C&E services are generally educational services that focus on the prevention of mental illness, the identification of mental health problems, and on what to do if mental health problems occur.

In 1975 amendments to the Community Mental Health Act mandated more essential services, including special programs for children and the elderly, after-care and halfway house services for patients discharged from mental health hospitals, and services to courts and related agencies to screen persons who may be in need of treatment. CMHCs were mandated to spend 2 percent of their annual budgets on program evaluation, but this requirement has recently been eliminated. State governments may now assume more responsibility in determining CMHC evaluation requirements.

Community cooperation is essential if CMHCs are to successfully provide services. Attitudes toward the mentally ill are especially important. Law enforcement officers must be able to recognize when a person is behaving in an unusual manner because of mental illness and needs mental health care rather than incarceration. The school system should be able to identify a child who is doing poorly in school because of personal and family problems. Physicians, clergy, and neighbors must also know that services are available. In addition, the CMHC must be willing to respond to the mental health needs of poor clients. Critics have charged that

> The human service professions—psychiatry, psychology, social work, the ministry—have been more concerned with their own development than with the needs of the people. The professionals have put most of their time and effort into working with low risk clients—the stable, slightly neurotic middle class. The "others" have been considered either incurable or not educated enough to benefit from therapeutic services.[19]

The Rights of Mental Health Patients

Sometimes treatment cannot be provided to persons with mental health problems on an outpatient basis or in community facilities. (The same is true for the severely mentally retarded and physically handicapped.) Community mental health programs may not be equipped to assist persons whose mental health problems are very severe, or specialized facilities may not exist in a community. Treatment in an inpatient mental health facility may be necessary. This type of treatment restricts an individual from moving about in the community and conducting everyday affairs. In the nineteenth century and in the early twentieth century, mental health patients had few rights. Today there is a greater concern for laws and policies which protect the rights of persons hospitalized in mental health facilities. The federal and state governments are responsible for protecting the rights of mental health patients. Patients must be informed of their rights to obtain and refuse treatment, and those who are not able to read must have this information explained to them.

Some obstacles prevent patients from receiving the best treatment in mental health facilities. Patients should always be treated in a way that respects their individual dignity, but this manner of treatment is contingent on the quality of the treatment facility and of its staff. Facilities are often crowded and caseloads high. Some are located in remote areas where there may be an inadequate number of persons trained to provide mental health services. Thus, qualified staff may be difficult to recruit and retain. Yet the decisions about a patient's day-to-day activities are largely staff decisions. The patient may have little influence in choosing these activities, short of refusing to participate. Moreover, when patients refuse to participate in activities, they are often considered to be uncooperative and resistant to treatment. This may serve to prolong their stay in the mental health hospital.

Patients have the right to know the reason for their admission and what must happen before release can be granted. They should be provided access to mental health laws and legal assistance. Patients should be afforded privacy when they have visitors, and visits should not be denied unless there is reason to believe that this might be harmful to the patient or others. Unfortunately, when hospitals are located far from the patient's home, it is more difficult for family to visit or for the patient to visit family on short leaves of absence from the hospital. Well-intentioned policies relating to the care of the mentally ill persons may not always be implemented to serve the best needs of the client.

Deinstitutionalization

Persons with mental health problems frequently face social rejection. While the public agrees that treatment should be provided to the physically and mentally handicapped and to the mentally ill, the public does not always believe that this treatment should be provided in their neighborhood. This belief persists for several reasons. Some people fear the mentally ill and believe they might endanger the safety of their families. Others believe that community-based facilities will cause their neighborhoods to become rundown if these facilities are not well maintained. There is also the fear that when community programs move in, neighborhood residents will decide to sell their homes, perhaps at a loss. We have reproduced a story about the problems faced in locating community treatment programs for the physically and mentally handicapped (see p. 130).

The phrase "treatment in the least restrictive manner" means that the freedoms of the individual receiving treatment should be preserved whenever possible. It is not appropriate to confine someone to treatment in a state hospital when a community facility can meet the individual's needs. Hospitals may compound patients' problems by making patients "institutionalized." They may be forced to get up at certain times and to eat at certain times; their meals may be prepared for them and their clothes washed for them; they may be told when to bathe and when to take their medication. As a result, patients become increasingly dependent on others for survival. When and if they return to their homes and communities, they may not have the skills to live independently.

But "deinstitutionalization" —reliance on community facilities—may also present problems. Some communities do not have enough local treatment and residential facilities. The discharge of large numbers of patients from state institutions to their home communities, in cases where the communities lack enough resources for newly released patients, may result in added stress for both patients and communities. Families are often not equipped to care for patients who may need supervision or special services within the home. Other families do not want or know how to cope with the burdens placed on them by family members returning from institutional care.

ILLUSTRATION: MENTAL HEALTH AND LOCAL POLITICS

LaMar Silver is no rabble-rouser....

His home in Orlando's Bel Aire Woods subdivision is a reward he worked hard to attain before retiring....

When two group homes for the mentally retarded opened within a block of his home, LaMar Silver felt his neighborhood was changed, even ruined. He was determined to fight.

Bill Brandt, a data processing consultant in his early 30s, is a family man with a sense of civic duty.... When a detoxification program for alcoholics moved into his neighborhood, Brandt too came out fighting.

The same alcoholic treatment facility was bitterly fought again when mental health officials tried to move it into another location. This time, the main opponent was a self-styled conservative and opponent of big government. A 38-year-old businessman, he was—and still is—convinced the facility will ruin his business. He challenged the move legally and lost. Still angry about his new neighbor, he doesn't want his name published but he'll discuss his objections at length....

Community acceptance—or lack of it—is a force to be reckoned with in the 1980s. As human service programs push to deinstitutionalize and open a gamut of community based programs, firefights are erupting in neighborhoods throughout the state and the nation.

At the very least, angry neighbors can cause costly delays and disrupt programs. Or, in the extreme, they can stop the opening of a facility and bring community programming to a grinding halt....

Silver ... said... "As far as I'm concerned and as far as the neighborhood's concerned, we have no objection to the clients. We don't object to the homes if they're not concentrated...."

According to Silver, after the second home opened, "For Sale" signs began springing up in the neighborhood. He estimated that about a half-dozen homes were sold in the area adjacent to the group homes and said he was told the houses sold for $10,000 to $20,000 less than comparable homes in the other areas. Silver maintains that the reduced prices brought undesirable people into the neighborhood. Yet he said he has not actually surveyed prices of homes sold in the area....

Two separate Tallahassee neighborhoods fought to stop the opening of an inpatient treatment program for alcoholics by the Apalachee Community Mental Health Center. One neighborhood won, the other lost. Yet the time-consuming and expensive battles caused the center to close the program for seven months....

Bill Brandt, president of the Lafayette Park Neighborhood Association, said the detox center was the final straw for residents. He said many people were unhappy with the short-term psychiatric care program already located in the center. And with five other group homes and related facilities in the immediate area, they felt their social consciousness stretched thin....

Apalachee officials said the move might have met less resistance had it not been for negative publicity about patients leaving the detox center and wandering through the neighborhood. No crimes were linked to detox clients and changes were made to prevent clients from wandering. But neighbors were unconvinced and feared clients might disturb them or their children.

Lafayette Park residents and Apalachee officials became adversaries, first before a zoning appeals board and then in court. Zoning officials said that the detox center—and the inpatient psychiatric unit—were prohibited in the area. The court agreed and gave Apalachee six months to move the programs

As Apalachee looked at other sites, opposition spread to every area considered. When six months were up, a new site had not been firmed up and the agency had to close the two treatment programs. It would be seven months before they reopened in their new home.

Apalachee officials finally zeroed in on a building located on commercially-zoned land east of Tallahassee. Across the street from a small cluster of businesses, it is about a half-mile from Eastgate, one of Tallahassee's newer single family subdivisions and home for many young families.

Although the zoning allowed for "clinics," Apalachee officials were geared for opposition. They went to work immediately to offset it by winning support from Eastgate residents and others. "We set up a Neighborhood Advisory Board of 14 people who live in Eastgate and nearby," said Apalachee's medical and educational consultant, Linda Cooper. "We educated them on the programs, who the supervisors were, who the clients were. We gave them honest, matter-of-fact answers to questions. We also stressed the fact we are a *resource* for their neighborhood—that one of them or a neighbor might need our services."

The advisory board formed a core of support for the treatment facility and members successfully overcame the objections of many of their neighbors.

But the welcome wasn't unanimous. A small group of businessmen fought the facility before the zoning appeals board and in court. At times their tactics were less restrained. "Do you want Mental patients and Drunks across from your children?" read the sign in front of a neighborhood skating ring.

Their efforts were unsuccessful. The center opened in December....

But the conservative businessman who asked not to be named said he questioned the need for the programs as well as objecting to them being located across from his business....

He said his concerns were twofold: the impact on his business and the safety of the children who often wait outside his skating rink for their parents.

So far, he said, there have been no incidents involving patients from the treatment facility. But he was skeptical about the future and vowed to take things in his own hands if an incident occurred....

The man's anger is not atypical. And threats of violence can become very real. A recent CBS "Sixty Minutes" show featured a segment on efforts to locate a group home in a Michigan community. The same night the house was burned to the ground—the apparent victim of arsonists....

Numerous studies have looked at the problem of community opposition to residential treatment facilities. Most conclude that neighbors oppose facilities because they believe:

—They will devalue property.

—Criminal activity and disturbances will increase.

—The character of the neighborhood will be negatively affected.

Yet, recent studies both in Florida and other states have concluded that these fears are generally unfounded.

A number of studies have examined the impact homes for the handicapped and other clients have on property values. They indicate there is no relationship between these facilities and property values—regardless of the age of the neighborhood, its relationship to downtown or the characteristics of its residents. In general, property values in communities with group homes had the same increase or decrease in market prices as comparable neighborhoods without such facilities.

One recent study, completed last summer by the Jacksonville Community Council, Inc., looked at the impact of residential treatment facilities on criminal activity. The study found that clients were more often the *victims* rather than suspects in criminal investigations....

Most studies also advocate that social services agencies take a "high profile" approach and educate the community before moving into a neighborhood rather than the "low profile" approach, where the goal is to move in unnoticed. But those with first-hand experience say what works in theory may fail in practice....

Richard Baron, project director for the Horizon House Institute of Research and Development in Philadelphia, said his organization favors the "community education" approach. Baron readily admits, however, that there's no conclusive data as to which approach is best and said there's much at stake in answering that question.

Baron said he believed the longterm solution lies in dispelling myths about handicapped and other clients and in educating the public as to their right to treatment in a community setting. Given an enlightened public, the task of overcoming pockets of opposition in specific neighborhoods would be easier, he said.

Client advocates believe that many confrontations can be avoided through implementation of the group home amendment to Florida's Local Government Comprehensive Planning Act. The amendment requires local governments to provide for group and foster homes in their local zoning plans.

Some client advocates, however, are fearful that special zoning may result in limiting residential facilities to "social services ghettos." And some advocates say special zoning shouldn't be necessary. "The purist position is that, constitutionally, these people have a right to live anywhere they want," said Linden Thorn of the Developmental Services Program office. "He [Mr. Silver] didn't have to have permission from his neighbors to buy his house."

Source: Pat Harbolt, "The Fight Against Community Programs" *Access: A Human Services Magazine* 4, no. 4, Feb. 81/Mar. 81/State of Florida, Department of Health & Rehabilitative Services, pp. 14–18.

CHILD WELFARE POLICY

The family has always been viewed as a sacred entity. Governmental interference in family life is generally viewed as an unnecessary intrusion. As a result, the United States has no official national family policy. Instead, there are many federal, state, and local laws that govern various aspects of family relations. There are also more than twenty separate federal government agencies that provide some type of services for children.[20] In this section we focus on one area of family relations—child welfare, especially child abuse and neglect.

According to Title IV–E of the Social Security Act, child welfare policy and services are aimed at accomplishing a number of purposes, including

1. Protecting and promoting the welfare of all children, including handicapped, homeless, dependent, or neglected children;
2. Preventing or remedying, or assisting in the solution of problems that may result in the neglect, abuse, exploitation, or delinquency of children;
3. Preventing the unnecessary separation of children from their families by identifying family problems, assisting families in resolving their problems, and preventing break-ups of the families where the prevention of child removal is desirable and possible;
4. Restoring to their families children who have been removed, by the provision of services to the child and the families;
5. Placing children in suitable adoptive homes in cases where restoration to the biological family is not appropriate; and
6. Assuring adequate care of children away from their homes in cases where the child cannot be returned home or cannot be placed for adoption.

Children Who Receive Social Services

Nearly two million children receive social services.[21] Slightly more boys (52 percent) than girls are served. The median age of these children is nine years. The majority of children are white, but about 30 percent are black, and 9 percent are Hispanic, Asian-Pacific, and Indian-Alaskan. Over half of the children receiving services attend school, while the rest are not attending school or are too young to attend.

Only 15 percent of the children receiving services live with both parents. Forty percent of these children live only with their mothers, and 5 percent only with their fathers. Almost one quarter live in foster homes, while the remainder live with adoptive parents, with relatives or guardians, or in institutions or group homes.

Thirty percent of the children have parents who are married; 25 percent have divorced parents. The remainder either have a deceased parent or parents who are legally separated or were never married. Thirty-eight percent of the children are recipients of AFDC.

The primary reasons children receive social services are neglect and abuse. Other reasons are financial need, emotional problems of the child or of a parent, conflict between child and parent, abandonment, and a parent's unwillingness to care for the child (see Table 7–1). In response to these problems, the services most often provided to children are protective services, health services, foster care, counseling, and day care (see Figure 7–2). The services provided most frequently to the child's principal caretaker are counseling, financial aid, and health services.

Child Abuse and Child Neglect

No one wants to think that there are adult members of society who would inflict harm on children, but the reality is that over one-half million cases of child neglect and abuse are reported each year.

Neglect and abuse are two different phenomena. Neglect results when a parent or caretaker does not provide a child with the essentials needed to live adequately. Neglect may be because of the failure or inability of parents or caretakers to provide adequate food, shelter, or clothing for a child. It can also occur when parents or caretakers fail to see that a child receives an adequate education or adequate health care. Neglect may also result from psychological deprivation. Children who are isolated from others, locked in rooms, and denied normal social stimulation may also be called neglect.

In contrast to child neglect, child abuse occurs when severe physical harm is inflicted on a child. Children who are beaten by parents or caretakers, and children who suffer broken bones, burns, lacerations, or other injuries as a result of such attacks, may be said to be abused.

What are the causes of child neglect and abuse? Many abusive parents

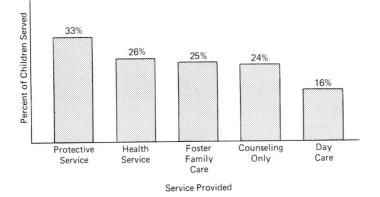

Figure **7-2** Social Services most frequently provided to children by public agencies. (Ann W. Shyne and Anita G. Schroeder, *National Study of Social Services to Children and Their Families Overview.* Washington, D.C.: U.S. Department of Health, Education and Welfare, July 1978, p. 21.)

suggests that these parents learn abusive behavior because this is the method of child rearing they experienced while growing up. There are other possible explanations for child neglect and abuse. Parents who are unable to cope with the stress of personal or economic problems, or who suffer from mental illness, may turn their frustrations toward their children. In other cases, parents may not be equipped to assume the responsibilities of child rearing. Young parents may underestimate the amount of time and attention a child requires. Like other social problems, child neglect and abuse are problems for which researchers will be unlikely to isolate a singe cause; it is likely that child abuse and neglect have multiple causes. In addition, there is no single profile of an abusive parent. Abusive parents do not fall into a specific age group, a specific social class, or a specific economic class. Neither are they all mothers or all fathers. Table 7–2 reviews some characteristics of reported cases of child abuse and neglect. According to these statistics, child abuse and neglect cases are reported by a variety of persons, including friends and neighbors, relatives, law enforcement agencies, medical professionals, and community and social service agencies. The vast majority of persons accused of perpetrating child abuse and neglect are the child's natural parents. Congenital drug addiction, along with minor physical injuries like cuts, bruises, and welts constitute the most frequently substantiated types of child abuse. In terms of substantiated child neglect, types of physical neglect including malnutrition, exposure to the elements, being locked in or out of the home, unintentional poisoning, abandonment, and lack of supervision are the most frequently occurring problems. These types of neglect constitute about half of all child abuse and neglect problems.

TABLE 7–1 Most Frequently Cited Primary Reasons for Children Receiving Social Services

REASON	PERCENT
Neglect of child	15
Abuse of child	7
Financial need	5
Emotional problems of parent	4
Emotional problems of child	4
Conflict in parent/child relationship	4
Abandonment of child	3
Unwillingness to care for child	3

Source: Ann W. Shyne and Anita G. Schroeder, *National Study of Social Services to Children and Their Families Overview,* U.S. Department of Health, Education and Welfare, July 1978, p. 17.

Discovering Child Abuse

Historically, children have been considered the possessions of their parents.[22] Parents who severely punished their children, even beat them, were not behaving deviantly; they were merely making sure that their children obeyed. The same tradition was true in America until the Industrial Revolution brought an abundance of new social problems. Among these social problems were the conditions of urban cities, which were often overcrowded and unsanitary and where hunger and disease were not uncommon. During this period it was thought that children from poor homes might be better raised in institutions where they might learn proper societal values. Poverty and a poor living environment were thought to be faults which children would learn from parents. Institutions such as the New York House of Refuge were established for neglected, abandoned, and delinquent youth. But the emphasis was not on protecting children from parents who harmed or neglected them. It was thought that placing children in institutions would help reverse the trend of poverty.

In the early twentieth century, the prevailing philosophy toward child care remained the "house of refuge." Even the establishment of juvenile courts in the early twentieth century did little to change this. Emphasis was on removing children from their homes, not on rehabilitating or treating parents. As the century progressed, though, more concern was expressed for children. They were removed from adult institutions, and new mothers' aid programs provided financial security to children in their natural homes. But abusive parents were not themselves the targets of social policies or social programs; in fact, the public continued to sympathize with parents who used physical force on their children.

It was not the social reformers, nor the judicial personnel of the juvenile courts, nor the public at large that discovered child abuse. It was *pediatric radiologists* who identified child abuse as a problem or "syndrome," gave it legitimacy, and aroused public concern. In 1946 John Caffey was the

TABLE 7–2　Child Abuse

Total Number of Reports of Neglect and Abuse	512,494
Source of Reports	
Friends, neighbors	17.2%
Relatives (includes siblings)	13.6
Law enforcement agency (includes courts)	11.6
Educational (includes school nurses, teachers, and other school personnel)	12.3
Medical (includes private and hospital physician, medical examiners, hospital personnel and nurses)	11.7
Community agency (includes public and private social agencies and preschools)	11.6
Parents/parent substitutes	7.1
Others (includes victims and anonymous reporters)	14.9
Alleged Perpetrators	
Natural parents	86.3
Other Parents (step, foster, adoptive)	8.8
Relatives	2.9
Other	2.0
Types of Substantiated Abuse Reported[a]	
Minor physical injuries[b]	13.0
Major physical injuries[b]	2.0
Burns, scaldings	0.9
Sexual abuse[b]	5.8
Types of Substantiated Neglect Reported[a]	
Physical neglect[c]	47.0
Emotional neglect[c]	16.6
Medical neglect	5.8
Educational neglect	5.0
Other abuse and neglect	6.0

[a]More than one category may have been recorded in each report.
[b]Categories included under *Major Physical Injuries* are: brain damage/skull fracture, subdural hemorrhage/hematoma, bone fracture, dislocation, sprain or twisting and internal injuries. Categories included under *Minor Physical Injuries* are: cuts, bruises, welts, and congenital drug addiction. *Sexual Abuse* includes rape, molestation, unnatural acts, incest, and unspecified sexual abuse.
[c]*Physical Neglect* includes: malnutrition, exposure to the elements, locking in/out, unintentional poisoning, abandonment, and lack of supervision. *Emotional Neglect* includes failure to thrive.

Source: *National Analysis of Official Child Abuse and Neglect Reporting, 1977,* September 1979, U.S. Department of HEW, Office of Human Development Services, Administration for Children, Youth and Families, Children's Bureau, National Center on Child Abuse and Neglect, DHEW Publication No. (OHDS) 79-30232, p. 59.

first to search for a cause of many of the bone fractures in children; his work led to the identification of parents as a cause of these fractures. However, Caffey and other pediatric radiologists were not the first to recognize child abuse. Emergency room physicians were the first to come into contact with these children, but at least four factors prevented them from discovering the problem. First, child abuse was not a traditional

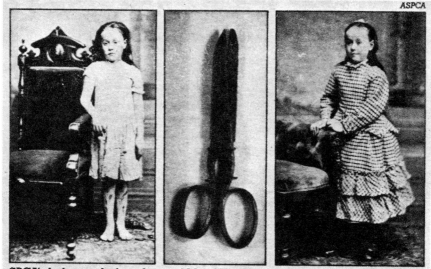

SPCA's *before-and-after* photos of Mary Ellen, with scissors used to punish her

Little Mary Ellen

Before 1875, U.S. authorities had no legal means to interfere in cases of battered children. The laws were changed with the help of the Society for the Prevention of Cruelty to Animals (SPCA).

A 9-year-old named Mary Ellen became the exemplar of the battered children's plight. Indentured to Francis and Mary Connolly (and rumored to be the daughter of Mary's ex-husband), the girl was whipped daily, stabbed with scissors and tied to a bed. Neighbors reported the situation to Etta Wheeler, a church worker, in 1874. When Wheeler found that there was no lawful way to rescue the child from her brutal guardians, she went to Henry Bergh of the SPCA for help.

Under the premise that the child was a member of the animal kingdom, the SPCA obtained a writ of habeas corpus to remove Mary Ellen from her home. On April 9, 1874, she was carried into the New York Supreme Court, where her case was tried. She was pitifully thin, with a scissor wound on her cheek. Mrs. Connolly was sentenced to a year in prison. Mary Ellen was given a new home. The following April, the New York Society for the Prevention of Cruelty to Children (NYSPCC) was incorporated.

Before-and-after photos of Mary Ellen (as a pathetic waif upon her rescue and as a healthy child a year later) still hang at the New York SPCA, framed with Mrs. Connolly's scissors.

(Reprinted with permission from Irving Wallace, David Wallachinsky, and Amy Wallace, "Significa," *Parade* magazine. Photos courtesy of ASPCA Archives.)

diagnosis. Second, doctors may not have believed that parents would abuse their children. Third, if the family, rather than just the child, was the doctor's patient, reporting abuse may have constituted a violation of patient confidentiality. Fourth, physicians may have been unwilling to report criminal behavior because of the time-consuming nature of criminal cases and their roles as witnesses in those proceedings.

Pediatric radiologists, rather than other physicians, discovered child abuse because they do *not* deal directly with the child and the family. Issues regarding confidentiality, who the client is, and court proceedings are not their primary concerns. The discovery of child abuse also served to elevate the status of pediatric radiologists. Radiologists were not highly regarded among members of the medical profession because they did not provide direct care to patients. Discovering child abuse allowed pediatric radiologists to develop closer collegial relationships with physicians with whom they consulted.

It was important to the medical profession that the discovery of child abuse be kept under its control. Child abuse had to be labeled a medical rather than a social or legal problem, or else physicians would be relegated to a subordinate role in its diagnosis and treatment. Child abuse was labeled "The Battered Child Syndrome" in 1962. Labeling child abuse as a medical syndrome legitimatized its recognition by physicians. Magazines, newspapers, and television programs, such as "Ben Casey" and "Dr. Kildare," publicized the discovery.

Between 1962 and 1965, every state passed legislation on child abuse. Today, child abuse legislation is aimed more at rehabilitating parents than punishing them. Most cases are reported to welfare rather than law enforcement agencies. Few persons are prosecuted and fewer are convicted. The social services that neglectful or abusive parents are most likely to receive are individual and group treatment. Self-help groups, such as Parents Anonymous, are also valuable sources of support. Social services for abusive and neglectful parents are directed at keeping the family unit intact. Most children in these families (80 percent) continue to remain at home.[23]

National Child Abuse Legislation

In January 1974 Congress passed the Child Abuse Prevention and Treatment Act and established the National Center for Child Abuse and Neglect. The purposes of the act are to assist the states in developing programs for abused and neglected children and to conduct abuse and neglect research.

To qualify for federal funds under this act, states' child abuse and neglect laws must (1) cover all children under eighteen years of age, (2) provide assistance in cases of mental, physical, and sexual abuse, (3) cover both neglect and abuse cases, (4) insure confidentiality of client records, and (5) see that a guardian ad litem (a guardian appointed for a specific purpose) is provided for children in cases which come before the court.

Since child abuse and neglect statutes are the prerogative of the states, there remains no single definition of child abuse or neglect. There is also no single piece of legislation that uniformly addresses abuse and neglect throughout the United States. Although available model legislation often serves as the basis for state statutes, it is still difficult to achieve consensus on definitions of child abuse and neglect. Even if simple definitions could be achieved, the problem of applying these definitions in specific cases would remain a problem. Child rearing and discipline practices also vary among communities and among those from different cultures, further compounding the problems of applying uniform definitions.[24]

SERVICES FOR OLDER AMERICANS

In many cultures, the senior members are respected and revered for their wisdom and knowledge. As important members of society, their decisions are most influential in shaping the direction of that culture. But such is not the case in America, where youth is cherished and where people spend money, time, and effort to prolong their youth. A society that worships youth and dreads old age tends to isolate older persons. The elderly are a vulnerable group. They are poorer than the population in general; they require greater amounts of health care; they are often excluded from pursuing gainful employment; they are prime targets for crimes like theft; their mobility is limited.

The proportion of elderly persons in America is growing. Advances in medicine and technology have prolonged the lives of Americans. As the elderly population grows, the elderly become more visible and their needs and demands upon society increase.

Earlier (in Chapter 4) we discussed the Social Security program and Medicare. These are important policy areas concerning the aged. However, in the 1960s, national policy began to recognize the social service needs of the elderly—especially in the Older Americans Act of 1965.

The Older Americans Act

The primary objectives of the Older Americans Act (OAA) are

An adequate income in retirement in accordance with the American standard of living.

The best possible physical and mental health that science can make available without regard to economic status

Suitable housing that is independently selected, designed and located, with reference to special needs and available at costs older citizens can afford

Full restorative services for those who require institutional care

Opportunity for employment with no discriminatory personnel practices because of age

Retirement in health, honor, and dignity—after years of contribution to the economy

Pursuit of meaningful activity within the widest range of civic, cultural, and recreational opportunities

Efficient community services including access to low-cost transportation, which provide a choice in supported living arrangements and social assistance in a coordinated manner and which are readily available when needed

Immediate benefit from proven research knowledge which can sustain and improve health and happiness

Freedom, independence, and the free exercise of individual initiative in planning and managing one's own life.

In order to qualify for services under the OAA a person must be at least sixty years old. Income is generally not used to determine eligibility, but the poor elderly are of special concern.

The OAA created an "aging network" to express the concerns of older Americans.[25] The network operates at the federal, regional, state, and local levels. At the federal level is the Administration on Aging (AoA) which is part of the Department of Health and Human Services. In addition to its advocacy function for older Americans, the AoA coordinates all federally operated programs for the aged. The AoA also provides technical assistance to state and local governments to help them develop and implement services for elderly persons, conducts evaluations of programs, conducts research on aging, and acts as a national clearinghouse on information about the elderly. To assist in its efforts, the AoA has ten regional offices across the United States.

At the state level, the aging network is generally found within the state's human services or welfare department, subordinate to an aging program office. The state offices assist in implementing federal policies and act as advocates for elderly citizens. They make the needs and problems of the aged known to the AoA and also to their own state legislatures, which have a great deal of influence on funding and administering state aging programs.

Most social services for the elderly are provided at the local level. At this level there are about 600 Area Agencies on Aging (AAAs). Each AAA is guided by an advisory council primarily composed of elderly persons. The AAAs perform their advocacy function by assessing the needs of the elderly in their communities. AAAs also distribute funds to community agencies that deliver services directly to the aged. Among the social services they provide are

Nutrition programs
Senior centers
Information and referral
Transportation
Homemaker and chore services
Legal counseling
Escort services
Home repair and renovation
Home health aid

Shopping assistance

Friendly visitation

Telephone assurance (phone calls to the elderly for reassurance and to check on their needs)

The OAA and the aging network are an important adjunct to the major financial programs (Social Security, SSI, and Medicare) for America's elderly. These social service programs provide important links for the elderly with the community. The OAA, for instance, represents an attempt to reintegrate elderly persons into the mainstream of American life. Social Security checks and Medicare services are helpful in relieving some of the financial burdens faced by America's elderly, but by themselves they are inadequate to alleviate many of the social problems faced by elderly citizens. The OAA helps round out financial assistance by responding to many of the needs of senior citizens, but the aging network is only as good as its reputation. Advocacy groups for older Americans are concerned that services be well publicized to insure they are utilized.

The Silver-Haired Legislatures

Several states have "silver-haired legislatures," where elderly citizens meet to discuss the problems of the aged and to recommend policies and problems to address these needs. The legislators meet and conduct a session similar to that of their elected state legislators, but the "laws" they "pass" are advisory.

Similar sessions have been conducted from time to time at the federal level. Several White House conferences on aging have been conducted, with elderly delegates from across the United States participating. The 1981 conference focused on the following issues concerning the elderly:

Improvement of their economic well being

Availability of quality health care

Establishment of a more comprehensive social service delivery system

Expansion of housing and long-term care facilities

Development of a national retirement policy

Offering of greater job opportunities

Overcoming of aging stereotypes

Stimulation of medical research on aging

The House of Representatives and the Senate each have special committees to address legislation concerning the elderly. Both the House and Senate committees were created in 1959. In the Senate, the committee is called the Special Committee on Aging and in the House it is called the Permanent Select Committee on Aging. State legislatures also have committees whose functions include addressing the financial and social needs of the elderly. In addition to these policy advisory groups, elderly people throughout the country have organized in an effort to make their needs known. Among the best known groups are the American Association of Retired Persons (AARP) and the Gray Panthers.

DO SOCIAL SERVICES REALLY WORK?

Do social services really help people? Evaluating any social welfare program or policy is difficult because social service programs are often without well-defined goals. There is a "confusion between policy ends and policy means. ... While federal and state governments are committed to 'doing something' about certain vulnerable populations, the end product of their efforts has not been specified."[26]

Even if we knew the specific goals of various social services, evaluating these services is not easy. There are two types of major obstacles to evaluation: political and methodological. Political obstacles operate at all levels of the social service delivery system. Evaluation is threatening to federal, state, and local government, to social service administrators, to social service workers, and last, but not least, to the recipients themselves. Evaluation is threatening to governments because it might imply that they have developed poor policies, passed inadequate laws in response to those policies, or funded ineffective programs. Evaluation is threatening to social service administrators because it might imply that they have done a poor job of implementing and managing the programs, laws, and policies developed by legislators. Evaluation is threatening to social service workers because it might imply that they are not adequately skilled in delivering and providing social services to clients. Finally, evaluation may be threatening to recipients because the process may invade their privacy, place pressure on them in times of personal crisis, and make them even more embarrassed about receiving social services.

A second major source of difficulty in conducting evaluations of social services is methodological. Methodological problems are problems found in the design of the evaluation. For example, there are difficulties in obtaining truly random samples and difficulties in generalizing from these special samples to the whole population. In addition, there is a "halo effect": Groups that are selected to receive services are more likely to improve because they are given attention, regardless of the quality of the service. Experimentation in the social services is also difficult since governments often cannot deny services to people. Many studies that are called *evaluations* are actually little more than a tabulation of the number of people seen, or the amount of services provided, rather than an evaluation of the actual effects or impacts of programs or services on these people.

But in spite of these political and methodological obstacles to evaluation, more efforts are being made to determine the effectiveness of social service programs. For example, one writer concluded that while there is very little empirical evidence of the overall effects of social service programs for the elderly, two demonstrable effects are "(1) an increase in the ability of the aged to maintain homes apart from younger relatives, and (2) an increase in proprietary nursing home beds for the sick aged."[27]

In the 1970s a number of studies were conducted to evaluate the success of community mental health centers.[28] A study conducted by the United States government's General Accounting Office spoke of the positive effects of CMHC programs. One effect cited was an increase in the availability of community care. In another report the Senate Committee on Labor and Public Welfare also discussed the positive results that have been achieved by CMHCs through provision of community-based care in lieu of institutional care. But other reports have not been as complimentary. A 1974 Nader Report states that community mental health centers have not reduced the number of persons admitted to state mental health institutions. The Nader Report accused psychiatrists of benefiting unfairly from the programs and of neglecting service to the poor.

A study of reports on child welfare services tells us that the effects of counseling services on families and children have not been clearly identified. Evaluation of services provided by family service and child guidance agencies has suggested "that the service is helpful, but available research does not establish this helpfulness at statistically significant levels."[29] Generally, half of those clients served by family service agencies show some improvement.[30] But the results of studies of child welfare services must be interpreted carefully.[31] Evaluative studies of child and family welfare programs suffer from the same methodological problems as other social service programs.

We see that it is difficult to determine the effects of social service programs. Studies that have attempted to evaluate the effectiveness of these programs often show mixed results. While there is no doubt that the number of social services available to those in need has increased, the demonstrable effects of these services are often limited or are ambiguous.

Should we conclude from this evaluation that social services are not very effective? This may be an unfair and premature assumption to make. Each of us can think of individuals who benefit greatly from social services: an elderly person who receives adequate meals through a nutrition program such as "Meals on Wheels," a friend whose depression has been relieved through services provided by a mental health center, a child whose adoption prevented transfer from foster home to foster home. In the aggregate, however, effects of social service programs cannot always be demonstrated easily. As attempts are made to perfect the delivery of these services to clients, researchers and program evaluators are also striving to develop evaluative strategies and techniques which take into account the political and methodological obstacles facing the evaluation of social service policies and programs.

SUMMARY

Social services include many types of programs, including day care, mental health care, juvenile delinquency prevention programs, child welfare programs, and nursing home care. Not all social services are directed toward the poor. People from all walks of life may require social services. Social services are provided by both public and private agencies. The federal government chose to reimburse the states at a generous rate for providing social services, especially those to public assistance recipients. Spending increased rapidly and the federal government exercised its option to control social service spending through Title XX of the Social Security Act.

Mental health services are one example of social services that may be needed by anybody regardless of economic and social status. Mental health services were first provided in large institutions where patients were often poorly treated. Better treatment methods such as "moral treatment," were regarded as too costly to provide. Reformers like Dorothea Dix helped improve institutional treatment, but it was not until the 1960s that greater emphasis was placed on community care. Two factors that paved the way for improved mental health legislation were (1) the identification of many young men with mental health problems during World War II and (2) the improvement of drugs which help the mentally ill function in society. The Community Mental Health Act of 1963 was the landmark legislation which encouraged the building and staffing of community mental health centers (CMHCs). CMHC services are available in most communities today.

One of the biggest obstacles faced by CMHCs is the fear that community residents have of mental health clients. Residents may oppose locating a mental health facility within their community because they believe that clients may harm their children, that the neighborhood will deteriorate, and that they will be forced to sell their property for less than it is worth. While these claims have not been substantiated, residents may resort to adopting zoning ordinances that prohibit the location of mental health facilities within their communities.

The United States has no official social policy for families and children, largely because of the belief that families should be relatively free from governmental intervention. In the United States a variety of policies govern family relations; some of these laws are used to intervene in cases of child abuse and neglect. Child abuse was not "discovered" in the United States until the 1960s when pediatric radiologists began looking for the cause of bone fractures and other unexplained traumas suffered by children. Prior to that time, punishment of children was considered a parental right. Children whose parents were incapable of caring for them were often sent to institutions to learn appropriate societal values, but parents were not the focus of treatment. Today public social service agencies are largely responsible for intervening in cases of neglect and abuse and for providing services to abusive parents.

The most important legislation which recognizes the social service needs of the elderly is the Older Americans Act of 1965. The act emphasizes a variety of services for the elderly, including nutrition programs and services which increase the capacity of the elderly to remain in the community. The Administration on Aging is the federal agency that is primarily responsible for administering this act by determining the needs of America's elderly and insuring that services are provided to address these needs. Some elderly persons may not be aware that a network of services is available to them within their communities.

Some attempts to evaluate the effectiveness of social services have produced positive results while others have been unclear about the benefits of social services. Social service providers and program evaluators can work together to develop better methods of assessing the effectiveness of social services.

NOTES

1. Alfred J. Kahn, *Social Policy and Social Services* (New York: Random House, 1979), pp. 12–13.
2. Robert Morris, *Social Policy of the American Welfare State: An Introduction to Policy Analysis* (New York: Harper & Row, Pub., 1979), p. 120.
3. U.S. Department of Health, Education and Welfare, *First Annual Report to Congress on Title XX of the Social Security Act,* 1977, p. 1.
4. Section 2001 of the Social Security Act as amended.
5. David Mechanic, *Mental Health and Social Policy,* 2nd ed. (Englewood Cliffs, N.J.: Prentice-Hall, 1980), pp. 15–16.
6. U.S. Department of Health and Human Services, Public Health Service, Alcohol, Drug Abuse, and Mental Health Administration, *Report of the Administrator, Alcohol, Drug Abuse, and Mental Health Administration,* 1979, p. 1.
7. Thomas R. Vischi, Kenneth R. Jones, Ella L. Shank, and Lowell H. Lima, U.S. Department of Health, Education and Welfare, Public Health Service, *The Alcohol, Drug Abuse, and Mental Health National Data Book: A Reference Book of National Data on Incidence and Prevalence, Facilities, Services Utilization, Practitioners, Costs, and Financing,* January 1980, p. 6.
8. Ibid.
9. Ibid.
10. Mechanic, *Mental Health and Social Policy,* pp. 51–52.
11. Ibid., p. 52.
12. Ibid., p. 53.
13. G. Grog, *The State and the Mentally Ill* (Chapel Hill, N.C.: University of North Carolina Press, 1966), cited in ibid., p. 54.
14. Ibid.
15. Ibid., p. 61.

16. See ibid., pp. 55–56 for a discussion of these psychiatric screenings.
17. Ibid., pp. 61–62.
18. Clara Claiborne Park with Leon N. Shapiro, *You Are Not Alone: Understanding and Dealing with Mental Illness—A Guide for Patients, Families, Doctors, and Other Professionals* (Boston: Little, Brown, 1976), pp. 93–94.
19. Bruce Denner and Richard H. Price, *Community Mental Health: Social Action and Reaction* (New York: Holt, Rinehart & Winston, 1973), p. v.
20. For a description of these programs see U.S. Department of Health, Education and Welfare, *Report on Federal Government Programs That Relate to Children,* 1979 prepared by the Representatives to the Federal Interagency Committee on the International Year of the Child, no. (OHDS) 79–30180.
21. These data are taken from U.S. Department of Health, Education and Welfare, Office of Human Development Services, National Center for Child Advocacy, U.S. Children's Bureau, Administration for Children, Youth, and Families, *National Study of Social Services to Children and Their Families. Overview,* prepared by Ann W. Shyne and Anita G. Schroeder, (Washington, D.C.: Government Printing Office, 1978), pp. 1, 3, 5, 6, 9, 12, 13, 17, 21, and 22.
22. This section relies on Stephen J. Pfohl, "The Discovery of Child Abuse," *Social Problems,* no. 3 (February 1977): 310–323.
23. Alfred Kadushin, *Child Welfare Services,* 3d ed. (New York: Macmillan, 1980), p. 199.
24. Ibid., pp. 214–220.
25. This section relies on Linda Hubbard Getze, "Need Help? What The Aging Network Can Do For You," *Modern Maturity* (March 1981): 33–36.
26. Morris, *Social Policy of the American Welfare State,* p. 133.
27. Ibid., p. 150.
28. See Lucy D. Ozarin, "Community Mental Health: Does It Work? Review of the Evaluation Literature," in Walter E. Barton and Charlotte J. Sanborn, eds., *An Assessment of the Community Mental Health Movement* (Lexington, Mass.: Heath, 1977), pp. 122–123.
29. Kadushin, *Child Welfare Services,* pp. 107–108.
30. Ibid., p. 99.
31. Ibid.

8

Fighting Hunger: Federal Food Programs

DO AMERICANS REALLY GO HUNGRY?

Hunger, malnutrition, undernutrition, and starvation are words that are often used interchangeably but actually have separate meanings. Consider the following definitions of these terms:

> *Hunger* is the subjective feeling that results from an individual's lack of food at a particular point in time.
>
> *Malnutrition* is an impairment or risk of impairment to mental or physical health resulting from the failure to meet the total nutrient requirements of an individual.
>
> *Undernutrition* is the consumption of an insufficient quantity of food or of one or more of the essential nutrients.
>
> *Starvation* is the state of advanced undernutrition, the effects of which are wastage of body tissue and ultimate death.[1]

Today, acute malnutrition is not commonplace among Americans, but problems of undernutrition, such as anemia, are more common.[2] One group of authors suggests that in America malnutrition should be re-defined as follows:

A person should be considered malnourished if for economic or other reasons beyond his control he experiences repetitive periods of prolonged hunger even though his total intake of nutrients is sufficient to protect him from symptoms of deficiency disease.[3]

This means that we cannot simply add up the amounts of calories, proteins, and vitamins a person consumes, and let the grand total suggest that a person is well nourished. Americans consume about the same amount of calories daily, regardless of whether they are poor, and most get more than enough of the essential nutrients, except for iron (see Table 8–1). Only whites above the poverty level take in 100 percent of the standard for iron. But for all other nutrients, everyone, rich or poor, receives more than 100 percent of the standard. For example, whites above the poverty line receive 82 percent more calcium than the standard for this nutrient, and blacks above the poverty line receive 32 percent more calcium than the standard. Whites below the poverty line receive less calcium than whites above the line, but those below the poverty line still receive more than the standard by 71 percent. Blacks below the poverty line receive less calcium than other groups but still get 29 percent more calcium than the standard.

However, in the United States, *patterns* of eating are more important than counting grams of protein or other numbers on the backs of food packages.[4] For example, in the United States poor people may eat adequately at the beginning of the month, but when food stamps, AFDC checks, or SSI checks run out near the end of the month, eating habits may change.[5] Or, the poor may have to decide between "heating and eating." Other patterns are also important. Children may attend school without breakfast and without money to buy lunch; supper may be their only full meal.[6] Parents may go without food in order to feed their children.[7] The poor elderly are sometimes unable to get to the store or have no teeth with which to chew food. In other cases people may not be able to obtain necessary nutrients from common food.[8] Some elderly persons have resorted to eating pet food to survive when finances have run low. When low-income families in southeast Washington, D.C., were asked what they would purchase if they had an additional $50 per month, eight out of twelve said, "food!"[9] Starvation may be rare or nonexistent in the United States, but patterns of inadequate nutrition do exist.

EARLY POLICIES: COMMODITY FOOD DISTRIBUTION

Prior to the 1930s, states and communities used their own devices to feed their "deserving" poor. But with the advent of the Great Depression, more and more people were unable to obtain enough food to eat. For many, the Great Depression conjures up pictures of men and women standing in bread lines and waiting in soup kitchens to obtain their only means of

TABLE 8–1 Average Daily Per Capita Consumption of Nutrients of Americans

	ALL PERSONS		PERSONS BELOW POVERTY LEVEL		PERSONS ABOVE POVERTY LEVEL	
	White	Black	White	Black	White	Black
Calories	2017	1825	1858	1742	2032	1885
Proteins (g)	78.92	69.65	70.42	65.65	79.67	72.50
Calcium (mg)	897	654	849	658	903	652
as % of Standard	181	131	171	129	182	132
Iron (mg)	12.10	10.80	10.90	10.26	12.21	11.21
as % of Standard	99	86	90	81	100	91
Vitamin A (I.U.)	4802	4613	4286	4587	4837	4714
as % of Standard	150	150	142	152	151	151
Vitamin C (mg)	86.99	80.01	69.33	75.97	88.83	83.31
as % of Standard	168	159	140	157	171	163

Source: *Statistical Abstract of the United States, 1979*, p. 128.

ILLUSTRATION: POLITICS DISCOVERS HUNGER

"Hunger in America was conceived as a national issue in April 1967 by two Northern senators in an alien rural south. On a mission guided by politics, they came to study poverty programs, but in the small Delta town of Cleveland, Mississippi, they found more than they had bargained for.

The United States Senator from New York felt his way through a dark, windowless shack, fighting nausea at the strong smell of aging mildew, sickness, and urine. In the early afternoon shadows, he saw a child sitting on the floor of a tiny back room. Barely two years old, wearing only a filthy undershirt, she sat rubbing several grains of rice round and round on the floor. The senator knelt beside her.

'Hello … Hi … Hi, baby…, he murmured, touching her cheeks and her hair as he would his own child's. As he sat on the dirty floor, he placed his hand gently on the child's swollen stomach. But the little girl sat as if in a trance, her sad eyes turned downward, and rubbed the gritty rice.

For five minutes he tried: talking, caressing, tickling, poking—demanding that the child respond. The baby never looked up.

The senator made his way to the front yard where Annie White, the mother of the listless girl and five other children, stood washing her family's clothes in a zinc tub. She had no money, she was saying to the senator, couldn't afford to buy food stamps; she was feeding her family only some rice and biscuits made from leftover surplus commodities.

For a few moments Robert F. Kennedy stood alone, controlling his feelings, which were exposed to the press entourage waiting outside the house. Then he whispered to a companion, 'I've seen bad things in West Virginia, but I've never seen anything like this anywhere in the United States.'

Senators Kennedy of New York and Joseph Clark of Pennsylvania discovered hunger that day, raw hunger imbedded in the worst poverty the black

South had known since the Depression of the 1930s. Driving along muddy, forgotten roads, the two senators and their aides stopped at shack after shack to see with their own eyes hungry, diseased children; to hear with their own ears the poor describe their struggle for survival."[1]

At the same time that political figures such as Robert F. Kennedy were discovering hunger, others were also investigating the problem of hunger. The Field Foundation, supported by the Field family of Chicago's Marshall Field department store, also documented the problems of eating, or not eating, in America.[2] Ten years later, in 1977, the Field Foundation conducted a follow-up study. The findings show that there are fewer cases of malnutrition today. And the doctors who conducted the study, four of whom had conducted the original 1967 study, suggest that federal food programs are responsible for much of the difference.[3]

Political conflict has played a large part in attempts to achieve the goal of reducing hunger. The goals of rational planning suggest that no American should go hungry; the politics of hunger in America suggest that nutrition programs remain part of the political struggle over welfare.

[1] Nick Kotz, *Let Them Eat Promises: The Politics of Hunger in America* (Englewood Cliffs, N.J.: Prentice-Hall, 1969), pp. 1, 2.
[2] Ibid,. pp. 7–9.
[3] Nick Kotz, *Hunger in America: The Federal Response* (New York: The Field Foundation, 1979), p. 9.

survival. These means of providing food for the poor were some of the first widespread attempts to deal with poverty and hunger in the United States. But this method of feeding needy persons was inadequate to meet the country's needs. In 1933 Congress established the Federal Surplus Relief Corporation to provide surplus commodity foods as well as coal, mattresses, and blankets to the poor.[10] Overproduction of food and encouragement by farmers to utilize surplus goods helped prompt the federal government to feed the poor. The Federal Surplus Relief Corporation provided as much relief to the agricultural industry as it did to the hungry.[11] The early commodity distribution program was characterized by recipients waiting in long lines to receive food, an experience which public officials believed was degrading for beneficiaries.[12]

There were other problems with the commodity food distribution program as well. Perishables were difficult to preserve, and alternatives to helping the hungry were needed. As a solution, the nation embarked on its first Food Stamp program in 1939. The program used two types of stamps, blue and orange. Orange stamps could be used to purchase any type of food; blue stamps could be redeemed only for surplus commodities. For every dollar spent on orange stamps, the beneficiary received fifty cents worth of blue stamps free.[13] Four years later, in 1943, the program ended. The American Enterprise Institute for Public Policy Research believes the program was terminated for three reasons: (1) Families who were poor but not receiving other public assistance payments were not eligible to receive assistance; (2) widespread participation was discouraged by purchase requirements which were believed to be too high; and (3) products other than surplus foods were sometimes purchased with the stamps.[14] These factors contributed to the early demise of the program.

With the termination of the original Food Stamp program came a return to the commodity food distribution method. Commodity distribution had been a popular method for feeding poor persons for at least two reasons. First, it insured that surplus foods would be utilized. Second, the poor were given foods which were supposed to meet minimum nutritional requirements. But the new commodity food distribution program left unsolved the problems of the original commodity program; food preservation remained a problem.

Alternatives to commodity distribution were continually considered. In 1961 President John F. Kennedy was able to begin a new Food Stamp program on a pilot basis. There was some early evidence that recipients purchased more and better goods under the program. This provided encouragement for passage of the Food Stamp Act of 1964.[15]

THE FOOD STAMP PROGRAM

Today's Food Stamp program is the responsibility of the United States Department of Agriculture (USDA), but local welfare agencies certify eligible recipients and provide them with the stamps. Recipients are given an allotment of stamps based on their income, assets, and family size. The stamps or food coupons, like money, come in various denominations and may be exchanged for food products in regular retail stores that choose to accept the coupons. Eligibility requirements and coupon allotments are established at the federal level.

The Food Stamp program was designed to be broader than the commodity distribution program. The states were to give food stamps to any persons whose income prevented them from acquiring an adequate diet. This meant that persons who were not welfare recipients but whose incomes were low (the near-poor) could also qualify.[16]

But food stamps have not always been provided at no charge. At first, the program worked like this: Those persons who qualified for benefits paid a specific price for their stamps, the amount depending on income, assets, and family size. The amount paid was supposed to be the amount the family would have spent on food. Recipients received stamps which had a greater value than the amount they paid. The difference between the amount paid and the value of the stamps was called the "bonus."

"In theory," says one observer, "the food stamp plan 'sounded' simple and workable, and should have been an enormous improvement over commodity distribution."[17] But, he says, what really happened was "extortion."[18]

> It was no accident that the stamp payment formula produced the outcries "We can't afford the stamps" and "The stamps run out after two weeks." Following their congressional leaders' twin desires of helping the farmers but not providing welfare to the poor, Agricultural Department bureaucrats had designed a Food Stamp program so conservative that reformers called the plan "Scrooge stamps."[19]

A number of changes were made in the Food Stamp program in the 1970s. Benefits were increased and eligibility and application procedures were standardized so that applicants are now treated similarly regardless of where they live or where they apply for stamps. Unemployed adult recipients who are capable of working are required to register for and accept work if a suitable job can be found.

A troublesome requirement had been that recipients were required to buy either all the stamps to which they were entitled or none at all. This requirement was modified so that a portion, rather than all of the stamps, could be purchased. The price of stamps could not exceed 30 percent of the household's income and in the poorest cases families could receive the stamps at no charge. Efforts were made to increase participation rates through advertising campaigns and outreach to nonparticipating eligible persons. In addition, communities were not immediately forced to choose between food stamps and commodity distribution. They could operate both programs until 1973, when food stamps had to be the program available in all communities.

THE ELIMINATION OF PURCHASE REQUIREMENTS

The most significant change in the Food Stamp program since its inception has been the elimination of the purchase requirements in 1977. Critics had held that the Food Stamp program did not necessarily make eating better or easier for the poor. For many families the amount they had to spend for food stamps was more than they could actually afford—without taking from the rent or other necessities. Other reasons for low participation have been the stigma attached to "being on welfare," lack of knowledge of the program, and inability to get to the Food Stamp office to apply. The elimination of the purchase requirement helped to increase participation rates. In the Southeast participation rose by over 32 percent, in the Mountain Plains by almost 32 percent, and in the Southwest by almost 31 percent. These areas include many rural states. In New England participation increased by only 7 percent.[20] Although all eligible persons do not participate, the Food Stamp program comes closer to being available to all needy Americans than any other welfare program.[21]

Rising food stamp expenditures, attributable to the increase in participation, have caused concern in Congress and the nation (see Figure 8–1). In 1965 the program cost a modest $32 million. By 1970 costs had risen to $473 million, still a relatively reasonable figure. But by 1980 costs exceeded $9 billion and were still rising. Even after controlling for inflation, program costs have risen dramatically, but many eligible persons still do not apply. Full participation would mean even greater program costs.

WHO GETS FOOD STAMPS?

The "working poor" and the "near-poor," as well as the poor, are eligible for food stamps. About twenty-two million persons, or approximately 10 percent of all Americans, receive food stamps. Table 8–2 shows some general characteristics of food stamp households. Public assistance recipients are automatically eligible for food stamps, and others must meet specified financial eligibility requirements. About 60 percent of food stamp recipients receive public assistance payments like AFDC or SSI. In determining eligibility for food stamps, family size is considered and certain

Figure 8-1 Food Stamp program—federal government contributions in billions of dollars, 1965-1981. *(Statistical Abstract of the United States, 1977,* p. 121; *1979,* p. 130; *Congressional Quarterly,* "Congress to Decide Fate of Food Stamps," February 7, 1981, p. 277.)

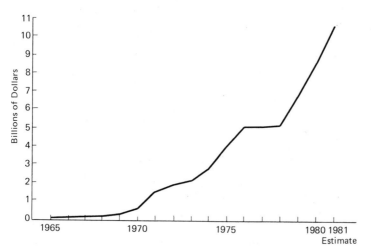

items are deducted from the family's income. Deductions include income taxes and OASDHI taxes, contributions to pension programs, union dues, excess medical costs, the cost of child care while a parent or parents are employed, and educational costs. Once an individual or family is declared eligible, the amount of stamps to be allotted is calculated. A family of four with no income receives $233 worth of foods stamps per month. The average monthly benefit per person is $38.95 per month or 44 cents per meal.

Much of America's poverty is concentrated in the South. The South has the highest participation rates in the Food Stamp program (39 percent). The Northeast ranks second in food stamp households with 24 percent, compared to 22 percent in the North Central United States, and 15 percent in the West.

The sizes of the households receiving food stamps vary. Unlike the AFDC program, single and married persons without children are eligible for food stamps. Twenty-two percent of all food stamp households contain only one person, while 17 percent have six or more persons. Eighty percent of all food stamp households report incomes of under $6,000 per year and 43 percent have annual incomes under $3,000.

Food stamp households tend to be headed by young persons. Almost forty percent are headed by persons under thirty-five years of age. Only 17 percent of food stamp households are headed by persons sixty-five years of age or older. These figures may represent a reluctance on the part of older people to participate in welfare programs, especially if they are not receiving other forms of public assistance and have never before received public assistance benefits.

Food stamp recipients tend not to be part of the labor force. Almost 60 percent of recipients are not employed because of advanced age or illness, or because they are caring for small children or others needing full-time attention. To qualify to receive food stamps, all able-bodied persons in the household who are not employed must register for work with the state employment agency and accept suitable employment if found. Thirty percent of recipients are employed, while 12 percent are currently unemployed but seeking work. At one time students who were not employed but who were self-supporting were eligible for food stamps. The new work requirement has disqualified many students who do not wish to accept employment.

Almost 60 percent of food stamp households are headed by women. This is especially true of black households. Seventy percent of black food stamp households are headed by women as compared with half of white food stamp households.

Taking a closer look at the racial composition of food stamp households, 37 percent of all food stamp households are black. A slightly greater proportion of black food stamp households than white food stamp households receive public assistance, and black food stamp households tend to be found in cities rather than rural areas. On other variables such as age, income, size of household, and employment status, blacks and whites who receive food stamps do not differ very much.

Some special categories of people can also receive food stamps. For example, alcohol and drug abusers receiving treatment in residential facilities can qualify for stamps. Victims of disasters like floods and fires may also be entitled.

PURCHASING HABITS OF FOOD STAMP RECIPIENTS

Do food stamp recipients shop differently from other people? An exploratory study conducted in Cookeville, Tennessee in 1978 compared food stamp with non–food stamp recipients and found the differences shown in Table 8–3. According to this study, there are a number of differences between food stamp shoppers and those who do not receive stamps. Food stamp shoppers are less likely to prepare for trips to the grocery store by making shopping lists. They shop in small nearby stores, unlike other shoppers who generally buy in supermarkets. In addition, food stamp recipients shop in stores that are located close to home, rather than in stores that charge lower prices. Food stamp shoppers are more satisfied with their local stores and appear to be less concerned about price, although they do buy in larger quantities than non–food stamp shoppers. But we cannot necessarily blame the poor for their shopping habits. They may have less access to information about sales and other shopping values. The poor are less likely to own automobiles, preventing them from attending shopping sales at far away supermarkets. Neighborhood stores tend to offer less selection at higher prices than large chain grocery stores, but without transportation the poor may be forced to shop in these nearby establishments.

In contrast to the study represented in Table 8–3, other studies suggest that food stamp shoppers spend their money and stamps in the same fashion as middle-class shoppers. For example, one study reports that the poor and the middle-class spend about the same percentage of their shopping dollar on meat and dairy products, but that the poor buy less expensive foods within these categories.[22] The accompanying illustration tells us about the diet of food stamp recipients. Stamp allotments allow recipients to purchase only the most economical foods under the "basic thrifty food plan" established by the United States Department of Agriculture. The illustration which follows tells us what receiving food stamps is like for one mother.

TABLE 8–2 Characteristics of Households Participating in the Federal Food Stamp Program

	% OF ALL HOUSEHOLDS RECEIVING FOOD STAMPS	% OF WHITE HOUSEHOLDS RECEIVING FOOD STAMPS	% OF BLACK HOUSEHOLDS RECEIVING FOOD STAMPS
Northeast	24.4	26.7	20.7
North-Central	21.7	21.6	22.5
South	38.6	33.0	49.4
West	15.2	18.7	7.4
Size of household			
1 person	21.7	23.5	19.2
2 persons	18.7	20.8	14.7
3 persons	17.6	16.7	19.0
4–5 persons	23.7	23.8	23.9
6 or more persons	16.8	14.0	21.5
Annual money income			
under $2,000	20.7	19.1	23.4
$2,000–$2,999	22.0	20.7	24.1
$3,000–$3,999	17.3	18.0	16.2
$4,000–5,999	20.1	18.6	22.4
$6,000–$9,999	11.6	13.1	8.8
$10,000 and over	5.4	6.7	3.1
Received Public Assistance	60.4	55.1	69.5
No Public Assistance	39.6	44.9	30.5
Head of household			
under 35 years	38.8	38.8	38.7
35–54 years	32.3	30.2	35.8
55–64 years	11.7	11.4	12.3
65 years and over	17.2	19.6	13.2
Employed	28.8	20.8	25.0
Unemployed	12.5	12.9	12.0
Not in labor force	58.6	56.3	63.0
Male head of family	41.7	48.9	29.5
Female head of family	58.2	51.2	70.5
Metropolitan area			
SMSA (Standard Metropolitan Statistics Area)	64.7	59.7	73.1
in central cities	44.8	34.7	61.5
outside central cities	19.9	25.0	11.6
Nonmetropolitan and farm	35.3	40.3	26.9

Source: United States Bureau of the Census, *Statistical Abstract of the United States, 1979*, p. 130.

THE NATIONAL SCHOOL LUNCH PROGRAM

The National School Lunch Act became law in 1946. Under this program, school age children obtain hot lunches at reduced prices or free if their parents are unable to pay. The program operates in the following way: The

TABLE 8–3 **Comparison of Food Shopping Behavior of Food Stamp Recipients and Nonsubsidized Food Purchasers**

FOOD STAMP RECIPIENTS	NONSUBSIDIZED SHOPPERS
1. Engage in less prepurchase preparation	1. Engage in extensive prepurchase preparation
2. Have less shopping experience	2. Have wide shopping experience
3. Shop in small, nearby stores	3. Shop in supermarkets, traveling as necessary
4. Choose a store on basis of location	4. Choose a store on basis of price
5. Are relatively unconcerned with selection	5. Are highly concerned with selection
6. Are not inclined to believe that supermarkets offer price, quality, or selection advantages	6. Believe that supermarkets offer price, quality, and selection advantages
7. Are well satisfied with their regular store	7. Express frustration and suggest store improvements
8. Do not perceive private brands favorably	8. Believe private brands offer acceptable quality at lower prices
9. Buy larger unit sizes	9. Buy smaller unit sizes
10. Are not very price-conscious	10. Are highly price-conscious

Source: Gerald Underwood Skelly, *A Study of the Differential Food Purchasing Behavior of Federal Food Stamp Recipients and Non-Subsidized Food Purchasers,* Dissertation, Florida State University, 1978, p. 231.

ILLUSTRATION: DOROTHY: "HAVING TO ASK, AND ASK, AND ASK"

Dorothy used food stamps off and on for six years. At the time of the interview, she was supporting her six children through a CETA job program and was no longer getting food stamps.

She first applied for the program when her husband left several years ago. Having had no previous training, she found it hard to find a job. "It was a difficult time," she said, "but we all stayed together. We figured that was the only way we were going to make it.

"Food stamps were good for me," she continued. "I'd get them once a month and I'd know I had that much food money coming to me that month, and I just had to budget accordingly.

"The family helped out a lot. The children wouldn't go into the refrigerator on their own. When they wanted something, they would ask. And although that's a good thing, that's bad, too. It's not a normal way to live, really. But being on assistance makes things different anyway.

"You have to live different than other people," she said, pausing. "You feel different. You feel different going into the store and pulling out food stamps rather than money. It's a terrible way to live. It really is."

Even though she no longer participates in the Food Stamp program, Dorothy continues to be active in a food stamp client relations group sponsored by the local department of social services. Her work as chairman of the group has given her a lot of insight into the problems of food stamp users.

People keep hoping, she said, that somehow, somewhere, money is going to turn up, and they won't have to ask for assistance. "You just keep thinking something's going to happen to relieve the situation. By the time people show up at the food stamp office, it's often a last ditch measure and the pressure's on.

"It's frightening. It's so frightening. You almost forget what you're doing, and you almost can't fill that form out."

The new application forms, she said, are an improvement, however. They are "easier to read. They're printed up better. They're written better. Easier to understand."

A crisis facing Dorothy at the time of the interview was whether or not she would be able to keep the CETA job that had kept her off assistance and food stamps for the past year.

"Employment is bad right now," she said, "and I'm still in the job market where just about everybody has more skills than me.

"But I have a better feeling now after having worked in the CETA program for a year. I've learned some things and I've gotten more respect for myself—my children have and my family has, too.

"If I have to go back on assistance," said Dorothy, "I will be eligible for food stamps. And that's one thing that frightens me. I am not going back on assistance and that's all there is to it. No, I'm not, no matter what—not assistance or food stamps, no indeed."

And what if the CETA job doesn't come through and she can't find another one right away? Will the stigma she feels in using food stamps be too high a price to pay?

Dorothy smiled and shook her head slightly. "Not for going hungry. You have to swallow your pride. I've had to do it enough. But I don't like it. I never will get used to it. I don't know whether people ever really do. They may say they do but ... you don't really get used to having to ask, and ask, and ask."

Source: Dianne D. Jenkins, "People Talk About Using Food Stamps", *Food and Nutrition* 9, no. 4 (August 1979), p. 3.

ILLUSTRATION: WHAT FOOD STAMP RECIPIENTS EAT

The massive overall spending totals for the Food Stamp program come down, at the individual family level, to a supplement for a rather spartan diet.

Food stamp benefit levels are based on the "Thrifty Food Plan," the lowest priced of the Agriculture Department's four family food plans. It outlines the cheapest types of food a family can eat and still get a nutritionally adequate diet.

Sample menus prepared by the department for the low-cost plan rely heavily on starches and sugar, with relatively small quantities of meat, fruits and vegetables. For example, one sample menu provides one-half pound of hamburger, two-thirds of a pound of liver, a small ham, a chicken, a can of tuna and some bologna as the meat for a family of four for a week.

The department estimates that it costs $233 a month to feed a family of four (two adults, two grade-school children) on the Thrifty Plan. No allowance is made for types of people in a family, whether teenagers with big appetites or old people with small ones.

The department assumes families should spend 30 percent of their net incomes on food. To compute food stamp allotments, it subtracts 30 percent of net income from the cost of the Thrifty Food Plan. Thus a family of four with no net income gets $233 a month in stamps, a family with $100 a month in income gets $203, and one with a $500 monthly income gets $83.

Some nutritionists criticize the Thrifty Food Plan as inadequate. Even in the best of circumstances, it provides certain age groups with less than the Recommended Daily Allowance (RDA) for nutrients such as vitamin B_6, magnesium, and iron. And many poor people do not have the nutritional knowledge to obtain an ideal diet with limited resources. Agriculture Department studies have shown that less than 10 percent of families spending at Thrifty Food Plan levels get 100 percent of the RDAs for nutrients; less than half get even two-thirds of the various RDAs.

Source: Harrison Donnelly, "Congress to Decide Fate of Food Stamps," *Congressional Quarterly*, Feb. 7, 1981, p. 278.

federal government, through the Food and Nutrition Service of the Department of Agriculture, provides cash assistance and food commodities to state departments of education. The departments of education then distribute the cash and food to public and private nonprofit schools that have agreed to participate in the program. Annual expenditures for the program exceed $2 billion and over 4 billion lunches are served each year to about 27 million children.[23] These 27 million children represent 60 percent of all school children.[24] Some 93,000 schools participate in the program.[25]

These figures sound impressive, but they might be more impressive if we could know for certain that the bulk of the program's benefits go to poor children. Middle-class children have often been the beneficiaries of the program.[26] And for two reasons, some poor children do *not* benefit from the National School Lunch program. First, in areas where parents must pay for the lunches, the cost per week, which is now as much as $3.75 in some communities, may still be more than some parents can afford. Second, in order to participate schools must have kitchen facilities to prepare the meals and areas in which to serve the meals. Schools in poor neighborhoods have often lacked these resources. Meals could be catered to these schools, but school lunch administrators have been known to lobby against earmarking federal funds for free meals to poor children, for fear that private caterers will take over their jobs.[27] The administrators contend they can take care of poor children out of general federal school lunch aid, yet, critics argue that these administrators have provided free lunches to less than half of the poor children in school.[28]

The School Breakfast program is operated in a similar fashion to the School Lunch program. Families pay as they are able, and the poorest do not pay at all. But because resources allocated for the program are not enough for all school districts, a priority system has been established. Schools in the poorest areas and schools to which children must travel long distances are given preference. While this is a rational approach to providing school breakfasts, the School Breakfast program, like the School Lunch program, has sometimes defied rationality. As with other programs, school districts must choose to participate in the program. Why would schools choose *not* to participate in a program that would benefit hungry children? First, the program means more administrative responsibilities for school personnel. Second, adoption of the program may mean that teachers and other school personnel must monitor the breakfasts and come to school earlier when the breakfasts are served before class. These factors may make the program unpopular among school personnel who do not wish to see the school day lengthened.

We have stated that one purpose of food programs for poor people has been to help agri-business sell its surplus foods. The Special School Milk program which began in 1954 was no different. Having begun at a time when the market was full of surplus dairy products, the program subsidizes the cost of the sale of milk to school children. Over 2 billion half pints of milk are distributed each year under this program.[29]

MEALS ON WHEELS

The Meals on Wheels program, begun in 1972, is part of a federal program to improve the nutrition of the elderly. States receive funding and coordinate administration of the program with local agencies. The agencies are responsible for seeing that the meals are prepared and delivered to the elderly persons. Elderly individuals who receive food stamps can pay for these meals with stamps and a donation amount is suggested for those who can afford to pay cash. In other cases, meals are provided at sites such as senior citizens' centers. In addition to improved nutrition, there is a positive spillover effect from these meal programs for the elderly. Often isolated, the elderly are provided a means to maintain contact with others in their community. A visit by the Meals on Wheels volunteer provides a check, in case the elderly individual has become ill or needs other assistance.

WIC

The Special Supplemental Nutrition Program for Women, Infants, and Children is informally referred to as WIC. The purpose of WIC is to upgrade the nutrition of low-income women, infants, and young children. The Food and Nutrition Service of the Department of Agriculture operates this program in cooperation with local health clinics and departments. Pregnant women, women with newborns, and those who wish to breast-feed are given food high in important nutrients. Infants and children under five years old can also receive food commodities. Some of the foods available through the program are eggs, juices, cheese, cereals fortified with iron, and fortified formulas for infants.

CASH vs. IN-KIND:
THE CONTINUING DEBATE

The older of the major welfare programs—for example, AFDC and SSI (formerly Old Age Assistance, Aid to the Blind, and Aid to the Permanently and Totally Disabled)—are *cash* assistance programs. The newer welfare programs—for example, Food Stamps and Medicaid—are *in-kind* programs. Why are the benefits of newer welfare programs administered differently from older welfare programs?

It might be argued that administering all welfare programs on a cash basis would be more efficient. AFDC and SSI recipients who qualify for food assistance would simply have their checks increased as a more efficient means of providing nutritional benefits. While the use of food stamps does allow recipients greater choice of food products than commodity distribution, the use of stamps is still stigmatizing to recipients as they stand in grocery store check-out lines. A cash allowance equal to the value of the stamps would reduce or eliminate this stigma and still allow the beneficiary a choice of food products.

But the choice of a cash allowance has been rejected. Part of the explanation is found in the nature of in-kind programs. Politicians who allot funds to the poor may believe that the use of stamps will insure a more adequate diet for the poor, since the stamps may be spent only to purchase food. Proponents of the use of stamps believe that this plan reduces the chances of food allowances being used for other purposes. Most food stamps are used to purchase food, although from time to time we hear reports of recipients who use stamps to buy expensive food or sell the stamps for cash. On the other hand, there is little evidence to suggest that a cash allowance would not be used to purchase food, and neither cash nor stamps can insure that recipients will purchase the most nutritious foods. In fact, many Americans, rich and poor, need guidance in obtaining a healthy diet.[30]

HOW MUCH FRAUD AND ERROR
IN WELFARE?

Do a large number of welfare clients cheat? Would recipients rather collect benefits than work? Are merchants who accept food stamps profiting unfairly from the Food Stamp program by overcharging food stamp recipients? Do the doctors who accept Medicare and Medicaid payments order more diagnostic tests and treatments than patients need? In addition to fraud, are welfare program administrators concerned about reducing errors in processing welfare applications? Are payments workers careful in their calculations of eligibility and payments to recipients? When we talk about fraud and error in welfare, we cannot limit our concerns to welfare clients alone. Those who provide services to welfare clients and those who administer welfare programs must also be considered.

Figures on the number of clients who "cheat" vary. Several years ago the Department of Health, Education and Welfare reported that less than 1 percent of welfare clients were reported for possibly committing fraud and that even fewer were prosecuted for fraud.[31] Admittedly, methods of detecting welfare fraud are limited, and those who believe that there are larger numbers of welfare cheats could argue that fraud often goes undetected or ignored. Studies have shown that the number of ineligible persons who receive AFDC and food stamps does not exceed 10 percent; in addition about 23 percent are receiving overpayments and 8 percent are receiving underpayments.[32] The National Food Stamp Information Committee believes that fraud and error rates are lower for the Food Stamp program, with only 4 percent of beneficiaries ineligible.[33] And it is unlikely that ineligibles who receive payments are financially well-off. In other words, stories about recipients who drive to the welfare department in Cadillacs are largely sensationalistic.

One charge leveled against welfare recipients is that they could really work if they wanted to and that many able-bodied persons are receiving welfare payments unfairly. Actually, many welfare recipients are not able to work because they are the mothers of small children or because they are too old, disabled, or ill to hold a job. Able AFDC mothers must register to work; the same is true for able-bodied food stamp recipients. Failure to accept suitable employment can result in loss of benefits.

Error rates may be attributed in part to welfare administrators and payment workers—the people who process welfare applications and determine eligibility, amounts of payments, and the conditions under which welfare clients must apply if they wish to receive benefits. Some reports suggest that about half of administrative errors are made by caseworkers.[34] Administrative errors such as overpayment and underpayment can be attributed to miscalculations by workers, failure by workers to understand the complicated rules which govern eligibility, the large number of cases to be processed, the volume of paperwork, and other unintentional or careless mistakes.

"Quality control" is a term and a method borrowed from business and industry.[35] In industry it refers to a process whereby samples of products, for example cars, are taken and checked or tested to insure that they perform adequately. In welfare the term quality control refers to the process of taking a sample of cases to insure that welfare recipients are actually eligible and that they are neither being paid too much nor too little. Sampling is based on scientific techniques to assure that the cross section of cases reviewed truly represents the range of recipients.

The federal government sets the standards and procedures for quality control, and the state welfare agencies actually review and investigate the cases by interviewing clients and verifying records such as rent receipts and pay check stubs. In any system which serves large numbers of people, some error is bound to occur. The federal government, however, believes that only a certain amount of error is tolerable. Error tolerance levels are 3 percent for ineligible persons receiving AFDC and 5 percent in cases where persons are eligible but are receiving overpayments. When a state determines that its error rate is too high, it is required to take steps to reduce error.

Some recent accounts of welfare fraud have focused on the "vendors" of welfare services. Vendors are those persons such as doctors who provide care to Medicare and Medicaid patients, food store retailers who exchange food stamps for groceries, and landlords who receive rent payments for those who qualify for subsidized housing. Television programs and newspaper reports have exposed doctors and operators of health clinics for overcharging for Medicare and Medicaid services and for charging for services that patients never received. Some individuals question whether grocers might overcharge those food stamp recipients who are forced to shop at a neighborhood store or not at all. Also landlords may collect the rent in subsidized housing units but fail to provide adequate heating or needed repairs.

The problem we face in trying to determine if there is a great deal of fraud and needless error in welfare programs is that different people can study the same welfare programs but obtain different findings and interpret the data differently. There is no single formula for determining whether the rates of fraud and error are extraordinarily high. Certainly, we would all like to see fairly administered welfare programs that cover those in need, result in few errors and no fraud, and actually help people! We often produce welfare policies that sound rational but result in unfair treatment of people, thus raising public concern that programs are poorly administered and that benefits sometimes go to persons who do not qualify.

POLITICS AND FOOD

The early commodity distribution programs were closely tied to federal agricultural policy. The U.S. government purchased agricultural products to guarantee a minimum income for farmers; the distribution of these products from federal stockpiles to the poor was viewed as a means of disposing of food surpluses. The federal government's community distribution programs had the support of the powerful farm lobby, the American Farm Bureau Federation, and the nation's farmers.

The current Food Stamp program, initiated in 1964, was also tied to agricultural policy—at least in its early years. The Food Stamp program began as a modest part of the activities of the U.S. Department of Agriculture. Initially the program had the support of farmers and of organizations who viewed the program as a means of increasing the demand for farm goods. But by the mid–1970s the Food Stamp program had outgrown all other farm programs and was on its way to becoming a $12 billion enterprise. The Food Stamp program eventually grew much larger than all other programs of the U.S. Department of Agriculture. Agriculture interests came to believe that the Food Stamp program was not directly linked to farm prices, farmers' incomes, and farm surpluses; the stamps were used for a wide variety of packaged foods sold at retail stores. At the same time, U.S. farmers began to acquire major markets for surplus foods in foreign trade. Indeed, by 1980 nearly half of U.S. farm production was sold in international markets. Farmers became less dependent on federal purchases of surpluses. Thus, the Food Stamp program lost an important political base—farmers and farm organizations.

Politically, it is easier to win support for an in-kind program, which distributes food to the poor, than a cash program, which distributes money to the poor. "Feeding the poor" appeals to nearly everyone. But cash payments do not carry the same urgency. Money can be spent for many purposes; not all of these purposes are viewed as "worthy" by the taxpayers whose money is being spent. It is true that it might be more "natural" to provide the poor with cash to purchase whatever they need most. But food stamps focus the aid on a recognized need—eating. No one really wants to see hunger or malnutrition in America. Thus, we can expect the Food Stamp program to continue, although its rate of growth may be slowed.

The Reagan administration has attempted to "reform" the Food Stamp program "to re-focus the program on its original purpose—to insure adequate nutrition for America's needy families." The administration believes that the program grew too large during the 1970s by allowing many families with higher than poverty-level incomes to participate. The result was "to divert the Food Stamp program away from its original purpose toward a generalized income transfer program, regardless of nutritional need."[36]

The Reagan reforms have included (1) tightening eligibility requirements so that only those families near or below the poverty line can participate; (2) calculating family income partly on the basis of past income rather than current income; (3) monitoring programs to reduce fraud and error; and (4) altering or eliminating cost-of-living adjustments in the program.

SUMMARY

Food is the most basic necessity of life. The United States has more than enough food for all of its people, and starvation is rare in America. Programs such as commodity distribution and Food Stamps have helped to improve the nutrition of poor Americans, but not all Americans eat adequately every day. Some do not eat well because they select foods that are not nutritious. Others do not eat well because they cannot afford enough food. Due to high food prices, food stamp allotments may be insufficient for recipients to afford enough food at the end of the month. Parents may go without food so their children can eat properly. The poor elderly may eat uncommon foods to survive. Most poor people say that if they were provided with additional income, they would spend it on food.

The first food programs provided surplus commodity foods to the poor. The programs were as much welfare programs for farmers, who were unable to sell their surplus foods, as they were for the poor. Commodity food programs were replaced by the Food Stamp program because perishables were difficult to keep and because the poor had been restricted in selecting foods. Stamps are a cumbersome method of providing food to the poor, but the idea of a cash allotment had been rejected by those who want to insure that the money goes to buy food. There is little evidence, however, to suggest that the poor would use a cash allotment for other purposes.

The major revision of the Food Stamp Act of 1964 came in 1977 with the elimination of the requirement that recipients pay for the stamps. Eliminating this requirement has increased low participation which had been blamed on the recipients' inability to afford the stamps.

The Food Stamp program is still criticized by those who insist the program is riddled with fraud. They accuse food stamp recipients of using the stamps to buy expensive food products that the average American cannot afford. They have also accused beneficiaries of selling the stamps for cash, an illegal practice. Research shows that less than 10 percent of recipients do not actually qualify for welfare assistance.

The Food Stamp program has come closer to covering all poor persons than any other welfare program. Some proposals, however, may limit the number of eligible persons. Examples of these proposals are enforcing "workfare"; reducing payments to families that also benefit from school breakfast and school lunch programs; and raising income limitations.

NOTES

1. The confusion in meanings of these terms is clarified by the Senate Select Committee on Nutrition and Human Needs as noted in Nick Kotz, *Let Them Eat Promises: The Politics of Hunger in America* (Englewood Cliffs, N.J.: Prentice-Hall, 1969), p. 35.
2. Barbara Bode, Stanley Gershoff, and Michael Latham, "Defining Hunger Among the Poor" in Catherine Lerza and Michael Jacobson, *Food For People, Not For Profit* (New York: Ballantine, 1975), pp. 299–300.
3. Ibid., p. 301.
4. Ibid., pp. 301–302.
5. Ibid., pp. 300–302.
6. Ibid., p. 301.
7. Ibid., p. 302.
8. Ibid., p. 301.
9. Ibid., p. 302.
10. Lucy Komisar, *Down and Out in the USA* (New York: New Viewpoints, 1977), p. 51.
11. Ibid., p. 51 and Kotz, *Let Them Eat Promises*, p. 45.
12. Komisar, *Down and Out*, p. 51.
13. Paul A. Brinker, *Economic Insecurity and Social Security* (Englewood Cliffs, N.J.: Prentice-Hall, 1968), pp. 390–391.
14. American Enterprise Institute for Public Policy Research, *Food Stamp Reform* (Washington, D.C.: 1977), p. 3.
15. American Enterprise Institute, *Food Stamp Reform*, p. 4.
16. Laurence E. Lynn, Jr., "A Decade of Policy Developments in the Income-Maintenance System" in Robert H. Haveman, *A Decade of Federal Antipoverty Programs: Achievements, Failures, and Lessons* (New York: Academic Press, 1977), p. 75.
17. Kotz, *Let Them Eat Promises*, p. 52.
18. Ibid., pp. 52–53.
19. Ibid., p. 53.
20. U.S. Department of Agriculture, "Food Stamp Changes Help the Rural Poor," *Food and Nutrition* 10, no. 1 (February 1980): 2.
21. Robert M. Ball, *Social Security Today and Tomorrow* (New York: Columbia University Press, 1978), p. 363.
22. Donald A. West, "Food Expenditures by Food Stamp Participants and Non-Participants," *National Food Review*, U.S. Department of Agriculture, June 1978, cited in Kotz, *Hunger in America: The Federal Response*, (New York: The Field Foundation, 1979), p. 16.
23. William Lawrence and Stephen Leeds, *An Inventory of Federal Income Transfer Programs* (White Plains, N.Y.: The Institute for Socio-economic Studies, 1978), cited in Ronald C. Federico, *The Social Welfare Institution: An Introduction*, 3rd ed. (Lexington, Mass.: D. C. Heath, 1980), p. 345.
24. U.S. Department of Commerce, Bureau of the Census, *Statistical Abstract of the United States, 1979*, p. 129.
25. Ibid.

26. Dorothy James, *Poverty, Politics and Change* (Englewood Cliffs, N.J.: Prentice-Hall, 1972), pp. 58–59.
27. Kotz, *Let Them Eat Promises*, p. 59.
28. Ibid.
29. U.S. Department of Commerce, Bureau of the Census, *Statistical Abstract of the United States, 1979*, p. 129.
30. Kotz, *Hunger in America: The Federal Response*, p. 16.
31. Department of Health, Education and Welfare, "Welfare Myths vs Facts," pamphlet SRS–72–02009 cited in Federico, *Social Welfare Institution*, p. 83.
32. *The Federal Budget of the United States Government*, Fiscal Year 1975, pp. 128–129.
33. National Food Stamp Information Committee, *The Facts About Food Stamps* (November/December 1975), p. 9.
34. Ibid.
35. U.S. Department of Health, Education and Welfare, *Quality Control in Aid to Families with Dependent Children*, no. (SRS) 74–04009, revised 1973.
36. *America's New Beginning: A Program for Economic Recovery*, Washington, D.C., February 18, 1981, p. 1.

9

Warring
On Poverty:
Victories, Defeats,
and Stalemates

THE CURATIVE STRATEGY—
THE "WAR ON POVERTY"

American confidence in the ability of government to solve social problems was once so boundless that President Lyndon Johnson was moved to declare in 1964: "This administration today, here and now, declares unconditional war on poverty in America." And later when signing the Economic Opportunity Act of 1964, he added: "Today for the first time in the history of the human race, a great nation is able to make and is willing to make a commitment to eradicate poverty among its people."[1] Ten years later, after the expenditure of nearly $25 billion, Congress abolished the Office of Economic Opportunity. There were still 25 million poor people in the country; this was approximately the same number of poor as when the "war on poverty" began. The government had passed a law—the Economic Opportunity Act of 1964; it had created a new bureaucracy—the Office of Economic Opportunity; and it had thrown many billions of dollars in the general direction of the problem—poverty. But nothing much had happened. The failure of the war on poverty is an important lesson in policy analysis.

The Curative Strategy

The war on poverty was an attempt to apply a *curative strategy* to the problems of the poor. In contrast to the *alleviative strategy* of public assistance which attempts only to ease the hardships of poverty, and in contrast to the *preventive strategy* of social insurance which attempts to compel people to save money against the future possibility of old age, death, disability, sickness, and unemployment, the curative strategy stresses efforts to help the poor become self-supporting by bringing about changes in these individuals and in their environment. The curative strategy of the war on poverty was supposed to break the cycle of poverty and to allow the poor to move into America's working classes and eventually its middle classes. The strategy was "rehabilitation and not relief." The Economic Opportunity Act of 1964, the centerpiece of the war on poverty, was said to "strike at the causes, not just the consequences, of poverty."

Area Poverty and Case Poverty

The first curative antipoverty policies originated in the administration of President John F. Kennedy. Kennedy was said to have read socialist Michael Harrington's *The Other America*—a sensitive description of the continuing existence of a great deal of poverty that had gone unnoticed by the majority of middle-class Americans. But Kennedy, the Harvard-educated son of a multimillionaire business investor, was visibly shocked when he first saw the wooden shacks of West Virginia's barren mountains during his 1960 presidential primary campaign. And Kennedy's economic advisor, John Kenneth Galbraith, had in 1957 written an influential book, *The Affluent Society,* which called attention to the continued existence of poverty in the midst of a generally affluent society. Galbraith distinguished between *case poverty* and *area poverty.* Case poverty was largely a product of some personal characteristics of the poor—old age, illiteracy, inadequate education, lack of job skills, poor health, or racial discrimination—which prevented them from participating in the nation's prosperity. Area poverty was a product of economic deficiency relating to a particular sector of the nation, such as West Virginia and much of the rest of Appalachia. "Pockets of poverty" or "depressed areas" occurred because of technological change or a lack of industrialization—for instance, decline in the coal industry, the exhaustion of iron ore mines, the squeezing out of small farmers from the agricultural market, and so on.

Kennedy Initiatives

The initial forays in the war on poverty were begun in the Kennedy administration. The fight against area poverty began with the Area Redevelopment Act of 1961, which authorized federal grants and loans to governments and businesses in designated "depressed areas." This program was later revised in the Economic Development Act (EDA) of 1965; EDA continues today as a major effort to overcome geographically defined poverty. The fight against case poverty began with the Manpower Development and Training Act (MDTA) of 1962—the first large-scale, federally funded job-training program. Eventually, MDTA was absorbed into the Comprehensive Employment and Training Act (CETA) of 1973; CETA continues today as the major federal effort in job training, although its future is uncertain under the Reagan administration.

Enter LBJ

When Lyndon B. Johnson assumed the presidency in 1963, he saw an opportunity to distinguish his administration and to carry forward the traditions of Franklin D. Roosevelt. Johnson believed that government work and training efforts, particularly those directed at youth, could break the cycle of poverty by giving young people the basic skills to improve their employability and making them self-sufficient adults.

Johnson's war on poverty included

The Elementary and Secondary Education Act of 1965: The first major, general federal aid-to-education program, which included federal funds to "poverty-impacted" school districts and which remains today as the largest source of federal aid to education.

The Food Stamp Program: The development of a major in-kind benefit program, which continues today to provide major relief to the poor.

Medicare: Amendments to the Social Security Act to provide health care insurance for the aged.

Medicaid: The first major federal health care program for the poor.

Job Training: An expansion of the Manpower Development and Training Act and the initiation of a series of new job-training programs, including the Job Corps and the Neighborhood Youth Corps for young adults and the Work-Study program to encourage college attendance among the poor.

The Economic Development Act of 1965 and *The Appalachia Regional Development Act of 1965:* Efforts to encourage economic development in distressed areas.

THE ECONOMIC OPPORTUNITY ACT—"COMMUNITY ACTION"

The Economic Opportunity Act created a multitude of programs that were to be coordinated in Washington by a new, independent federal bureaucracy—the Office of Economic Opportunity (OEO). OEO was given money and authority to support varied and highly experimental techniques for combating poverty at the community level. As evidence of the priority given OEO, its first director was Sargent Shriver, brother-in-law of the slain President John F. Kennedy and later Democratic vice-presidential candidate with George McGovern in 1972. OEO was encouraged to bypass local and state governments and establish new "community action" organizations throughout the nation—semiprivate organizations with the poor participating in their own governance. OEO was *not* given authority to make direct grants to the poor as relief or public assistance. All of the OEO programs were aimed, whether accurately or inaccurately, at curing the causes of poverty, rather than at alleviating its symptoms.

Youth Programs

A number of OEO programs were oriented toward youth—breaking the cycle of poverty at an early age. The Job Corps was designed to provide education, vocational training, and work experience in rural conservation camps for unemployable youth between the ages of sixteen and twenty-two. Job Corps trainees were supposed to be "hard core" unemployables who could benefit from training away from their home environment—breaking habits and associations that were obstacles to employment, while learning reading, arithmetic, and health care, as well as auto mechanics, clerical work, and the use of tools. Another youth program was the Neighborhood Youth Corps, designed to provide work, counseling, and on-the-job training for young people in or out of school who were living at home. The Neighborhood Youth Corps was intended for young people who were more employable than those who were expected in the Job Corps. A work-study program helped students from low-income families remain in high school or college by providing them with federally paid, part-time employment in conjunction with cooperating public or private agencies. The Volunteers in Service to America (VISTA) program was modeled after the popular Peace Corps idea, but volunteers were to work in domestic poverty-impacted areas rather than in foreign countries.

Community Action

The core of the Economic Opportunity Act was a grass-roots "Community Action Program" to be carried on at the local level by public or private nonprofit agencies, with federal financial assistance. Communities were urged to form a "community action agency" composed of representatives of government, private organizations, and, most important, the poor themselves. It was originally intended that OEO would support antipoverty programs devised by the local community action agency. Projects might include (but were not limited to) literacy training, health services, homemaker services, legal aid for the poor, neighborhood service centers, vocational training, and childhood development activities. The act also envisioned that a community action agency would help organize the poor so that they could become participating members of the community and could avail themselves of the many public programs designed to serve them. Finally, the act attempted to coordinate federal and state programs for the poor in each community.

Community action was to be "developed, conducted, and administered with the maximum feasible participation of the residents of the areas and members of the groups served." This was one of the more controversial phrases in the act. Militants within the OEO administration frequently cited this phrase as authority to "mobilize" the poor "to have immediate and irreversible impact on their communities." This language implied that the poor were to be organized as a political force by federal antipoverty warriors using federal funds. Needless to say, neither Congress nor the Democratic administration of President Lyndon Johnson really intended to create rival political organizations that would compete for power with local governments in those communities.

The typical community action agency was governed by a board consisting of public officials (perhaps the mayor, a county commissioner, a school board member, or a public health officer), prominent public citizens (from business, labor, civil rights, religious, and civic affairs organizations), and representatives of the poor (in some cases elected in agency-sponsored elections, but more often hand-picked by ministers, social workers, civil rights leaders, and so on). A staff was to be hired, including a full-time director, and paid from an OEO grant for administrative expenses. A target area would be defined—generally it was the low-income area of the county or the ghetto of a city. Neighborhood centers were established in the target area, perhaps with counselors, employment assistance, a recreation hall, a child care center, and some sort of health clinic. These centers assisted the poor in contacting the school system, the welfare department, employment agencies, the public housing authority, and so on. Frequently, the centers and the antipoverty workers who staffed them acted as advocates for the poor and as intermediaries between the poor and public agencies. This activity was called *outreach*.

Head Start

Community action agencies also devised specific antipoverty projects for submission to the Washington offices of OEO for funding. The most popular of these projects was "Operation Head Start"—usually a cooperative program between the community action agency and the local school district. Preschool children from poor families were given six to eight weeks of special summer preparation before entering kindergarten or first grade. The idea was to give these disadvantaged children a "head start" on formal schooling. Congress (as well as the general public) was favorably disposed toward this program and emphasized it in later budget appropriations to OEO.

Legal Services

Another type of antipoverty project was the "legal services program." Many community action agencies established free legal services to the poor to assist them in rent disputes, contracts, welfare rules, minor police actions, housing regulations, and so on. The idea behind the project was that the poor seldom have access to legal counsel and are frequently taken advantage of because they do not know their rights. Congress amended the act in 1967 to insure that no OEO funds would be used to defend any person in a criminal case. But antipoverty lawyers using federal funds have been active in bringing suits against city welfare departments, housing authorities, public health agencies, and other government bodies.

More OEO Projects

Other kinds of antipoverty projects funded by OEO include family planning programs—the provision of advice and devices to facilitate family planning by the poor; homemaker services—advice and services to poor families on how to stretch low family budgets; job training—special outreach efforts to bring hard core unemployed into more established workforce programs; "Follow Through"—to continue Head Start efforts with special educational experiences for poor children after they enter school; "Upward Bound"—educational counseling for poor children; as well as other programs.

POLITICS AND THE WAR ON POVERTY

The war on poverty, specifically OEO, became an unpopular stepchild of the Johnson administration even before LBJ left office. The demise of the OEO programs cannot be attributed to political partisanship—that is, to the election of a Republican administration under Richard Nixon. Nor can the demise of the poverty program be attributed to the Vietnam War—since both "wars" were escalated and later deescalated at the same time. The Nixon administration "reorganized" OEO in 1973, transferring the Job Corps, the Neighborhood Youth Corps, and all job-training programs under a reorganized CETA to the Department of Labor. The administration also transferred the Work-Study Program, Head Start, and Upward Bound to the then Department of Health, Education and Welfare. VISTA became part of a larger federal volunteer program called ACTION. The Ford administration later abolished OEO in 1974. It turned over a greatly reduced community action program to an independent Community Services Administration; and it turned over legal services to an independent Legal Services Corporation.

The reasons for the failure of the war on poverty are complex; the Office of Economic Opportunity was always the scene of great confusion. Personnel were young, middle-class, and inexperienced, and there was always a high turnover among administrators. Community action agencies throughout the country appeared directionless. Aside from Head Start, there were no clear-cut program directions for most community action agencies. Many of the poor believed that the poverty program was going to provide them with *money;* they never really understood that community action agencies could provide only organization, outreach, counseling, training, and similar assistance. Many community action agencies duplicated, and even competed with, existing welfare and social service agencies. Some community action agencies organized the poor to challenge local government agencies. As a result, more than a few local governments called upon the Johnson administration and Congress to curb community action agencies using federal funds to "undermine" existing programs and organizations. There were frequent charges of mismanagement and corruption, particularly at the local level. Finally, some community action agencies became entangled in the politics of race; some big city agencies were charged with excluding whites; and in some rural areas, whites believed that poverty agencies were "for blacks only."

Perhaps the failure of the war on poverty can be explained by our lack of knowledge about how to *cure* poverty. In retrospect, it seems naive to believe that passing a law, creating a new bureaucracy, and passing out money to local agencies to find their own cures, could have succeeded in eliminating, or even in reducing, poverty. Can poverty be cured? Head Start was one attempt to cure poverty. Research on Head Start revealed that the program is very popular among parents. But after two or three years in school, there are *no* differences in the achievement or aspiration levels of poor children who attended Head Start and poor children who did not attend Head Start. Likewise, research on Job Corps enrollees suggests that after several years there is *no* difference between the employment records of young people who participated in the Job Corps and those who did not. In short, we may be forced to conclude that social science simply does not know enough about social behavior to be able to cure poverty.

It might be argued that the war on poverty was never funded at a level that would make substantial impact. OEO funds were spread over hundreds of communities. Such relatively small amounts could never offset the numerous, deep-seated causes of deprivation. The poverty program raised the expectations of the poor, but it never tried to cope with poverty on a dimension comparable to the size of the problem. Often the outcome was only to increase frustration.

In an obvious reference to public policies affecting the poor and the black in America, Aaron Wildavsky wrote:

A recipe for violence: Promise a lot; deliver a little. Lead people to believe they will be much better off, but let there be no dramatic improvement. Try a variety of small programs, each interesting but marginal in impact and severely underfinanced. Avoid any attempted solution remotely comparable in size to the dimensions of the problem you are trying to solve. Have middle-class civil servants hire upper-class student radicals to use lower-class Negroes as a battering ram against the existing local political systems; then complain that people are going around disrupting things and chastise local politicians for not cooperating with those out to do them in. Get some poor people involved in local decision-making, only to discover that there is not enough at stake to be worth bothering about. Feel guilty about what has happened to black people; tell them you are surprised they have not revolted before; express shock and dismay when they follow your advice. Go in for a little force, just enough to anger, not enough to discourage. Feel guilty again; say you are surprised that worse has not happened. Alternate with a little suppression. Mix well, apply a match, and run....[2]

It would be difficult to find a better summary of the unintended consequences of public programs for the poor and the black.

It is possible to view the war on poverty as failing because it promised too much, raised people's hopes, and delivered too little. Daniel P. Moynihan writes:

Over and again the attempts by official and quasi-official agencies...to organize poor communities led first to the radicalization of the middle-class persons who began the effort; next to a certain amount of stirring among the poor, but accompanied by heightened radical antagonism *on the part of the poor* if they happened to be black; next to the retaliation from the larger white community; where upon it would emerge that the community action agency, which had talked so much, been so much in the way of change in the fundamentals of things, was powerless. A creature of a Washington bureaucracy, subject to discontinuation without notice. Finally, much bitterness all around.[3]

CAN WE "CURE" POVERTY?:
CONFLICTING EVIDENCE
ABOUT HEAD START

Can we "cure" poverty? Is the curative strategy effective? The answer to this question is unclear, just as the answer to so many evaluative questions in public policy is unclear. Let us consider, for example, attempts to evaluate the effectiveness of one of the most popular anti-poverty programs, Head Start.

When the Economic Opportunity Act of 1964 first authorized the creation of local community action agencies throughout the nation to fight the war on poverty, the responsibility for devising community antipoverty projects was placed in the hands of local participants. But within one year, the Office of Economic Opportunity in Washington, and its director, Sargent Shriver, decided that Head Start programs were the most desirable antipoverty projects. OEO earmarked a substantial portion of funds for local community action agencies for Head Start Programs. The typical local Head Start project was a cooperative program between the community action agency and the local school district. Preschool children from poor families were given six to eight weeks of special summer preparation before entering kindergarten or first grade. The idea of helping to prepare disadvantaged children for school elicits more sympathy from the middle class than programs which provide free legal aid for the poor, help them get on welfare rolls, or organize them to fight city hall. Indeed, Head Start turned out to be the most popular program in the war on poverty. Nearly all of the nation's community action agencies operated a Head Start project, and over one-half million children were enrolled throughout the country at the height of the program in the late 1960s. Some communities expanded into full-year Head Start programs and also provided children with health services and improved daily diets. Head Start became OEO's showcase program.

Evaluating Head Start

Head Start officials within OEO were discomforted by the thought of a formal evaluation of their program. They argued that educational success was not the only goal of the program; that child health and nutrition, and even parental involvement in a community program, were equally important goals. After much internal debate, Director Shriver ordered an evaluative study, and in 1968 a contract was given to Westinghouse Learning Corporation and Ohio University to perform the research.

When Richard Nixon assumed the presidency in January 1969, hints of negative findings had already filtered up to the White House. In his first comments on the poverty program, Nixon alluded to studies showing the long-term effect of Head Start as "extremely weak." This teaser prompted the press and Congress to call for the release of the Westinghouse Report. OEO claimed that the results were still "too preliminary" to be revealed. However, after a congressional committee investigation and considerable political pressure, OEO finally released the report in June 1969.[4]

The report stated that the researchers had randomly selected 104 Head Start projects across the country. Seventy percent were summer projects and 30 percent were full-year projects. Children who had gone on from these programs to the first, second, and third grades in local schools (the experimental group) were matched in socioeconomic background with children in the same grades who had not attended Head Start (the control group). All children were given a series of tests covering various aspects of cognitive and affective development (the Metropolitan Readiness Test, the Illinois Test of Psycholinguistic Abilities, the Stanford Achievement Test, the Children's Self-Concept Test, and others). The parents of both groups of children were matched on achievement and motivation.

The unhappy results can be summarized as follows:

1. Summer programs were ineffective in producing any gains in cognitive and affective development that persist into the early elementary grades.

2. Full-year programs produced only marginally effective gains for certain subgroups, mainly black children in central cities.

3. However, parents of Head Start enrollees voiced strong approval of the program.

Political Reaction

Head Start officials reacted predictably in condemning the report. Liberals attacked the report because they believed that President Nixon would use it to justify major cutbacks in OEO. The New York Times reported the findings under the headline "Head Start Report Held 'Full of Holes.'" This newspaper warned liberals that "Congress or the Administration will seize the report's generally negative conclusions as an excuse to downgrade or discard the Head Start Program"[5] (not an unreasonable action in the light of the findings, but politically unacceptable to the liberal community). Academicians moved to the defense of the war on poverty by attacking various methodological aspects of the study. In short, scientific assessment of the impact of Head Start was drowned in a sea of political controversy.

Ten Years Later

It is difficult for educators to believe that education, especially intensive preschool education, does *not* have a lasting effect on the lives of children. The prestigious Carnegie Foundation decided to fund research in Ypsilanti, Michigan—research which would keep tabs on disadvantaged youngsters from preschool to young adulthood. In 1980 a report was released on an eighteen-year study of the progress of 123 low I.Q. children, fifty-eight of whom (the experimental group) were given special Head Start–type education at ages three and four and continued to have weekly visits throughout later schooling.[6] The others (the control group) received no such special educational help. Both groups came from low socioeconomic backgrounds; half of their families were headed by a single parent and half received welfare. Because the sample was small and local, researchers were able to track the children's progress to age nineteen.

The initial results were disappointing: Most of the gains made by the children with preschool educations disappeared by the time the children had completed second grade. As children in the experimental group progressed through grade school, junior high school, and high school, their grades were not better than the children in the control group.

However, throughout the years, children with preschool educations scored slightly higher (8 percent) on reading, mathematics, and language achievement tests than the control group. More important, only 19 percent of the preschoolers ended up in special classes for slow learners, compared to 39 percent for the control group. The preschoolers also showed fewer delinquent tendencies and held more after-school jobs. The key to this success appeared to be a better attitude toward school and learning among children with preschool educations. Finally, more preschoolers were likely to finish high school and find jobs than those in the control groups, and the preschoolers were less likely to end up on welfare.

The researchers end their report by arguing that a Head Start–type experience is a bargain to society in the long run, because it reduces the later need for social support systems such as welfare.

CETA: JOB TRAINING
OR MAKE-WORK?

The Comprehensive Employment and Training Act of 1973 (CETA) was originally proposed by the Nixon administration as a means of reforming and reorganizing the large array of job-training programs which had emerged from the "Great Society" programs of the 1960s. CETA was designed to accomplish two general goals: (1) *consolidation* of job programs from the Manpower Development and Training Act of 1962; the Economic Opportunity Act of 1962, including community action programs featuring job training, the Job Corps, and the Neighborhood Youth Corps; and a separate Job Opportunities in the Business Sector (JOBS) program; and (2) *decentralization* of these programs, giving control and implementation to local governments. The U.S. Department of Labor was given overall supervision for consolidating various job-training programs and distributing funds to city, county, and state governments, which serve as "prime sponsors" for the programs.

Initially, CETA was directed at "structural" unemployment—the long-term, "hard core" unemployed with few job skills, little experience, and other barriers to productive employment. But later, particularly in response to the economic recession of 1974–1975, Congress extended the targeted population to include "cyclical" unemployment—persons who were temporarily out of work because of depressed economic conditions. Indeed, Congress forced the Nixon and Ford administrations to accept more "public service jobs" through CETA than either administration requested.

CETA has provided job training for over three and one-half million persons per year. Programs include classroom training, on-the-job experience, and public service employment. "Prime sponsor" local governments may contract with private community-based organizations (CBOs) to help recruit poor and minority trainees, to provide initial classroom training, and to place individuals in public service jobs. Indeed, it is sometimes argued that CBOs do a better job of "getting down to the people" than local governments.

As it has turned out, a major share of CETA funds has been used by cities to pay individuals to work in regular municipal jobs. CETA offers local governments the possibility of substantially lowering their labor costs by "substituting" federally paid CETA workers for regular municipal employees. In addition, CETA enables many local governments to shift regular municipal employees (police, firefighters, refuse collectors, and others) to the CETA budget and off the city's payroll. Instead of creating new jobs, a substantial portion of CETA money flowing to cities has simply funded a continuation of existing jobs. Obvious substitution occurs when a government lays off employees and then rehires them in their old jobs with CETA funds.

Although CETA regulations officially prohibit such substitution, most observers agree that the practice is widespread. Indeed, it has been estimated that about half of all CETA jobs are jobs formerly paid for by local governments.

Defenders of CETA argue that substitution is not necessarily wasteful if municipal employees were going to lose their jobs without assistance from CETA. Substitution allows cities facing financial stress to cut back on their own spending and yet not force large numbers of their employees to go jobless.

On the other hand, it is clear that CETA funds are not all "targeted" to those who need the assistance most—the economically disadvantaged and long-term, hard core unemployed. One estimate is that only one-third of CETA workers come from welfare families. Prime sponsors tend to focus on the "cream" of the labor market—skimming off the most skilled of the unemployed. Nonetheless, according to federal figures, about 40 percent of federal jobs participants are minorities, about 45 percent have less than high school educations, 39 percent are age twenty-one or less, and 73 percent are classified as "low income" (see Table 9–1).

The Humphrey-Hawkins Act of 1978 "guarantees" jobs to every "able and willing" adult American. The ambitious language of the act reflects the leadership of its sponsor, the late Senator Hubert H. Humphrey (D. Minn.). The act views the federal government as "the employer of last resort" and pledges to create "public service jobs" to put the unemployed to work on public projects. Lowering the unemployment rate to 3 percent is to be a "national goal."

But the Humphrey-Hawkins Act is more symbolic of liberal concerns than it is a real national commitment. Doubtlessly, pressures on Congress and the president to increase the funding of public service jobs will increase during periods of recession. But it is unlikely that the national unemployment rate will ever be reduced to 3 percent. Increasingly, Congress and the president have become concerned with the creation of "real," permanent, private-sector jobs, rather than government-funded public service jobs.

THE U.S. EMPLOYMENT SERVICE: FINDING JOBS

The labor market does not always coordinate jobs with workers. This is particularly true at the levels of unskilled and semiskilled jobs. The U.S.

Employment Service (USES) consists of 2,400 state-operated, federally funded employment offices throughout the nation. USES claims to place about 5 million workers in jobs each year. The poor make up about one-quarter of these placements. Although federally funded, USES offices are staffed and administered separately in each state. As a result, services vary somewhat from state to state.

USES is supposed to service both employers and unemployed workers. It accepts job listings from private and public employers, and it accepts job applications from individuals seeking employment. For both employers and job-seekers USES is a "free" job service. But USES sometimes has difficulty in getting employers to list jobs with the service, especially highly skilled or professional jobs. The reason may be that most of the USES job applicants possess limited skills.

One reason for the difficulty confronting USES in placing people may be that some individuals list themselves as job-seekers only to fulfill requirements of food stamp, welfare, or unemployment insurance programs. Most state unemployment insurance programs *require* recipients to register with USES, to check with the service every week to see if there is a job opening in their field, and to state that they did not decline a job in their regular occupation as conditions of receiving their unemployment benefits. Moreover, increasingly, food stamps and welfare benefits are being distrib-

TABLE 9–1 Characteristics of the Unemployed, the Poor, and Training and Employment Program Participants[a]

	UNEMPLOYED WORKERS			POVERTY POPULATION[b]			PROGRAM PARTICIPANTS		
	1975	1977	1980	1975	1977	1980	1975	1977	1980
Average number (millions)	8.0	6.9	7.7	16.1	17.0	17.4	2.4	3.5	3.4
Percent:[c]									
Age 21 or less	35	35	34	26	26	24	29	33	43
Female	44	48	44	62	63	63	58	48	53
Less than high school education	49	43	40	67	65	64	38	38	52
Low income	21[d]	22[d]	22[d]	100	100	100	71	65	74
Public assistance recipients	n.a.	n.a.	n.a.	n.a.	n.a.	n.a.	42	23	37
Minority	19	22	22	30	30	31	40	36	43

[a]Unemployed and poor reported on a calendar year basis; program participants reported on a fiscal year basis.
[b]Data collected in March of year shown here, represents income of prior year. Source: Bureau of the Census data from the Current Population Survey.
[c]Program participant figures excludes summer employment programs for youth.
[d]Represents individuals living in poverty areas.
n.a. = Not available.

Source: *Budget of the United States Government 1982*

uted to employable adults, whether or not there is a real likelihood that they will be employed, only on condition that they register with the USES.

THE MINIMUM WAGE: HELPING OR HURTING?

Laws establishing minimum wages for working people have been an accepted strategy in fighting poverty since the federal Fair Labors Standards Act of 1938. The purpose of this law was to guarantee a minimum wage level that would sustain health and well-being and a decent standard of living for all workers. The minimum wage began in 1938 at 25 cents per hour; by 1981 it had been increased to $3.35 per hour. A basic work week of forty hours was established; employees can work longer, but overtime work requires additional pay. Today over 90 percent of nonsupervising personnel in the American work force are covered by the law, with certain exceptions in retail trade, services, and agriculture.

It is sometimes argued that the minimum wage is the most direct and comprehensive measure to increase the earnings of the working poor. Indeed, it might be argued that the minimum wage ought to be higher than it is. In 1981 a minimum wage worker earning $3.35 per hour on a forty-hour work week would earn $134 weekly, or $6,968 for a fifty-two–week year. The poverty level for an urban family of four for 1980 was $8,380. If there was only one worker in this family, and the worker was paid only the minimum wage, the family would still live under the official poverty line.

Certainly a high minimum wage helps the person who has a job, particularly an unskilled or semiskilled job which is likely to be affected by minimum wage levels. There are some persons, though, who actually believe that workers may not be hired by employers because government-imposed wage levels are too high to justify adding these people to the payroll. In other words, does a high minimum wage create unemployment by discouraging employers from taking on additional workers—especially workers who have few skills and whose labor is not "worth" the minimum wage?

The persons most likely to be excluded from jobs because of a high minimum wage are teenagers. They have not yet acquired the job skills to make their labor worth the minimum wage. With a high minimum wage, fast food chains, movie theaters, retail stores, and the like tend to cut back on their teenage help to save costs. At a lower minimum wage, more teenagers could be expected to find work. The teenage unemployment rate is approximately three times higher than the unemployment rate for adults. Some economists claim that this youth employment problem is partly a result of the minimum wage. But there is no real consensus about whether the reduction or elimination of the minimum wage for teenagers would substantially reduce youth unemployment.

One alternative that has been proposed to alleviate teenage unemployment and still maintain wage standards for adults is the "dual minimum" proposal. The Fair Labor Standards Act might be amended to permit all youths under eighteen years old, and youths between the ages of eighteen and twenty in the first six months of employment, to receive a lower minimum wage than the minimum wage fixed for persons over eighteen or with more than six months on the job.

ILLUSTRATION: LEGAL SERVICES UNDER FIRE

The federal government's Legal Services Corporation grew out of the early legal services provided as part of the OEO "community action" programs in the 1960s. Today the Legal Services Corporation is a separate nonprofit corporation, financed by Congress from tax dollars to provide legal services to the poor. The corporation is headed by an eleven-member board appointed by the president. More than 300 regional legal service groups around the nation are staffed by about 5,000 attorneys.

According to the Corporation, most of its work consists of advising the poor of their legal rights in everyday cases—rental contracts, loans, credit accounts, welfare rules, housing regulations, and other day-to-day civil law. The Corporation is prevented by law from representing the poor in criminal cases. (The states are required by the U.S. Constitution to provide legal counsel to persons accused of felonies.) The corporation reports that only 15 percent of its cases ever reach the courtroom. Others are resolved by the parties before litigation begins.

Defenders of the Legal Services Corporation argue that the poor require legal protection as much as or more than the affluent. Most case work, they claim, revolves around survival issues of food, shelter, or clothing. "We represent the most powerless people in America." Government-paid poverty lawyers are prohibited from taking fees, such as a percentage of damages in accident-injury suits. Moreover, legal service money cannot be used for political activity, public demonstrations, or strikes.

But opponents of the Legal Services Corporation say that it is irrational to establish a government agency to sue other government agencies. The Legal Services Corporation has been involved in several well-publicized "class action" suits. In these suits, lawyers from the corporation claim to represent a whole "class" of poor people, not just one individual or family, and they usually bring these suits against another government agency. For example, the Bay Area Legal Services in Tampa, Florida, using federal funds, sued the state of Florida to stop the state from requiring its high school graduates to pass a functional literacy test. Corporation lawyers argued that the test was discriminatory because larger proportions of black students failed it than white students. Should the Legal Services Corporation take on such "class action" cases? Even when the cause is just, it might be argued that taxpayers should not have to foot the bill for these "class action" suits. Or according to one critic of the Corporation: "Why should the taxpayers have to cough up $300 million a year for an elite corps of radical lawyers who want to move this country to the left?"[1]

Alternatives to the Legal Services Corporation have been proposed by those who agree that the poor need lawyers but complain that the government should not pay for "class action" suits:

A voucher system, similar to food stamps. Poor people would qualify for a certain number of vouchers to be redeemed at private law firms.

"Judicare," which, like Medicare, would be a national insurance program. Everyone would contribute a small amount and everyone would be insured against legal expenses.

A prohibition against "class action" suits by lawyers paid through the Legal Services Corporation.

The Reagan administration has tried unsuccessfully to abolish the Legal Services Corporation; Congress has continued to support it. The corporation is not only a subsidy for the poor; it is also a subsidy to the law profession. It creates legal work and it pays lawyers' fees. Since a majority of the members of Congress are lawyers, the benefits to this important "nontarget" group—the legal profession—appear to have saved the Legal Services Corporation from extinction.

[1]Congressional Quarterly, *Weekly Report,* April 18, 1981, p. 660.

SUMMARY

The curative strategy of the war on poverty was an attempt to eradicate many of America's social problems. But this attempt to combat poverty by creating a variety of new social welfare programs proved to be a dismal failure. Twenty-five million people remained poor in the United States. The groundwork for the war on poverty was laid during the administration of President John F. Kennedy with the passage of the Area Redevelopment Act, but it was President Lyndon B. Johnson who succeeded in establishing the Office of Economic Opportunity (OEO). The purpose of OEO was to assist the poor in establishing community action agencies to get at the causes of poverty rather than providing direct cash grants to the poor. Job programs, literacy programs, legal aid programs, and child development programs were among the many services offered. Community action agencies were to be operated with the "maximum feasible participation of the poor."

The war on poverty sounded like a rational approach to remedying poverty, but the war was plagued by a number of problems that led to its demise. Many OEO staff members were inexperienced at administering social programs. The goals of the many programs were not clear and services were often unnecessarily duplicated. Others contended that the war raised the expectations of poor Americans but provided so little funding for *each* community that it was doomed to failure. Accusations of racism toward whites and corruption of and mismanagement within the programs all contributed to pressures against OEO. The agency was abolished in 1974, with its remaining programs transferred to other federal departments.

Case studies of Head Start programs, the Comprehensive Employment and Training Act (CETA), and the Legal Services Corporation help to illustrate how politics interferes with rational approaches to policy-making. Conservatives attacked Head Start programs for having few long-term effects on participants. Liberals attacked conservatives for looking for a way to eliminate the Head Start programs. Conservatives believe that CETA funds jobs that local governments would pay for anyway. Liberals believe that paying for these jobs is better than allowing financially troubled city governments to lay off workers. Opponents of the Legal Services Corporation reject the idea of the federal government paying lawyers to sue itself. Proponents believe that all citizens should be entitled to legal services, regardless of their financial status.

NOTES

1. Quoted in Daniel Patrick Moynihan, *Maximum Feasible Misunderstanding* (New York: Free Press, 1969), pp. 3–4.
2. Aaron Wildavsky, "The Empty-Headed Blues: Black Rebellion and White Reaction," *The Public Interest* (Spring 1968): 3–4.
3. Moynihan, *Maximum Feasible Misunderstanding*, pp. 134–135.
4. Westinghouse Learning Corporation, Ohio University, *The Impact of Head Start* (Washington Office of Economic Opportunity, 1969).
5. James E. Anderson, *Public Policy-Making* (New York: Holt, Rinehart & Winston, 1975), p. 150.
6. *Newsweek*, December 22, 1980, p. 54.

10

Improving
Health Care:
Treating
the Nation's Ills

National health policy in America presents many examples of the problems of rational policy-making. Political issues intervene at every stage of the rational decision-making process—in defining the goals of health policy, in identifying alternative courses of action, in assessing their potential costs, and in selecting policy alternatives that would maximize the quality and accessibility of health care, while minimizing its cost.

In general, few would dispute the notion that health care is a basic human right. No one should be denied medical care for lack of money; no one should suffer or die for lack of financial resources to obtain adequate medical attention. But how much health care is "enough"? How much are people willing and able to pay for health care? If all of us cannot have all of the health care we want (that is, if health care is a "scarce resource"), then how do we decide who will get what care and how? As we shall see, these are largely *political* questions that do not lend themselves easily to rational planning.

Health care is an issue that affects all of us directly. But health care for the poor and elderly is a particularly worrisome issue, for several reasons. (1) The poor and the aged, on the average, require more medical attention than the general population. Indeed, health problems are a contributing cause of unemployment, inadequate income, and poverty. (2) Preventive health care for the poor is infrequent. In addition to nutritional deficiencies and other health risks facing the poor, even minor costs can delay treatment of health problems until they develop into major crises. (3) Health care facilities and personnel (the "delivery system" for health care) are particularly disorganized and inadequate in poor areas, both in inner cities and in poor rural areas.

GOOD HEALTH OR MEDICAL ATTENTION?

The first obstacle to a rational approach to health policy is deciding upon our goal. Is health policy a question of *good health*—that is, whether we live at all, how well we live, and how long we live? Or are we striving for good *medical care*—that is, frequent and inexpensive visits to a doctor, well-equipped and accessible hospitals, and equal access to medical attention by the rich and poor?

Good medical care does not necessarily mean good health. Good health is related to many factors over which doctors and hospitals have no control: heredity, life style (smoking, eating, drinking, exercise, worry), and the physical environment (sewage disposal, water quality, conditions of work, and so on). Of course, doctors can set broken bones, stop infections with drugs, and remove swollen appendices. Anyone suffering from any of these or similar problems certainly wants the careful attention of a skilled physician and the best of hospital facilities. But in the long run, infant mortality, sickness and disease, and life span are affected very little by the quality of medical care.[1]

If you want to live a long healthy life, choose parents who have lived long healthy lives and then do all the things your mother always told you to do: Don't smoke, don't drink, get lots of exercise and rest, don't overeat, relax, and don't worry.

Historically, most of the reductions in infant mortality and adult death rates, in the United States and throughout the world, have resulted from improved public health and sanitation—including immunization against small pox, clean public water supply, sanitary sewage disposal, improved diets and nutrition, and increased standards of living. Many of today's leading causes of death (see Table 10–1), including cancer, heart disease, stroke, cirrhosis of the liver, emphysema, accidents, and suicides are closely linked to heredity and personal habits.

The overall death rate in the United States (the number of deaths per 100,000 people) continues to decline. Considerable progress is being made by the nation in reducing both infant and adult death rates for many of the major killers—heart disease, stroke, pneumonia, diabetes, and emphysema. However, the cancer death rate continues to rise despite increased medical spending, as does the number of deaths attributable to alcoholism (cirrhosis), suicide, and homicide. Moreover, death rates for the poor and blacks, although declining over time, remain much higher than the death rates for the nonpoor and nonblack.

TABLE 10–1 Leading Causes of Death[a]

	1960	1965	1970	1975	1980
All Cases	954.7	943.2	945.3	888.5	878.1
Heart Disease	369.0	367.4	362.0	336.2	332.3
Stroke (cerebrovascular)	108.0	103.7	101.9	91.1	84.1
Cancer	149.2	153.5	162.8	171.7	178.7
Accidents	52.3	55.7	56.4	48.4	47.7
Pneumonia	37.3	31.9	30.9	26.1	23.7
Diabetes	16.7	17.1	18.9	16.5	15.2
Cirrhosis	11.3	12.8	15.5	14.8	14.3
Infant diseases	37.4	28.6	21.3	12.5	10.8
Emphysema, asthma	[b]	14.4	15.2	12.0	10.3
Suicide	10.6	11.1	11.6	12.7	13.3
Homicide	4.7	5.5	8.3	10.0	9.2

[a]Deaths per 100,000 population per year.
[b]Not separately recorded.
Source: U.S. National Center for Health Statistics, *Vital Statistics of the United States,* published annually (Washington, D.C.: Government Printing Office).

MEDICAID: HEALTH CARE
FOR THE POOR

The poor and the black in America have greater health problems than the affluent and the white. A case in point is the infant mortality rate, which is generally considered to be especially sensitive to the adequacy of health care and is therefore frequently used as a general indicator of well-being. Infant deaths have declined rapidly over the last thirty years for both whites and blacks. But black infant death rates, which have been consistently higher than those for whites, remain almost twice as high as white infant death rates (see Table 10-2). These and other health statistics clearly suggest that black Americans and the poor do not enjoy the same good health as affluent white Americans.

Prior to 1965 medical care for the poor was primarily a responsibility of state and local governments and private charity. But interest in national health care for the poor dates back to the turn of the century, when reform groups during the Progressive Era first proposed a national health insurance plan. In 1935 potential opposition from the American Medical Association (AMA) forced President Franklin D. Roosevelt to drop the idea of including health insurance in the original Social Security Act; he feared its inclusion would endanger passage of the entire act. Every year from

1935 to 1965, health insurance bills were introduced into Congress. But all of them failed, in part because of the opposition of the AMA. National health insurance became a major issue in the Truman administration in the late 1940s, but the AMA succeeded in branding national health insurance as "socialized medicine." (Proposals for national health insurance generally tried to "socialize" health *insurance* and did not call for government ownership of hospitals and employment of physicians as in Great Britain.) Fear of government interference in medical practice, along with opposition of the medical community, succeeded in defeating national health plans for thirty years. Nonetheless, in 1950, the federal government did authorize states to use federal-state public assistance funds (under Old Age Assistance, Aid to the Blind, Aid to the Permanently and Totally Disabled, and Aid to Families with Dependent Children programs) for medical services. In 1957 the Kerr-Mills Act began a separate federal and state matching program for hospital care for the elderly and the poor, but not all of the states chose to participate in the program.

Medicaid is the federal government's largest single welfare program for the poor. The costs of Medicaid now exceed the costs of all traditional welfare programs—including AFDC, SSI, and the Food Stamp programs. A combined federal and state program, Medicaid was initiated in 1965 and grew quickly into the nation's largest welfare program. The states exercise broad administrative powers and carry almost half of the financial burden. Medicaid is an in-kind public assistance program designed for needy persons: No prior contributions are required, monies come from general tax revenues, and most recipients are already on welfare rolls. Although states differ in their eligibility requirements for Medicaid, they must cover all AFDC families, and most states also cover SSI recipients. In addition, a majority of states extend coverage to other "medically needy"—individuals who do not qualify for public assistance but whose incomes are low enough to qualify for medical aid. About half of the states extend Medicaid to families headed by someone receiving unemployment compensation.

Approximately twenty-five million people per year receive Medicaid payments—a figure roughly comparable to the poverty figure for the nation. However, because of the tangle of separate state eligibility requirements, we cannot be sure that all of the poor are receiving Medicaid.

States also help set benefits under Medicaid. All states are required by the federal government to provide inpatient and outpatient hospital care, physicians' services, family planning, laboratory and x-ray services, nursing, and home health care. States must also develop an Early and Periodic Screening, Diagnosis, and Treatment (EPSDT) program for all children under Medicaid. However, it is the states that generally decide upon the rate of reimbursement to hospitals and physicians. Low rates can discourage hospitals and physicians from providing good care or any care at all under Medicaid. To make up for low payments, hospitals and doctors may schedule too many patients in too short a span of time or prescribe unnecessary tests and procedures designed to make treatment more expensive.

Medicaid costs have far exceeded original estimates. The rapid rise in welfare rolls in the late 1960s accounted for a large proportion of the increased costs of the program. Another factor has been the high rate of inflation in medical care prices. Hospital costs and physicians' fees have raced ahead of even the high inflation rate affecting all segments of the economy. Ironically, part of this medical inflation has been produced by the Medicaid and Medicare programs, which have created heavier demands for medical care. Finally, the one-third of all Medicaid payments which goes for nursing home care has spawned a large number of nursing homes and has resulted in larger numbers of aged people being placed in nursing homes. Thus, Medicaid costs have escalated because of (1) increases in welfare rolls, (2) inflation in medical costs, (3) increased use of nursing homes, and (4) greater accessibility to health care services.

TABLE 10–2   Infant Mortality Rates by Race, 1950–1980 (Deaths per 100,000 Live Births)

	1950	1960	1970	1975	1980
White	26.8	22.9	17.8	14.2	12.3
Black	44.5	43.2	30.9	24.2	21.7
Total	29.2	26.0	20.0	16.1	14.1

Source: *Statistical Abstract of the United States, 1981, p. 73.*

MEDICARE: HEALTH CARE
FOR THE AGED

The provision of adequate health care for the nation's aged is an issue of critical concern. The proportion of America's population which is over sixty-five is steadily increasing (see Table 10–3). More important, the process of aging is associated with increased incidence of chronic conditions and disabilities. The aged have about two and one-half times as many restricted activity days as the general population and more than twice as many days in bed and in hospitals.[2] While the need for medical care increases with age, the costs of that care become even more burdensome because the aged do not enjoy the same average incomes as younger age groups. The median income of families headed by persons sixty-five years of age or over is less than half of the median income of all other families.[3]

Medicare, like Medicaid, was enacted in 1965 as an amendment to the nation's basic Social Security Act. Medicare provides prepaid hospital insurance for the aged under Social Security and low-cost voluntary medical insurance for the aged, directly under federal administration. Medicare includes (1) Hospital Insurance (HI)—a compulsory basic health insurance plan covering hospital costs for the aged financed out of payroll taxes that are collected under the Social Security system; and (2) Supplemental Medical Insurance (SMI)—a voluntary, supplemental medical insurance program that will pay doctors' bills and additional medical expenses and is financed in part by contributions from the aged and in part by general tax revenues.

TABLE 10–3   Population over Age 65

	1950	1960	1970	1980
Millions	12.4	16.5	20.0	25.5
% of population	8.1	9.2	9.8	11.3

Source: *Statistical Abstract of the United States, 1981.*

Only *aged* persons (sixty-five years or older) are covered by Medicare provisions. Eligibility is *not* dependent on income; *all* aged persons eligible for Social Security are also eligible for Medicare. As part of the Social Security system, Medicare compels employers and employees to pay into the program during their working years in order to enjoy the benefits, including health insurance, after retirement. Benefits under HI include a broad range of hospital services (after the first day of care, which must be paid by the beneficiary) as well as nursing home care following hospital treatment. Benefits under SMI include physicians' services, outpatient hospital care, and other medical services. SMI is voluntary and open to all individuals over sixty-five, whether they are eligible for Social Security or not. No physical examination is required and preexisting conditions are covered. The costs of SMI are so low to the beneficiaries—approximately $100 per year—that participation by the elderly is almost universal. SMI insurance payments can be deducted automatically from Social Security payments. Beneficiaries of SMI must pay the first $60 of physicians' services themselves, after which SMI pays 80 percent of allowed charges for medical services.

Note that both the HI and SMI provisions of Medicare require patients to pay a small *initial* charge. The purpose is to discourage unnecessary hospital or medical care. HI generally pays the full hospital charge, but many doctors charge higher rates than allowable under SMI. Indeed, it is estimated that only about half of the doctors in the nation accept SMI allowable payments as payment in full. Many doctors bill Medicare patients for charges above the allowable SMI payments. Medicare does *not* pay for prescription drugs, eyeglasses, or hearing aids.

Medicare provides hospitalization and medical insurance for those ages sixty-five and over who are eligible for Social Security or railroad retirement benefits.

This coverage also extends to persons afflicted with chronic kidney disease, regardless of age. The Medicare program is divided into two parts:

Part A. Financed principally through a special hospital insurance tax levied on employees, employers, and the self-employed (in 1980 each paid a tax of 1.05 percent of the first $25,900 of covered earnings), Part A pays for 90 days of inpatient hospital care subject to $180 deductible. A $45 per day co-payment is required for the 61st through the 90th days. Additionally, a lifetime reserve of 60 days (subject to a $90 per day co-payment) may be drawn upon when a person exceeds 90 days in a benefit period (defined as beginning when the insured enters a hospital and ending when he or she has not been in a hospital or skilled nursing facility for 60 days). Part A also pays for 100 days of posthospital skilled nursing facility care (subject to a $22.50 per day co-payment after the first 20 days) and 100 medically necessary posthospital home health visits. Part A does not cover doctors' services, even when they are performed in the hospital.

Part B. Part B is an optional supplementary insurance plan covering doctors' fees and other outpatient services. Those who enroll pay a monthly premium ($8.70 in 1980). All persons ages sixty-five and older and all persons enrolled under Part A can choose to participate in Part B. The plan pays 80 percent of "reasonable charges" for the following covered services after the insured pays the first $60: services of independent practitioners (primarily physicians), 100 home health visits (exempt from co-insurance), medical and related services, outpatient hospital services, and laboratory services.

In general, reimbursement under the Medicare program is based on "reasonable costs" for hospitals and other institutional providers, and "reasonable charges" for physicians and other noninstitutional providers of health care.

Medicaid is a public assistance program that uses state and local tax money as well as federal funds to provide medical care for the poor. Each state is required to provide health care benefits to those persons who qualify for public welfare. If they desire, states may also extend coverage to the "medically indigent"—those persons who do not qualify for public assistance but whose incomes are too low to cover medical expenses. The federal share of state Medicaid funds ranges from 50 percent to 78 percent depending upon the state's per capita income. Each state administers and operates its own program and, subject to federal guidelines, determines eligibility and the scope of benefits to be provided. The programs vary considerably from state to state, with Arizona having no Medicaid program.

HOW MUCH MEDICAL CARE IS ENOUGH?

No health care program can provide as much as people will use. Each individual, believing that his or her health and life is at stake, will want the best trained medical specialists, the most thorough diagnostic treatment, the most constant care, and the best and most sophisticated facilities available. And doctors have no strong incentive to try to save on costs; they want the best and most advanced diagnostic and treatment facilities for their patients. Doctors can always think of one more thing that might be done for any patient—one more consultation with another specialist, one more diagnostic test, one more therapeutic approach. Any tendency doctors might have to limit testing or treatment is countered by the threat of malpractice suits; it is always easier to order one more test or procedure than to risk even the remote chance that the failure to do so will someday be used as cause for a court suit. So both patients and doctors are encouraged to push up the cost of health care, particularly when public or private insurance pays the cost.

Approximately *90 percent* of the population is covered by some sort of health insurance—most by private insurance companies that provide group insurance for workers and their families through employers, and the rest by Medicaid and Medicare, both of which provide federal health insurance for the poor and the aged. But this method of "third party financing" of health care has vastly increased the nation's medical bill. Neither the doctor nor the patient has any strong incentive to keep the bill low when it seems that "someone else" is paying the tab. Moreover, the traditional method of payment for both doctors and hospitals is "after the fact." That is, the patient does not know ahead of time what the bill will be. The patient, after all, has already paid the insurance premium; the cost of a particular service does not hit his or her pocketbook in a direct, immediate fashion. The result in this nation, as more and more people have come under private insurance or Medicaid or Medicare, has been a skyrocketing of health care costs.

It is perfectly rational for *individuals* to demand costly medical care, particularly when these costs are paid by government or private insurance companies. But is it rational for *the public as a whole* to support a health care system which includes little or no incentive to limit costs?

Total national health care expenditures have risen from $26.9 billion in 1960 to $244.6 billion in 1980—an increase of nearly 1,000 percent (see Figures 10–1 and 10–2). Instead of spending 5 percent of the nation's Gross National Product (the total of all goods and services produced) for health care, we are now spending 10 percent. Future projections point upward—both in terms of dollars and percentages of the Gross National Product.

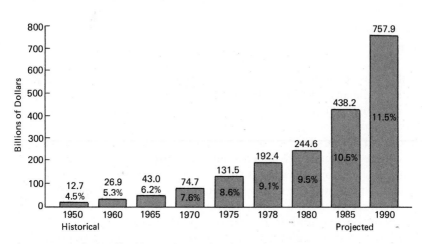

Figure 10-1 Total national health expenditures, selected years 1965 to 1990, in billions of dollars and percentage of gross national product. (Congressional Quarterly, *Health Policy*. Washington, D.C.: Congressional Quarterly, Inc., 1980, p. 3.)

The causes of this "medical inflation" are diverse:

1. Certainly "third party financing" has contributed to these rapidly increasing health care costs. This includes the expansion of private insurance plans, as well as the rapid expansion of the federal government's Medicaid and Medicare programs.

2. The growing number of the nation's elderly population (persons over sixty-five) has contributed to rising expenditures in all areas of health care. The elderly spend more time in hospitals, visit doctors more often, purchase more drugs, and need more nursing services than the rest of the population.

3. Advances in medical technology have added to health care expenses. These advances have enabled us to diagnose and treat illnesses—including cancer and heart disease—that were considered surely fatal a decade ago. Yet the installation of such equipment as CAT scanners (which are able, by computer, to take a detailed x-ray of a person's entire body) and intensive cardiac care units have dramatically increased hospital costs.

4. The nation has also experienced a vast expansion of hospital facilities—an expansion which has created an excess of expensive-to-maintain hospital beds. It was the federal government, through the Hill-Burton Act, that encouraged new and modernized hospital facilities throughout the 1950s, 1960s, and early 1970s. Now the complaint is that the nation is "overbedded." (Although some rural areas may not have a hospital or even a doctor.)

While medical "cost containment" remains on the national policy agenda, a growing number of economists and physicians have defended the increased costs of medical care. If people place a high value on medical care, they should be free to make this choice. Perhaps the nation *should*

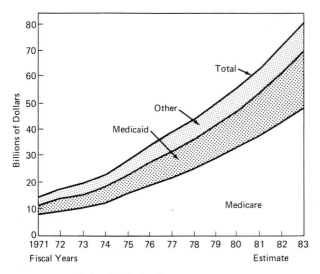

Figure 10-2 Federal outlays for health. (Fiscal 1981 budget.)

spend 10 or 15 percent of the Gross National Product on medical care. After all, so the argument goes, the combined revenues of the alcohol and tobacco industries amount to almost as much as medical care. Medicaid and Medicare have enabled the poor and the aged to enter the marketplace for medical care; it is understandable that this increased demand will raise prices. And who does *not* want a sophisticated cardiac intensive care unit close by when they become the victim of a heart attack?

WHAT AILS MEDICINE?

What has national health policy accomplished for the poor in America? There is no doubt that *access to medical care* for the poor has improved with Medicaid and Medicare. Contrary to popular stereotypes, the poor in America see doctors more often than the nonpoor. Indeed, the poor see doctors about 20 percent more often than the nonpoor. We must assume, then, that the poor are receiving more, if not better, medical care than the nonpoor.

Yet despite the increase in medical care for the poor, the *health* of the poor remains worse than that of the nonpoor. That is to say, infant mortality rates, death rates due to specific causes, and average life spans of the poor remain below those of the nonpoor. It is true that these measures of health are improving over time for both groups, but there is no indication that Medicaid and Medicare have been mainly or even partly responsible for these improvements. Indeed, improvements in health statistics were just as

195

great prior to the enactment of Medicaid and Medicare as they have been after the enactment of these programs.

So we are faced with a paradox in rational health care policy: We can increase access to medical care, but we cannot improve health. As Aaron Wildavsky observes:

> If the question is, "Does health increase with government expenditure or medicine?" the answer is likely to be "No." Just alter the question: "Has access to medicine been improved by government programs?" and the answer is most certainly with a little qualification, "Yes."[4]

Another problem with the current health care system in America is the inadequate coverage provided by health insurance programs—particularly the private insurance programs which cover the greatest proportion of the population. These private health insurance plans often leave gaps in medical coverage. These "medigaps" include: limitation to the first thirty or sixty days of hospital care; overall dollar limits on payments that will be made to hospitals and physicians for particular services; exclusion of various diagnostic tests, outpatient care, or office visits, and so on. (Some minor medigaps also exist in Medicare, particularly "out-of-pocket" deductibles which must be paid by the patient. But some unscrupulous insurance companies sell unnecessary private policies to the elderly.[5]) Moreover, private insurance often will not cover individuals initially found to be in poor health. And perhaps the most serious concern about private insurance is that it frequently fails to cover "catastrophic" medical costs—costs that may run to tens or hundreds of thousands of dollars for serious, long-term illnesses. Many middle-class families can lose their life savings and become "medically indigent" because of serious illness.

Again paradoxically, Medicare and Medicaid have contributed directly to "medical inflation" by increasing demand (adding patients), making more money available for medical care, and removing many cost control constraints from patients and doctors. Thus, national health policy has helped to create a new problem: spiraling health care costs, which in turn require new policies. It is not clear, however, given the record of Medicaid and Medicare, that the federal government is really capable of holding down medical inflation. One method to curb inflation would be to require all hospitals to keep rate increases under federal guidelines. Federal payments could be denied to hospitals that exceed these guidelines. But hospital administrators object that such a sweeping measure would hurt the quality of health care and limit the availability of high technology medical diagnostic and treatment facilities. Another method would be to allow the Social Security Administration to enter into specific agreements with hospitals to pay for services at predetermined rates. Indeed, some states already have rate-setting agencies for hospitals.

One previously tried approach to cost containment can be found in the National Health Planning and Resources Development Act of 1974.

The act creates two hundred *health systems agencies* (HSAs) across the nation with authority to grant or withhold "certificates of need" for new medical facilities. These HSAs are designed to prevent duplication of facilities, overbuilding, and unnecessary costs. Withholding a "certificate of need" can lead to a withholding of Medicaid and Medicare payments to a hospital. But to date there is little evidence to suggest that HSAs have made any significant contribution to reducing medical inflation.

The federal government has also experimented with health costs and health care delivery by supporting *health maintenance organizations* (HMOs). HMOs are membership organizations that hire doctors and other health professionals at fixed salaries to serve dues-paying members. HMOs typically provide comprehensive health care for enrolled members. The members pay a regular fee and they are entitled to hospital care and physicians' services at no extra cost. Advocates of HMOs say that the organizations are less costly than fee-for-service medical care because doctors have no incentive to overtreat patients. Moreover, HMOs emphasize preventive medicine and therefore attempt to treat medical problems before they become serious illnesses. In 1973 Congress endorsed the HMO idea by passing a Health Maintenance Organization Act offering federal assistance to the development of HMOs. Surprisingly, however, there has been no rapid expansion of HMOs. Many of the complaints about the organizations are similar to complaints about service in other bureaucratic settings: Patients see different doctors on different days; doctors in HMOs do not work as hard as private physicians; and care is "de-personalized."

THE HEALTH CARE INDUSTRY

As mentioned previously, the health care industry dwarfs all other sectors of the American economy. The largest portion of these health care expenditures (39.8 percent) go to hospitals (see Table 10–4). Physicians' services make up the second largest portion of all health care expenditures (18.4 percent). Nursing home care is the third largest category of health care expenditures (8.8 percent), followed by drugs (7.4 percent), dentists (7.3 percent), and administration (4.8 percent). Public health accounts for only 2.9 percent of total health care expenditures, and research accounts for only 2.1 percent.

The proportion of total health care expenditures paid for by the government has risen from 24.9 percent in 1965 to 41.1 percent in 1980. Thus, the government's role in health care has expanded rapidly.

The health care industry, then, consists of hospitals, physicians, dentists, nurses and other professionals, drug companies, and nursing home operators, together with private medical insurance companies. The health care providers—hospitals, physicians, nursing homes—are opposed to most government efforts at cost containment; they fear that government

TABLE 10–4 Health Care Spending

	1965	1980
Total	$43.0 billion	$244.6 billion
Personal Health Care %	86.7	88.1
Hospitals	32.4	39.8
Physicians	19.7	18.4
Dentists	6.5	7.3
Other professionals	2.4	2.3
Drugs	13.4	7.4
Eyeglasses	4.3	1.9
Nursing homes	4.8	8.8
Other	3.0	2.1
Administration	3.4	4.8
Public Health	1.9	2.9
Research	3.4	2.1
Construction	4.7	2.2
Percent of GNP	6.2	9.5
Public health care percent	24.9	41.1
Private health care percent	75.1	58.9

Source: Congressional Quarterly, *Health Policy* (Washington, D.C.: Congressional Quarterly, Inc., 1980), p. 12.

"price setting" will curtail their freedom and reduce the quality of medical care. Only the insurance companies have an interest in holding down health care costs. However, the insurance companies do *not* want to increase the role of government, particularly in health insurance. The insurance companies have led the opposition to proposals for national health insurance.

THE POLITICS OF NATIONAL
HEALTH INSURANCE

When the original Social Security Act of 1935 was passed, efforts were made in Congress to include "a comprehensive national health insurance system with universal and mandatory coverage." But President Franklin D. Roosevelt was forced to back off from this program when he became fearful that its inclusion in the original Social Security bill would bring about defeat of the entire bill. Representatives of the AMA contended that the plan would not work without the political support of the nation's physicians. President Harry S. Truman pushed hard for a national health insurance program tied to Social Security, but again opponents in the medical community succeeding in branding it "socialized medicine" and defeated the proposal. President Lyndon B. Johnson chose to pursue a somewhat narrower goal—compulsory health insurance for the aged, Medicare, and a related program for the poor, Medicaid. Johnson was successful in amending the Social Security Act to achieve these goals in 1965. But the decades-old dispute over national health care continues.

NHI—Protecting the Nation's Health

The United States remains one of the few industrial nations in the world where medical care expenses can cause poverty. Even though most people are covered by some kind of private or public medical insurance program, there are major gaps in this coverage. Many American families whose incomes are too high to qualify for Medicaid either do not purchase insurance at all or they purchase inadequate coverage—perhaps $25 or $50 per day against $100 or $150 per day hospital room charges. Or sometimes private insurance runs out after the first thirty or sixty days of hospital care, and eventually the seriously ill are impoverished by medical bills.

One careful 1980 study of the nation's health insurance produced the following information:[6] (1) About 85 percent of the population is covered by private insurance or public medical programs for basic hospital room and board costs, *but* only 29.4 percent have coverage protecting them adequately against catastrophic or major medical expenses; (2) only 40 percent of the population is covered for outpatient doctor costs and only 44 percent for nursing home care, and (3) fewer than 20 percent of the population has insurance protection for prescription drugs. Health care is a right. Whatever other goals we may pursue, most Americans agree that lack of money should not be a barrier to adequate medical care. Access to doctors, hospitals, and drugs is necessary for a decent life.

A comprehensive and mandatory national health program for *all* Americans would be the best way to guarantee that everyone has equal access to medical care. Moreover, a comprehensive federal health insurance program could also provide a means of placing a ceiling on rising medical costs.

A variety of national health insurance (NHI) plans have been introduced in Congress over the years; the program submitted by U.S. Senator Edward M. "Ted" Kennedy is one of the more comprehensive plans. The Kennedy plan includes the following provisions:

1. A National Health Board would be appointed by the president to set policy guidelines, oversee the program, and calculate the federal health budget each year.
2. A national insurance corporation would be formed to collect tax premiums from workers and allocate them to private insurance companies. These companies would process all claims. (Some supporters of NHI do not believe that private companies should play any role at all in national health insurance and that insurance claims should be paid directly by the federal government.)

3. Every American would be required to have health insurance coverage. (The Kennedy bill was officially named the "Health Care for All Americans Act.") Workers and their families would be covered by plans developed through their employers. All others would be insured through a special federal insurance fund.

4. NHI would be funded in part by a new tax on employers (who would pay 65 percent of the cost of this insurance) and employees (who would pay 35 percent). Additional federal and state appropriations might be required to meet the expected costs.

5. Benefits would include full coverage of inpatient and outpatient hospital care, physicians' services including office visits, laboratory and x-ray services, nursing home care, and prescription drugs.

6. In order to contain costs, physicians' fees and hospital charges would be determined by the government for each year. The annual budget for NHI would have to be approved by Congress.

Comprehensive, universal health insurance, including the Kennedy NHI plan would eliminate the need for separate Medicare and Medicaid programs for the aged and the poor. *All* Americans would be covered by national health insurance.

NHI would not be "socialized medicine" in the sense that hospitals would be government owned or doctors public employees. The analogous program is Canada's, not Great Britain's. The Canadians established universal hospital insurance in 1958 and universal physician insurance in 1968. Their rate of "medical inflation" over the last twenty years has been roughly the same as ours. This suggests that NHI need not be especially inflationary.

NHI—A Giant Step Sideways

Some people believe that national health insurance would be "a giant step sideways" in health care, if not an actual health hazard.[7] It would encourage the United States to continue to put scarce resources into even more sophisticated, elaborate, and costly medical care, whether or not this care had much impact on the nation's health.

We know that nearly 90 percent of the population is covered by some form of private or public health insurance. Medicaid currently serves the poor; the poor now see doctors more often and stay in hospitals longer than the nonpoor. Medicare serves the aged; they also enjoy greater access to medical care than the rest of the population. The national "need" is *not* for more medical care. Indeed, Americans may be receiving too much medicine. The "need" is for a rational means of distributing a scarce resource— medical care—in an efficient fashion which would actually improve the nation's health.

Medical care is a "scarce resource" in that there will never be enough of it available to satisfy the unlimited demands of each individual and each physician. If all costs were eliminated, each patient and doctor could order the most elaborate diagnostic procedures (extensive lab work, CAT scanning, consultations with specialists), extraordinary treatments (renal dialysis, organ transplants), long hospital stays, extensive nursing care, frequent office visits, and so on. With potential unlimited demand, medical care must be "rationed" in *some* fashion. It is difficult to assert that "health care is a right" when we know that some method of controlling aggregate demand for medical services will continue to be imposed on Americans. In Great Britain, under socialized medicine, health care is "rationed," in part by *time* rather than money: Patients are required to wait many hours to see a doctor and months to undergo most types of surgery. It is persons who are willing and able to *wait*, rather than pay, that are served. And, of course, the press on patients may result in a poorer quality of care, although conclusive evidence on this point is not available.

It is really impossible to estimate what the total cost of medical care would be if NHI were adopted. If 10 percent of our GNP is devoted to health now, what can we expect when *all* Americans are covered by a government program? What happens when virtually all incentives to control costs are removed? The total cost of health care could rise to 15 or 20 percent of the GNP, and *government* expenditures for health could rise to $200–$300 billion annually, or 40 percent of the entire federal budget. Yet there is no evidence that spending such a large share of the nation's resources on medical services, through the federal government or otherwise, would improve the nation's health.

Americans would be required to sacrifice *something* for such an increase in medical services--whether it would be other social services, including Social Security, or education, or defense, or private spending. There is no "free" medical care.

Yet, once again, health studies generally suggest that medical care does not always imply good health. Often one encounters the comparisons of Utah and Nevada, two state populations with similar incomes, education, urbanization, climate, and numbers of physicians and hospital beds. Yet Utah enjoys one of the highest levels of health in the nation—lower death rates, fewer days lost to sickness, longer life spans. Nevada, on the other hand, is at the opposite end of the ranking of states by these measures of health.

> The answer almost surely lies in the different life styles of ... the two states. Utah is inhabited primarily by Mormons ... who do not use tobacco or alcohol and in general lead stable, quiet lives. Nevada ... has high rates of cigarette and alcohol consumption and very high indexes of marital and geographic instability.[8]

The adoption of a limited alternative program of "catastrophic" health insurance could protect most Americans from becoming impoverished by large medical bills. "Catastrophic" health insurance, as opposed to "comprehensive" health insurance, would pay medical bills *over* some limit—for example, any bills over $5,000 per year. Individuals would be responsible for their care up to this limit; the government would relieve individuals of additional medical costs. The results would be to relieve Americans of the fear of major medical costs, while at the same time relying on the private market to help contain unnecessary medical treatment and cost.

In addition to catastrophic health insurance for all Americans, health specialists have proposed that the nation adopt a "Kiddie Care" program for children under age seven and their mothers.[9] According to Theodore Marmor, Kiddie Care is necessary because (1) poor children are disadvantaged, even more than poor adults, in receiving medical care,[10] and (2) "the care that children need most is readily producible, relatively cheap, and reasonably likely to improve the health of preschoolers."[11] Kiddie Care focuses on routine services needed by children such as immunizations which will likely reduce the need for more expensive care later in life. Since the target of the program is children, Kiddie Care may be likely to gain popular support.

MEDICAID, MEDICARE, AND THE REAGAN ADMINISTRATION

The Reagan administration came into office promising that Medicare would be untouched by its budget cutting efforts. Medicare was included among the Reagan "safety net" programs, programs which would be protected from budget reductions. However, Medicaid was *not* included in the safety net. According to the Reagan officials, "High federal matching, excessive benefit provisions, and overly-generous eligibility have made the Medicaid program a very poorly managed social program that fails to provide cost-effective services to those most in need."[12] The administration claims that Medicaid costs have escalated alarmingly and that combined federal and state expenditures under Medicaid exceeded $1,300 per year for each eligible beneficiary. As the reason for those excessive costs, the administration cited the "insulation" of patients, doctors, and hospitals from the cost consequences of their decisions.

The Reagan administration did not propose any large-scale reform or rearrangement of the Medicaid program. Instead, the Reagan budget office called for a cap on federal matching money to the states for Medicaid. Currently, the federal government pays between 50 and 78 percent of each state's Medicaid expenditures. A federal cap on matching money would provide incentives to the states to tighten their own Medicaid programs.

SUMMARY

Health care for aged and poor Americans has been on the social policy agenda since the early twentieth century. Health care proposals have received strong public backing, but political opposition from the powerful American Medical Association helped to delay large-scale federal government involvement in medical assistance for fifty years!

The largest medical care programs are in-kind programs called Medicare and Medicaid. Medicaid is the single *most* expensive public assistance program. It is operated jointly by the federal and state governments. All AFDC recipients and many SSI recipients are automatically eligible for Medicaid. Other medically indigent persons may also qualify. Twenty-five million Americans are Medicaid recipients.

Medicare is a social program financed by the government through payroll taxes. Medicare serves the nation's aged population. The elderly are more susceptible to illness and disease than other segments of the population and require more health services. Social Security beneficiaries are automatically eligible for Medicare, regardless of their income.

Health care expenditures make up a continually increasing amount of the federal budget. Rising medical costs can be attributed to the expansion of private insurance coverage, growth of the Medicaid and Medicare programs, the growing population of elderly persons, advances in medical technology, and the expansion of hospital facilities.

The access of the poor to medical care has increased, but the health of poor Americans has not improved in direct proportion to expenditures. The poor see doctors more often than the nonpoor, but their infant mortality rates are higher and their life spans are shorter. Providing more health care does not necessarily counteract the negative effects of the disadvantaged environments in which the poor live.

Another paradox in the quest for a rational health policy is that persons with private medical insurance are generally not protected against catastrophic, long-term illness that can lead to financial ruin.

The goals of a rational health care policy are to provide adequate health care for Americans while containing health care costs. Federally-established health systems agencies (HSAs), designed to keep health costs down by helping communities avoid duplication of medical services, have had little impact on cost containment.

Health maintenance organizations (HMOs) represent another attempt at keeping medical costs under control. Members pay fixed fees that are supposed to discourage doctors from providing too much care. HMOs have not been as popular as anticipated.

National health insurance (NHI) is a controversial plan for alleviating the nation's health care problems. Proponents believe that all Americans should be entitled to health care services, but others argue that most

Americans are already covered by private insurance companies and that such sweeping changes in the health care delivery system are not needed. They believe that catastrophic health care insurance, which would prevent Americans faced with large health care bills from financial ruin, is a more cost-efficient alternative to national health insurance. NHI does not appear to be in the offing.

NOTES

1. Although this point may seem arguable, the research literature is extensive. See, for example, Victor R. Fuchs, *Who Shall Live?* (New York: Basic Books, 1974); Nathan Glazer, "Paradoxes of Health Care," *The Public Interest* (Winter 1971): 62–77; and Leon R. Kass, "Regarding the End of Medicine and the Pursuit of Health," *The Public Interest* (Summer 1975): 11–42.
2. National Center for Health Statistics, figures cited in John L. McCoy and David L. Brown, "Health Status Among Low-Income Elderly Persons: Rural-Urban Differences," *Social Security Bulletin* 41, no. 6 (June 1978), p. 14.
3. U.S. Department of Commerce, Bureau of the Census, *Statistical Abstract of the U.S., 1980.*
4. Aaron Wildavsky, *Speaking Truth to Power* (Boston: Little, Brown, 1979), p. 286.
5. See Report of House Committee on the Aging in Congressional Quarterly, *Health Policy: The Legislative Agenda* (Washington, D.C.: Congressional Quarterly, Inc., 1980), pp. 78–79.
6. Ibid., p. 4.
7. The phrase is courtesy of Peter Steinfels, "National Health Insurance: Its Politics and Problems," *Dissent* 24 (Winter 1977): 61–71.
8. Fuchs, *Who Shall Live?*, p. 53.
9. Theodore R. Marmor, "The Politics of National Health Insurance: Analysis and Prescription," *Policy Analysis* 3, no. 1: 25–48. Also reproduced in John E. Tropman, Milan J. Dluhy and Roger M. Lind (eds), *New Strategic Perspectives on Social Policy* (New York: Pergamon Press, 1981), pp. 30–50.
10. Karen Davis and Roger Reynolds, "The Impact of Medicare and Medicaid on Access to Medical Care" (Washington, D.C.: Brooking's Institution, n.d.), p. 3; published also in *The Role of Insurance in the Health Services Sector,* Richard Rosett, ed. (New York: National Bureau of Economic Research, 1976), and cited in Marmor, "The Politics of National Health Insurance," p. 38.
11. Marmor, "The Politics of National Health Insurance," p. 38.
12. Office of Management and Budget, *A Program for Economic Recovery*, February 18, 1981, pp. 1–15.

11

Challenging
Social Welfare:
Racism
and Sexism

SOCIAL WELFARE: RACISM
AND SEXISM

Poverty and other social problems are not random events. These problems plague some groups more than others. Prejudice and discrimination against racial, ethnic, and cultural minorities, and against women, the elderly, and the handicapped all contribute to perpetuating poverty and other social problems.

Racism and sexism have long been a part of American society. Blacks are expected to live in certain areas of the community, but not others. Women are expected to occupy some jobs, but not others. Women and members of minority groups are often treated in ways that reflect myths and misconceptions. For example, women are expected to be the primary child rearers; blacks are expected to excel in sports or dancing.

Prejudice and discrimination occur every day. *Prejudices* are stereotyped *attitudes* that are harbored toward a group of people. *Discrimination* consists of *actions* that have negative consequences for a group of people. Prejudice and discrimination often occur simultaneously. A landlord believes that Mexican-Americans make poor tenants and refuses to rent to them. An employer avoids hiring women based on a belief that mothers are unreliable employees because they miss time from work to care for their children. A civic club leader omits blacks from the annual membership recruitment drive because "other members" will not like the idea. In this chapter we explore disadvantages that accrue to women and minorities and look at policies that seek to alter these problems.

WOMEN AND WELFARE

When we trace the origins of public assistance, we see that some of the earliest welfare programs were directed toward dependent children and their mothers. Women became public assistance beneficiaries because they were expected to remain at home to care for their young children when their husbands were unable to support them because of death, divorce, or desertion. Even when women wanted to work to support themselves and their families, they were generally forced into low-paying jobs. These factors contributed to a pattern of female dependency on welfare which continues to exist. Most AFDC recipients are still women and their children. While fathers qualify for AFDC in some states, the number of fathers who are part of the program remains very small. Attempts to prepare AFDC mothers to work have not produced many positive results. Short-term training has but a limited capacity to raise earnings. The jobs obtained may pay very little, while the costs of clothing, transportation, and child care are rising. Women are also overrepresented in the SSI program. Twice as many women as men receive SSI.

The historical patterns of inequities in education, status, employment, and pay have made women and their families much more dependent upon welfare than men. While 6 percent of male-headed families are at or below the poverty level, 35 percent of all female-headed households are poor.[1] In other words, women are six times as likely as men to be poor. In recent years these figures have remained relatively stable.

Black women are especially susceptible to poverty and dependence upon public assistance payments. While 20 percent of white women receive public assistance payments, approximately 46 percent of black women are on the public assistance rolls. Six percent of white women receive SSI, but 12 percent of black women are SSI recipients. However, white women are more likely to receive Social Security insurance payments than black women. Table 11–1 compares governmental sources of income of white and black women.

FIFTY-NINE CENTS

Women lack the earning power of men. For every dollar earned by men, women earn only fifty-nine cents. Women earn less for a number of reasons. (1) Traditionally, many women have not been the major wage earners in the home. (2) The wages of working women have been

TABLE 11–1 Sources of Government Income for White and Black Female-Headed Households

	PERCENTAGE OF HOUSEHOLDS	
	White	Black
Income from government	58.1	69.0
Social Security	34.6	22.4
SSI	6.0	11.5
Public Assistance	19.8	46.5
Other income (includes unemployment and worker's compensation, and veteran's payments)	12.0	7.8

Source: U.S. Bureau of the Census, *Current Population Reports,* series P-609, No. 124 cited in Bureau of the Census, *Statistical Abstract of the United States, 1980,* p. 468.

considered as secondary to their husband's wages. (3) Women have been considered temporary employees who would leave their jobs to marry and have children. (4) Women's paid work has been considered as extracurricular activity to fill free time. (5) Women have had fewer opportunities for education that would lead to better-paying jobs. (6) Women have been forced to accept jobs that do not conflict with family schedules. (7) Career-oriented women have been thought of as selfish or neglectful of their families. (8) "Women's work" —cleaning, child rearing—are not wage-earning jobs.

Today each of these eight assumptions about women's work has been widely challenged. Many families rely on the work and wages of their female head for support, whether she is the primary wage earner or she shares this responsibility with her spouse. Women make up an ever-increasing portion of the permanent work force. In the early 1980s, more than half of all females age sixteen and older held paid jobs. Since 1950 the number of employed, married women has nearly tripled. Fifty-two percent of all wives have jobs outside the home.[2] For many women, working is neither a sideline nor a means of filling free time. Women are earning more advanced degrees and are obtaining technical training that qualifies them for better-paying jobs, although access to job opportunities continues to be a problem. A number of changes—more day care facilities, men assuming greater marital and parental responsibilities, flex-time (flexibility in arranging work schedules), creative employment opportunities—have made it easier for women to go to work. Fewer women are being bound by tradition, and more are seeking careers out of necessity or desire or both. Finally, women who perform numerous duties at home are beginning to demand recognition that they are also contributing to the labor force.

The social forces that have shaped the low earning status of women have begun to change, but progress is sometimes slow. The National Organization for Women (NOW) reports that women's wages in relation to men's wages have actually declined since 1955 (see Table 11–2). In 1955 women earned 63.9 cents for every dollar earned by men. Today, women's earnings have dropped to 59.6 cents. Even after controlling for education, women make less than men (see Table 11–3). College-educated women continue to earn less than men with eighth-grade educations. Women also earn less than men in professions like elementary and secondary education, and in clerical jobs where large numbers of women are employed (see Table 11–4). The same is true of the social work profession. Women have continued to earn less despite Title VII of the Civil Rights Act of 1964, the Equal Pay Act of 1963, and other laws which prohibit sexual discrimination in employment and compensation. This inequality is a primary explanation of their overrepresentation in welfare programs.

TABLE 11–2   Women's Earnings for Every Dollar Earned by Men

1955	63.9¢
1959	61.8
1960	60.8
1962	59.5
1965	60.0
1967	57.8
1970	59.4
1972	57.9
1973	56.6
1975	58.8
1977	58.9
1978	59.4
1979	59.6

Source: "ERA and the 59¢ Wage Gap," (Washington, D.C.: National Organization for Women, 1981), based on data from the Bureau of Labor Statistics, U.S. Department of Labor and the Census Bureau of the U.S. Department of Commerce.

EQUAL RIGHTS FOR WOMEN

Women have been striving for equality through political participation since the suffragette movement. This movement culminated in 1920 in the Nineteenth Amendment to the United States Constitution, which gave women the right to vote. Since then a number of other pieces of federal legislation have attempted to address the inequities women face in employment, education, and the marketplace.

1. The Equal Pay Act of 1963 requires employers to compensate male and female workers equally for performing the same jobs under similar conditions. The law does not cover all groups, but amendments to the act have added to the types of jobs and employers who must comply.

TABLE 11–3 Wage Gap by Education

EDUCATION	MEN	WOMEN	WOMEN'S PAY TO MEN'S $
Less than 8 years	$11,034	$ 7,425	67¢
8 years	14,475	7,766	54
High School:			
1–3 years	15,205	8,552	56
4 years	18,111	10,506	58
College			
1–3 years	19,376	11,861	61
4 years	23,338	13,430	57
5 + years	25,858	16,694	65

Source: "ERA and the 59¢ Wage Gap," (Washington, D.C.: National Organization for Women, 1981), based on data from the Bureau of Labor Statistics, U.S. Department of Labor, and the Census Bureau of the U.S. Department of Commerce.

TABLE 11–4 Wage Gap by Full-Time Occupations and Job Titles

OCCUPATION	MEN	WOMEN	WOMEN'S PAY TO MEN'S $
Clerical Workers	$16,503	$ 9,855	60¢
Typists	12,122	9,248	76¢
Cashiers	11,244	7,645	68¢
Service Workers	11,925	7,319	61¢
Private Household	12,991	3,618	28¢
Health Services	11,238	8,346	74¢
Professionals	21,310	13,701	64¢
Teachers	18,158	13,431	74¢
Grade & High School	16,905	13,107	78¢
College	22,958	16,219	71¢
Computer Specialists	21,774	18,342	84¢
Operatives	14,921	8,562	57¢
Manufacturing	15,109	8,725	58¢
Sales Workers	17,084	8,880	52¢
Sales Clerks	10,994	7,208	66¢
Retail Trade	12,245	7,297	60¢
Managers	21,835	11,705	54¢
Finance/Insurance	24,127	12,044	50¢
Public Administration	20,401	14,753	72¢
Laborers, except farm	11,974	8,985	75¢
Manufacturing	13,457	9,217	68¢
Construction	10,916	7,821	72¢
Craft Workers	17,106	10,585	62¢

Source: "ERA and the 59¢ Wage Gap," (Washington, D.C.: National Organization of Women, 1981), based on data from the Bureau of Labor Statistics, U.S. Department of Labor and the Census Bureau of the U.S. Department of Commerce.

2. Title VII of the Civil Rights Act of 1964 prohibits sexual discrimination in employment practices and provides the right to court redress. The Equal Employment Opportunity Commission is the agency charged with interpreting and enforcing Title VII.
3. Executive Order 11246, as amended by Executive Order 11375, prohibits employers who practice sexual discrimination from receiving federal contracts. Employers are also required to develop plans for "Affirmative Action" (positive steps taken to recruit and promote women to remedy inequities).
4. Title IX of the Education Amendments of 1972 prohibits sexual discrimination by elementary, secondary, vocational, professional and higher education institutions that receive federal funds.
5. The Equal Credit Act of 1975 prohibits discrimination by lending institutions based on sex or marital status.

The Equal Rights Amendment (ERA) attempted to guarantee women equal rights through the U.S. Constitution. The Equal Rights Amendment stated:

Section 1.   Equality of rights under the law shall not be denied or abridged by the United States or by any state on account of sex.

Section 2.   Congress shall have the power to enforce by appropriate legislation the provisions of this Article.

Section 3.   This amendment shall take effect two years after the date of ratification.

Proponents of the ERA argued that this guarantee of sexual equality under law should be part of the Constitution— "The Supreme Law of the Land." It is true that a number of existing federal and state laws prohibit sexual discrimination, but are these laws adequate to address the problem? ERA proponents contend that, like many other social policy issues, sexual discrimination is best addressed by a national policy rather than by a multitude of federal, state, and local laws that are each subject to change, modification, and repeal. Proponents continue to contend that women have long been disadvantaged and that the ERA can only contribute to more equitable treatment for women.

However, opponents of the ERA were successful in halting this constitutional amendment just three states short of the thirty-eight states (three-quarters) needed for ratification. In 1972 the United States Congress passed the ERA and set a 1979 deadline for state ratification. But by 1978 the amendment had not been ratified. Congress granted an extension of the deadline until June 30, 1982. Despite the endorsement of 450 organizations with 50 million members—unions, churches, civil rights groups, legal associations, educational groups, medical organizations[3]—the ERA failed.

The "Stop ERA" movement was based on fears about what might happen if the ERA passed. It was argued that the ERA would lead to an extension of military registration, and perhaps even a military draft and combat duty for women. The ERA did not specifically address the role of women in the armed services. Other issues—marriage, divorce, child custody, inheritance—were also not specifically mentioned in the ERA. It was thus difficult to predict the long-range consequences of the ERA. Some feared that passage of the amendment would cause laws governing relationships between men and women to change in ways that might disadvantage women. Others claimed that the ERA would not have much of an impact at all. "Stop ERA" Chairperson Phyllis Schafly announced to women:

> ERA won't do anything for you. It won't make your husband do half the dirty diapers and dishes. It won't make your ex-husband pay support. I think the defeat of the ERA is a tremendous victory for women's rights.[4]

Do Americans want the ERA? Some national polls report that majorities of Americans—both men and women—support equal rights. (Support for ERA was reported at 71 percent by the NBC–Associated Press in 1980; 64 percent by Gallup, 1980; 61 percent by *Time* magazine, 1981; 61 percent by the *Washington Post*–ABC, 1981.[5]) Although the ERA was not ratified, supporters have vowed to keep the issue alive.

ABORTION POLICY

Before the 1960s, abortions were rarely permitted in any states, except in cases where the mother's life was in danger. Then, about a quarter of the states made some modifications in their abortion laws, extending them to cases of rape, incest, or when the physical or mental health of the mother was in jeopardy. Obtaining an abortion was still difficult because each case had to be reviewed individually by physicians and by the hospital where the abortion was to be performed.

In 1970 abortion policy began to change.[6] Four states (New York, Alaska, Hawaii, and Washington) liberalized their abortion laws, permitting women to obtain an abortion upon the woman's request with her physician's agreement. In 1973 the Supreme Court made decisions which fundamentally changed abortion policy. In the cases of *Roe* v. *Wade* and *Doe* v. *Bolton,* the Supreme Court ruled that the Fifth and Fourteenth Amendments to the Constitution, which guarantee all persons "life, liberty and property," did not include the life of the unborn fetus. In addition, the First and Fourteenth Amendments guaranteeing personal liberties were said to extend to child-bearing decisions. The Supreme Court did stipulate some conditions under which abortions could and could not be restricted by the states. (1) During the first three months of pregnancy the states cannot restrict the mother's decision for an abortion; (2) from the fourth to six months of pregnancy the states cannot restrict abortions, but they can protect the health of the mother by setting standards for how and when abortions can be performed; (3) during the last three months of pregnancy the states can prohibit all abortions except those to protect the mother's life and health.

ERA and Minority Women
Double Discrimination – Racism and Sexism

Minority women have long been the victims of double discrimination, suffering from effects of both racism and sexism. Women on the average are paid 59¢ for every dollar paid to men. But for Black women, the 59¢ shrinks to 54¢ and for Hispanic women, to 49¢. The treatment of race as a suspect class under the 14th Amendment and the statutory guarantees against race discrimination, while not a panacea, have had a significant effect. Black and Hispanic men on the average are paid 73¢ for every dollar paid to white males.

Just as the 14th Amendment was enacted to guarantee equal protection under the law for Blacks leading to the legal definition of race as a "suspect" classification, the Equal Rights Amendment must be passed to guarantee equal protection under the Constitution without regard to sex.

The Equal Rights Amendment which would guarantee equal justice under the law for *all* women is a vitally important tool in the fight for minority women's rights.

Diversity Among Women

The backgrounds and experiences of all women vary by race, ethnicity, economic status, religion and culture. But specific problems become especially clear when racial and ethnic data are made available by sex. For example:

Black women over the years have had higher rates of participation in the employment ranks than any other group of women. A majority of Black adult females have been in the labor pool since about 1975. These high job rates, however, do not spell success for Black women in the labor force. Their unemployment rates have generally been the highest of any category. This is true despite the strides Black women have made in recent years in closing the education gap. In 1979, the median years of education attained by black women were 11.1, compared to 12.3 for white women and 9.3 for hispanic women.

Mexican-Americans constitute the second largest minority in the United States today.

Census projections are that the Hispanic population will surpass the number of Black Americans during the next decade. Chicanas face not only economic and educational barriers, but language, religious and cultural blocks as well.

Puerto Rican women differ from other minorities who preceded them to the United States: they came as American citizens. Nevertheless, numerous problems, differences in customs, racial and ethnic biases and limited knowledge of English, have restricted their social, economic and educational success. Other women of Spanish origin, including *Cuban women*, face similar discrimination, but have varied backgrounds and cultures.

In any discussion of *Native American women*, it is necessary to keep in mind the diversity among the nearly 800 tribal entities in existence today. Despite the availability of free schools, in parts of the Southwest less than 10% of Native American women have completed eight years of schooling. Census data show, however, that women in the total Native American population have completed a median of 10.5 years of school.

Asian American women, like Native Americans, are a highly diversified ethnic group. The Asian American population includes Koreans, Vietnamese, Indonesians, Thais, Malaysians and a wide representation of Pacific people such as Samoans, Guamanians and native Hawaiians, and Americans of Chinese, Japanese and Filipino origins. Although many Asian American women are educated, having attended or completed college, they are still concentrated in lower-paying clerical positions. The segment of the Asian population most at a disadvantage, however, is composed of those women who cannot speak, read or write English. Illiteracy in English is generally a problem for Asian American women over 55.

A serious barrier when defining the problems of minority women for lawmakers is the lack of adequate employment and education data. This is especially true for Native American, Asian American women, and the many Spanish-origin populations. 1980 census data has not yet been

3

212

tabulated, and government figures between census years are based on estimates at best.

Below is an analysis of available data by race and sex. The figures graphically show how minority women are victimized by both race and sex discrimination. Regrettably, the available data are adequate only to explore the plight of Black and Hispanic women.

Minority Women Face Severe Economic Discrimination

Minority women are victims of the lowest wage rate and highest unemployment rates of all categories of persons. The following chart shows the Wage Gap—the real picture of double discrimination faced by minority women.

The Wage Gap

	1979 Annual Earnings	
White Males	$17,427	$1.00
Black Males	12,738	73¢
Hispanic Males	12,658	73¢
White Females	10,244	59¢
Black Females	9,476	54¢
Hispanic Females	8,466	49¢

The Workforce is Changing But Women Are Still at the Bottom

The needs of the modern workplace are shifting. The previously labor intensive manufacturing industries, traditionally male dominated, need fewer and fewer workers. At the same time, traditional female occupations are experiencing a great increase, especially in the area of clerical and service industries. These "women's jobs" however, are low paying and have little advancement opportunity. Minority women are especially overrepresented in these fields.

Today's educational system channels women into traditional female occupations. A greater proportion of minority women hold service, household and operative jobs than other groups. Hispanic and Black women hold few managerial and professional jobs.

A large majority of people living in poverty in the United States are women and children. A study by the National Advisory Council on Economic Opportunity calls the trend the "feminization of poverty," and predicts that by the year 2000 the poor population will be composed entirely of women and children.

In 1979, 12% of all persons were below the poverty line; of those, 9% were whites and 31% blacks. Only 7% of male heads of household were so impoverished, while 32% of female heads of households were below the poverty line.

Forecast for the Future

The budget cutbacks by the Reagan Administration hit women with special force. Aid to Families with Dependent Children (AFDC), food stamps, health care for poor women and children, CETA job training programs—all face drastic cuts or elimination. And these budget cuts have the greatest effect on those least able to afford it: minority women who already bear the burden of double discrimination.

Most minority women understand the need for Equal Rights Amendment. Support for ERA as reflected in public opinion polls is higher among minority women than white women.

Opponents of abortion, generally called the "right to life" groups, oppose the freedom to obtain an abortion. They often base their arguments on religious and moral grounds. Proponents of abortion, who often call themselves the "prochoice" movement, believe that a woman has the right to make decisions about her own body, including the decision to terminate an unwanted pregnancy. Without recourse to legal abortions they fear that women may turn to illegal abortions that can result in health risks or even death for the mother. Proponents believe that misery and suffering may be saved when a parent or parents can make a decision about unwanted children. Abortions are being used increasingly as a method of birth control. The number of abortions has more than doubled from over one-half million in 1972 to nearly one and one-half million today.[7]

Today, one of the most pressing abortion issues has to do with the use of federal funds to finance abortions for poor women.[8] Under the Medicaid program, poor pregnant women could qualify for federally funded abortions. But in 1976 antiabortion groups were able to tack an amendment on to the appropriations bill for the Department of Health, Education and Welfare. The amendment, known as the Hyde Amendment, prohibited the federal government from incurring the costs of abortions, except in cases that endanger the mother's life. The amendment does not restrict women from obtaining a privately funded abortion.

The National Abortion Rights League lost a Supreme Court battle to change Congress's decision. The Supreme Court upheld the Hyde Amendment by declaring that the poor do not have the right to abortions financed by the federal government, except in cases endangering the mother. In 1977 the federal funding ban was lifted in promptly reported cases of rape and incest and in cases where "severe and long-lasting" harm would be caused to the woman. These extensions of the law are important because definitions of severe and long-lasting harm are open to interpretation. Interpreted liberally, the change in the law can affect federally funded abortions for many poor women.

WOMEN, MEN, AND SOCIAL SECURITY

When the Social Security system was first adopted, the roles of men and women were different from the way they are today. Women were less likely to work outside the home, and divorce was much less common. The Social Security system reflected the social conditions of the 1930s when most women received Social Security benefits because they were "dependents" of their working husbands.

Since women are poorer than men, they rely more heavily on transfer payments such as Social Security. Three-quarters of women ages sixty-five and older live on annual incomes of less than $5,000; Social Security is the sole source of income for 60 percent of elderly women.[9]

Rapid changes in the past few decades have left the Social Security system outmoded in a number of ways. "In 1980, less than 10% of all American husband-wife families fit the stereotype of an employed father, stay-at-home mother and two or more children under 18."[10] Today, women make up about one-half of the labor force. Some women work to supplement their husband's wages or because they enjoy being productive outside the home, but an increasing number of women work because they are the family's primary breadwinner. High divorce rates and increases in the number of women raising families without husbands have contributed to the number of households headed solely by women.

The Social Security system has not kept pace with the changing roles of men and women.[11] Women have been inadequately treated by the Social Security system for a number of reasons. First, women's wages are generally lower than men's wages, resulting in lower benefits paid to women when they retire. Second, women are likely to spend less time in the work force because they also carry the responsibilities of home and children. This also results in lower benefits paid to women. Third, divorced women are entitled to only one-half of their former husbands' benefits. If this is the woman's only income it is generally not adequate. Fourth, widows generally do not qualify for benefits unless they are sixty years old, or unless there are children under age eighteen in the home. Fifth, homemakers are not covered on their own unless they have held jobs in the labor force. Sixth, Social Security benefits are often based on the earnings of the primary worker, generally the husband. The wages of a secondary earner may not raise the couples combined Social Security benefits very much. Seventh, couples in which one worker earned most of the wages may receive higher benefits than those in which the husband and wife earned equal wages. Eighth, and finally, married workers benefit from Social Security more than single workers. An individual who has never worked can benefit from Social Security payments based on the work of a spouse. Single workers do not receive additional benefits, even though they have made Social Security payments at the same rate as married workers.

Two major options have been suggested for remedying inequities in the Social Security system. The "earnings sharing" option would divide a couple's earnings equally between the husband and wife for each year they are married. This option would allow benefits to be calculated separately for the husband and the wife and would eliminate the ideas of the "primary wage earner" and the "dependent spouse." This option would also recognize that the spouse who takes care of the home is an equal partner in the marriage. A second option is the "double decker plan." Under this option everyone would be eligible for a basic benefit, whether or not they have worked. Individuals who have also contributed to the paid labor force would receive a payment in addition to the basic benefit.

BLACKS AND WELFARE

The living conditions of black and white Americans differ markedly. On the average, blacks do not live as long as whites; they are in poorer health; they earn less, and they are overrepresented in public assistance programs.

Table 11–5 compares the incomes of blacks, whites, and those of Hispanic origin. Sixteen percent of black families earn less than $5,000 annually, compared with 12 percent of Hispanic and 5 percent of white families. Twice as many whites as blacks earn $25,000–35,000 annually. Hispanic families have better earning records than black Americans. In 1980 the median income of black families was $12,674, compared with an Hispanic median income of $14,716 and a white median income of $21,904.

TABLE 11–5   Income Levels for White, Black, and Hispanic Families, 1980

INCOME	% OF TOTAL WHITE	% OF TOTAL BLACK	% OF TOTAL HISPANIC ORIGIN
0 to $4,999	4.9	16.4	11.5
$5,000 to $9,999	11.3	23.8	20.8
$10,000 to $14,999	13.9	16.8	20.3
$15,000 to $19,999	14.1	12.8	14.9
$20,000 to $24,999	14.2	10.2	11.3
$25,000 to $34,999	20.8	11.8	14.2
$35,000 to $49,999	13.6	6.3	6.1
$50,000 and over	7.2	1.7	2.5
Median Income	$21,904	$12,674	$14,716

Source: U.S. Bureau of the Census, Current Population Reports, Series P-60, No. 127, *Money Income and Poverty Status of Families and Persons in the United States: 1980* (Advance data from the March 1981 Current Population Survey), U.S. Government Printing Office, Washington, D.C., 1981, p. 13.

Since black Americans earn less than white Americans and those of Hispanic origin, they are also more likely to be poor. Table 11–6 compares poverty rates for these three groups from 1972 to 1980. For each year blacks were almost three times as likely to be poor as whites; those of Hispanic origin were less likely to be poor than blacks. While poverty rates gradually decreased for black and white Americans from 1972 to 1978, they rose by nearly two percent for both groups in 1980. Poverty rates for Hispanic persons have generally increased between 1972 and 1980, reaching 26 percent in 1980.

Even after controlling for education, blacks are more likely to be poor than whites and those of Hispanic origin. While educational attainment is closely related to income, the income of blacks in America is less likely than whites to increase with education (see Table 11–7). For example, 11 percent of whites with an eighth-grade education have incomes below the poverty level, compared with 37 percent of blacks and 28 percent of those of Hispanic origin. The difference persists at the high school and college levels. There are nearly four times as many poor black as poor white high school graduates. Even college attendance does not eliminate this difference in earning patterns.

TABLE 11–6   Percentage of White, Black and Hispanic Persons Below the Poverty Level, 1966–1980

	% OF TOTAL	% OF WHITE	% OF BLACK	% OF HISPANIC ORIGIN
1980	13.0	10.2	32.5	25.7
1978	11.4	8.7	30.6	21.6
1976	11.8	9.1	31.1	24.7
1974	11.6	8.9	31.4	23.2
1972	11.9	9.0	33.3	22.8
1970	12.6	9.9	33.5	—[9]
1968	12.8	10.0	34.7	—[9]
1966	15.7	12.2	41.8	—[9]

Source: U.S. Bureau of the Census, Current Population Reports, Series P-60, No. 127, *Money Income and Poverty Status of Families and Persons in the United States: 1980* (Advance data from the March 1981 Current Population Survey), U.S. Government Printing Office, Washington, D.C., 1981, p. 29.

TABLE 11–7   Poverty Status of Whites, Blacks and Hispanics by Educational Level, in Thousands, 1980

Education	WHITE		BLACK		HISPANIC ORIGIN	
	Number	% of Total	Number	% of Total	Number	% of Total
Elementary:						
Less than 8 years	739	20.6	345	35.8	262	32.5
8 years	417	10.8	141	36.6	72	27.5
High School:						
1–3 years	747	11.7	489	38.0	120	27.4
4 years	1144	6.4	417	22.7	99	14.1
College:						
1 year or more	526	3.0	147	11.9	46	8.0

Source: U.S. Bureau of the Census, Current Population Reports, Series P-60, No. 127, *Money Income and Poverty Status of Families and Persons in the United States: 1980* (Advance data from the March 1981 Current Population Survey), U.S. Government Printing Office, Washington, D.C., 1981, p. 35.

Considering the depressed income of black Americans, their over-representation in public assistance programs should come as no surprise. Although blacks comprise only 12 percent of the total U.S. population, they comprise 43 percent of all AFDC recipients, 28 percent of SSI recipients, and 36 percent of all food stamp recipients. (Table 11–8 compares black and white participation in public assistance programs.) The proportion of blacks in public assistance programs serves to reinforce stereotypes that blacks are less motivated to work than white Americans, despite widespread recognition of the effects of racial discrimination. In fact, patterns of racial

TABLE 11-8   Participation in Social Welfare Programs for Whites and Blacks, in Thousands

	WHITES		BLACKS	
	Number	% of All Recipients	Number	% of All Recipients
Aid to Families with Dependent Children (Families)	1853	53.6	1515	43.0
Food Stamps (families)	2763	62.5	1601	36.2
Supplemental Security Income (individuals)	2664	64.2	1141	27.5

Source: *Statistical Abstract of the United States, 1980,* 101st edition, Washington, D.C., 1980, p. 358, and 100th edition, 1979, p. 130.

discrimination are so firmly entrenched in American society that the term "institutional racism" has been used to refer to these practices.

However, we should not obscure the progress that blacks have made in recent years. While their income in relation to whites remains substantially lower, the proportion of blacks below the poverty level decreased from 56 percent in 1959 to 32 percent today. The quality of housing occupied by blacks has improved, and blacks are also more likely to hold professional jobs and to graduate from college.[12]

SEPARATE BUT NOT EQUAL

The Fourteenth Amendment guarantees all citizens equal protection under the law, but this amendment is also an example of how ideas that sound rational can be used to maintain and perpetuate racial discrimination. Until 1954 the Fourteenth Amendment served as legal grounds for equal but separate protection under the law. Segregation of blacks and whites in public schools, on public buses, and in other public (and private) places was condoned. Public facilities for blacks were supposed to be equal to facilities for whites (see *Plessy* v. *Ferguson),* but this was generally not the case. Yet it was not until the middle of the twentieth century that the Supreme Court exercised its power in overturning the separate but equal doctrine set forth in the case of *Plessy* v. *Ferguson.*

In 1954 a growing black dissatisfaction with the separate but equal doctrine resulted in a Supreme Court ruling that marked the official recognition of racial inequality in America. Schools in Topeka, Kansas, were segregated but essentially equal in terms of physical conditions and quality of education. However, in the case of *Brown* v. *Board of Education of Topeka, Kansas,* the Supreme Court ruled that separate was not equal. In its decision the Court took the position that "the policy of separating the races is usually interpreted as denoting the inferiority of the Negro Group." The

Court also stated that "segregation with the sanction of law, therefore, has a tendency to retard the education and mental development of Negro children." The *Brown* decision remains a landmark case in the history of equal rights.

However, "de facto" segregation of schools due to neighborhood segregation continues to exist.[13] When children from inner-city black neighborhoods attend their neighborhood schools, the schools are almost totally composed of black students. One solution to de facto school segregation is busing. In 1971, in the case of *Swann* v. *Charlotte-Mecklenburg Board of Education,* the Supreme Court approved of court-ordered busing of children to achieve integration in school districts that had a history of discrimination. However, in 1974, in *Milligan* v. *Bradley,* the Supreme Court ruled *against* busing across city-suburban boundaries to achieve integration. This decision means that de facto segregation will remain in areas where schools in largely black central cities are surrounded by predominately white suburbs.

Busing remains a bitter American controversy. Parents often reject the idea of sending a child to a school several miles away when a neighborhood school is nearby. Parents, generally white parents, who have purposely purchased homes in certain school districts, are often angered when their child must be bused to a school that they feel is inferior. On the other hand, without school integration poor children will continue to receive their education in disadvantaged situations.

Educational inequality also results from the way public education is financed. The major source of school funding is the local property tax. Schools in middle- and upper-class neighborhoods have larger financial bases, while schools in poor neighborhoods have more limited financial resources. These financial inequities have led to a call for equal educational expenditures for all school children, regardless of their families' economic status. Unequal educational opportunities continue to prevent minority persons from obtaining jobs that would increase their earning capacity and reduce their dependence on welfare programs.

CIVIL RIGHTS ACT

Since the 1954 *Brown* decision, the single most important reform with regard to racial equality has been the Civil Rights Act of 1964. The act states:

1. It is unlawful to apply unequal standards in voter registration procedures, or to deny registration for irrelevant errors or omissions on records or applications.
2. It is unlawful to discriminate or segregate persons on the grounds of race, color, religion, or national origin in any public accommodation, including hotels, motels, restaurants, movies, theaters, sports arenas, entertainment

houses, and other places that offer to serve the public. This prohibition extends to all establishments whose operations affect interstate commerce or whose discriminatory practices are supported by state action.

3. The attorney general shall undertake civil action on behalf of any person denied equal access to a public accommodation to obtain a federal district court order to secure compliance with the act. If the owner or manager of a public accommodation should continue to discriminate, he would be in contempt of court and subject to peremptory fines and imprisonment without trial by jury.

4. The attorney general shall undertake civil actions on behalf of persons attempting orderly desegregation of public schools.

5. The Commission on Civil Rights, first established in the Civil Rights Act of 1957, shall be empowered to investigate deprivations of the right to vote, study, and collect information regarding the discrimination in America, and make reports to the president and Congress.

6. Each federal department and agency shall take action to end discrimination in all programs or activities receiving federal financial assistance in any form. This action shall include termination of financial assistance.

7. It shall be unlawful for any employer or labor union with 25 or more persons after 1965 to discriminate against any individual in any fashion in employment, because of his race, color, religion, sex, or national origin, and that an Equal Employment Opportunity Commission shall be established to enforce this provision by investigation, conference, conciliation, persuasion, and if need be, civil action in federal court.

Amendments to the act in 1968 prohibited housing discrimination. It has been twenty years since passage of the first Civil Rights Act, yet the balance of racial power has not shifted as dramatically as many blacks would like. In many cases blacks are forced to use a case-by-case, courtroom approach to insure the rights that have been granted to them by law.

ILLUSTRATION: URBAN BLIGHT AT CABRINI-GREEN

More than ten years ago Henry Aaron, an authority on housing, wrote:
> Over the years public housing has acquired a vile image—highrise concrete monoliths in great impersonal cities, cut off from surrounding neighborhoods by grass or cement deserts best avoided after dark, inhabited by large, mostly black, families, exhibiting the full range of social and economic difficulties.[1]

Today Cabrini-Green, a Chicago housing project, still seems to fit this description.

Cabrini-Green became the focus of national press coverage when the mayor, Jane Byrne, decided to move in.[2] The project is a ghetto of its own composed of 78 towerlike buildings—some 19 stories high. There are 13,500 residents at Cabrini-Green who are black, poor, mostly children, and mostly welfare recipients. More than half the residents do not even have telephones. Cabrini-Green is one example of the condition of many large public housing projects.

One advantage of living at Cabrini-Green is that the rent is low. Some two bedroom apartments rent for as little as $50 a month. But Cabrini-Green's residents do not look at their home as a blessing. In fact, one is hard pressed to hear residents say anything positive about Cabrini-Green. Some call the place a prison. Crime is rampant at Cabrini-Green. Murders, shootings, rapes, robberies, and gang wars are nothing new to the neighbors at Cabrini-Green. Some residents go to work, come home, lock their doors, and do not venture out. Crime is a major problem, but there are others. Cockroaches and rodents are not uncommon. City exterminators come by, but some residents are not convinced that this helps. One little girl said she was afraid of mice so she liked to play on the front porch where she "can get away from them quick." Cabrini-Green's towers are equipped with elevators but complaints are that the elevators are often on the fritz—a major problem if you live on the ninth floor. One elderly resident broke an elevator door down to get a child out, because, he says, the repairman never came. Drugs are used by some of the young at Cabrini-Green, and drinking liquor at neighborhood taverns provides some escape for the adult population.

Cabrini-Green is very close to a wealthy Near North Side neighborhood. In fact, Mayor Byrne lives just a mile away from the project. Byrne agreed that Cabrini-Green needed cleaning up; so she and her husband moved into one of Cabrini-Green's apartments, and some conditions at the project changed. Cabrini-Green became cleaner, there were more police around and crime decreased, but Byrne's stay at the project lasted less than one month. She now keeps the apartment for occasional visits. Mayor Byrne was not the only one to move out of Cabrini-Green. The city has begun to evict residents who fail to pay their rents. Bruce Conn, who has lived 20 of his 31 years at Cabrini-Green, and his family were evicted, but Conn looked at the positive side of the situation. "This may be the best thing. I've been wanting to get out of the place for a while now, but once you're in it's almost impossible to get out."

[1] Henry J. Aaron, *Shelter and Subsidies, Who Benefits from Federal Housing Policies?* (Washington, D.C.: The Brookings Institution, 1972), p. 108.

[2] Information and quotations about Cabrini-Green rely on David J. Blum, "Cabrini-Green Project, Big Ghetto in Chicago, Fights a Losing Battle," *Wall Street Journal*, May 5, 1981, pp. 1 & 18.

HOUSING: A TOOL OF RACIAL DISCRIMINATION

One of the largest single items in the average household budget is housing. Whether payments come in the form of the monthly rent or the mortgage payment, housing costs are consuming an ever-increasing portion of the personal budget. As far back as the Housing Act of 1949, Congress acknowledged the need for "a decent home and a suitable living environment for every American family." Yet, the poor often have little choice except to rent apartments and homes that the more affluent have left behind.

Housing policy in the United States—public and private, formal and informal—is perhaps the most pervasive tool of racial discrimination. Despite laws which prohibit discrimination in the sale and rental of property, neighborhood segregation remains a fact of life in most communities. Integration, required by law in schools and work places, has not been realized in the area of housing. The integration of neighborhoods would essentially eliminate the need for busing or other aids to school integration. When the middle classes leave the inner cities to move to the bedroom communities of the suburbs, the poor are left to live in the deteriorating apartment buildings of the inner cities.

Even blacks who can afford to rent or buy suburban homes in a white community may be discouraged from doing so through a number of informal and illegal practices. Word-of-mouth advertising, rather than newspaper advertising, restricts the number and type of people who will learn that a particular home or apartment is for sale or rent. Another practice is not to advertise the cost or monthly rent of a home. If an "undesirable" person expresses interest in the property, the owner quotes an exorbitant figure that discourages the prospective minority buyer or tenant. There is a fear of neighborhood integration among whites who believe that property values and the quality of neighborhood life will suffer when minorities move in.

Housing segregation is also pervasive in government programs that have actually perpetuated racial boundaries. For example, Section 235 of the 1968 Housing Act became the "largest single subsidized housing program, and the most controversial."[14] Section 235 has been controversial for a number of reasons, among them the role it has played in maintaining segregation.[15]

> The U.S. Commission on Civil Rights has charged the FHA [Federal Housing Administration] with using the Section 235 program to perpetuate racially segregated residential patterns in metropolitan areas. The Commission found that the agency had delegated its legal responsibilities under the 1968 Fair Housing Law and the Civil Rights Act of 1964 to bar discrimination in any federally supported housing to the private housing and home finance industry, which has largely ignored the intent of the civil rights legislation ... The report stated that white and minority groups buyers were offered Section 235 housing on a segregated basis and that 'minority buyers received cheaper, inferior housing and smaller government subsidies than white buyers.'[16]

The sale of inferior housing to minority persons caused another unintended consequence of Section 235. Low-income families who had become the mortgage holders on shoddily constructed and poorly maintained homes could not afford to make needed repairs. The upshot was the abandonment of a large number of "235" homes. The federal government was left holding the bag on thousands of defaulted mortgages.[17]

Redlining

Redlining is another practice which has contributed to the inferior living arrangements of blacks and other minorities. Redlining occurs when a bank, mortgage company, home insurance company, or other enterprise refuses to finance or insure property in certain areas. Redlined areas are generally those occupied by poor and minority groups. Inability to obtain financing and insurance further depresses the community.

It is not only private enterprise that has been accused of redlining. The National Commission on Urban Problems argued that the "FHA has generally regarded loans to such groups [poor and blacks] as 'economically unsound'" and that the "FHA was not merely neutral with respect to the incidence of decay and blight; its policies actually aided, abetted, and encouraged it."[18]

> In 1968 Congress moved to halt FHA's acknowledged practice of "redlining" whole areas of central cities, usually those occupied by the poor and nonwhites, by authorizing the agency to insure mortgages for construction, rehabilitation, and purchase of properties in "declining urban areas" in which normal eligibility requirements cannot be met; but the past and present orientation of the agency makes it unlikely that a switch of emphasis and clientele can be effectuated.[19]

More minority families can afford to purchase decent homes today than ever before; yet, most neighborhoods remain segregated.

NATIVE AMERICANS AND WELFARE

Social welfare problems also plague other groups, with Native Americans among the most seriously affected. "Indians have the lowest income, worst health and the largest indice of social problems in the U.S."[20] Native Americans have faced unusual hardships. These hardships have been attributed to attempts to force Native Americans to assimilate into the majority culture, despite substantial differences of their culture—family, structure, religion, and communication patterns—from that of whites. Native Americans have also faced displacement from their own reservations and have encountered problems in adapting to urban life.

The Bureau of Indian Affairs (BIA) is responsible for assisting Native Americans in meeting their welfare needs, but the BIA has been criticized for its paternalistic or authoritarian attitude toward its clientele. According to some, "The BIA takes care of Indians' money, land, children, water, roads, etc. with authority complete as that of a prison."[21] One of the worst degradations has been the removal of Native American children from their families to be raised by others. This practice has been rationalized by welfare professionals who have viewed Native American child-rearing practices as overly harsh.[22] The Indian Child Welfare Act of 1978 was designed to remedy problems concerning the placement of Native American children by restoring greater control over child placement disposition to Indian tribes. Priority for placement of Native American children is now given to members of the child's own tribe, rather than to non-Indian families.

In recognition of the abuses experienced by these individuals, the Indian Self-Determination and Education Assistance Act of 1975 emphasizes tribal self-government and the establishment of independent health, education, and welfare services. The extent to which this act can address the needs of the Native American population is questionable. The act cannot serve as retribution to those whose survival and culture have been threatened over the years.

MINORITIES AND POLITICS

One reason for political conflict over solutions to problems of minority groups is that the definition of *minority groups* has grown broader. We once thought of minorities as being racial groups, but today women, Chicanos (Mexican-Americans), Puerto Ricans, and those of other national origins may also be included in this list. Other groups—the elderly, former mental patients, the physicially handicapped, homosexuals—may also be added. There is a concern that

> Society has now generated and accepted definitions which permit so many minorities that the term, the related problems, and the proposed solutions have lost all meaning ... It may be that the blurring of the nature and degree of their [minority groups] oppression serves neither their causes nor social justice.[23]

While the issue of which groups should be considered minorities is being debated so are a number of other issues that affect minorities. We consider here affirmative action legislation, the Voting Rights Act, and the status of the Legal Services Corporation.

Affirmative action refers to policies to achieve equality in admissions and employment among racial groups. The success of affirmative action programs is sometimes based on the notion that minority groups should be admitted, hired, and promoted in proportion to their representation in the population.[24] But to what extent should affirmative action policies be pursued? Why is it not enough to pursue policies which do not discriminate against persons because of racial background. Or should policies go much further in order to reduce inequities in employment? Originally the federal government pursued an approach of nondiscrimination. Examples of nondiscrimination are found in President Truman's decision to desegregate the military in 1946 and in Titles VI and VII of the 1964 Civil Rights Act. Nondiscrimination simply means will that preferential treatment will not be given to selected racial groups.[25]

But, the quest for civil rights among blacks brought dissatisfaction with this method of achieving racial equality. There was concern that a more aggressive approach should be taken to promote equality in college admissions and in employment. One aspect of this concern spurred a debate that quotas rather than goals be used to achieve racial equality. Quotas are defined as "imposing a fixed, mandatory number or percentage of persons to be hired or promoted, regardless of the number of potential applicants who meet the qualifications,"[26] while a goal is a

> Numerical objective, fixed realistically in terms of number of vacancies expected, and the number of qualified applicants available ... If the employer ... has demonstrated every good faith to include persons from the group which was the object of discrimination ... but has been unable to do so in sufficient numbers to meet his goal, he is not subject to sanction.[27]

In addition the employer is not obligated to hire an unqualified or less qualified person in preference to a prospective employee with better qualifications.[28]

The Philadelphia Plan of 1967 issued by the U.S. Office of Federal Contract Compliance was one of the first examples of an affirmative action plan. The plan required that those bidding on federal contracts submit plans to employ specified percentages of minority groups.[29] Another quota-type plan was adopted in 1971 by the Federal Aviation Administration. This plan essentially placed a freeze on hiring any additional employees if every fifth vacant position was not filled by a minority.[30] However, the Civil Service Commission has rejected the use of quota systems in favor of goal setting. Employers feel they should not be punished if they are unable to recruit qualified minority applicants. Yet others believe that minority applicants are available for many jobs if employers (1) make the effort to advertise in places where minorities are likely to be and (2) take the time to provide job development opportunities to those already in their employ.

Opponents of quota setting generally believe that giving preferential treatment to minorities constitutes a violation of equal protection of the laws provided in the Fourteenth Amendment to the U.S. Constitution. In 1974 a federal court upheld this belief in its decision that the University of Washington Law School should admit Marco DeFunis, Jr. DeFunis had protested the university's decision to reject his application while admitting blacks with lower grades and test scores. Other cases charging reverse discrimination have also been heard by the courts. Recently the Supreme Court ruled on the issue of admitting less qualified minority applicants over white applicants in the case of Alan Bakke. The Court determined that Bakke had been unfairly denied admission to the University of California's medical school because his qualifications were stronger than those of some minority candidates admitted to the school. Proponents of the decision believed that the Bakke case may help to change what they perceive to be a trend of reverse discrimination against whites. Opponents fear that the *Bakke* decision threatens the future of affirmative action. Some worry that affirmative action is fading from the limelight and that gains that blacks have made in employment may not be sustained. Yet we cannot totally ignore the gains that blacks have made in education and employment. While gains may never be made as quickly as we would like, "it is important that we do not mistake failure to progress fast enough with failure to progress at all."[31]

The 1980s have brought other concerns about minority rights such as renewal of the Voting Rights Act. When President Lyndon B. Johnson signed the Voting Rights Act in 1965, he stated that:

> The right to vote is the most basic right, without which all others are meaningless ... The vote is the most powerful instrument ever devised by men for breaking down injustice and destroying the terrible walls which imprison men because they are different from other men.

Since the 1940s a number of major steps have been taken to insure that minorities are provided the same opportunities to vote as whites. The Voting Rights Act was designed to further insure, protect, and encourage the right to a voice in the electoral process. The Act is periodically reviewed by Congress and was renewed in 1982. At times some have expressed concern that the support for the Act may be waning, but there is little chance that Congress would fail to voice its reapproval of this legislation. Of greater concern is the question of

> How much blacks can gain through the exercise of their vote. In the North, blacks have voted freely for decades, but conditions in the urban ghettos have not been measurably improved through political action ... It is probably true that people can "better" protect themselves from government abuse when they possess and exercise their voting rights, but the right to vote is not a guarantee against discrimination.[32]

Few blacks have served in Congress. Black mayors have been elected in some of America's larger cities—Los Angeles, Detroit, and Cleveland, for example—but there continues to be a lack of minority leadership in important political posts.

Finally, the Legal Services Corporation is in jeopardy. The Legal Services Corporation has provided free legal assistance to the poor (many are also minorities) in noncriminal cases—rent disputes, eviction, welfare application rejections. There is a growing concern, however, that the government is providing funds which are often used to pursue cases against other government agencies. Some believe there is a certain absurdity to the government, in essence, suing itself; yet others believe that if the Legal Services Corporation is abolished, one more vestige of recourse for the poor and minorities will be eliminated with no where else to turn for free legal assistance.

IMMIGRATION POLICY

Immigration and naturalization policy are also issues to consider in our discussion of discriminatory practices. The United States population is composed of people from virtually every country, every culture, every religion, and every race. In 1906 the Bureau of Immigration and Naturalization was established to assist persons entering the country. From time to time, however, immigration policies have prohibited certain groups from entering the United States. Laws such as the Chinese Exclusion Act of 1833 and the Oriental Exclusion Law of 1924 severely restricted the entrance of these groups of people. The Quota System Law of 1921 and the Immigration Act of 1924 also limited the number of Asians entering the United States. Immigration policies have been much more favorable to certain other groups, such as northern Europeans.

The treatment of Japanese-Americans after the Japanese attack on Pearl Harbor in 1941 serves as an example of the discriminatory treatment that was afforded to American citizens of foreign backgrounds. Following the Pearl Harbor incident, Japanese-Americans were interned in relocation camps for fear that they might threaten U.S. security. Another reason given for the relocation was to protect Japanese-Americans from potential attacks by Americans angered by the Japanese actions. However, interned Japanese-Americans did not believe this action was either necessary or benevolent.[33] To prove that they were indeed Americans, many Japanese-Americans volunteered to serve in the armed services. Internment ended in 1943 with the recognition that citizenship and loyalty to one's country makes one an American, not racial characteristics. However, that these American citizens were deprived of their freedom because of the military actions of a foreign government remains an important lesson in American history.

Vietnamese Refugees

In 1965 stringent national origin quotas limiting the number of entrants from various countries were abolished. But new issues are at the forefront of today's American immigration policy. The Vietnam War displaced and impoverished many Vietnamese people who later sought refuge in the United States and in other countries. Of special concern is the number of Amerasian children, children born to American servicemen and Vietnamese women. Many of these children live in poverty in Vietnam since they were not brought to the United States by their fathers. Considered "half-breeds" in the place of their birth, these children have found them-selves ostracized. Establishing their fathers' identities is difficult, thus many are without the option of coming to the United States. Squalid life conditions in Vietnam leave these children with little hope for a brighter future.

Cuban and Haitian Entrants

Since 1980 the plight of Cuban and Haitian refugees has also been brought to the attention of the United States. The entrance of these persons, however, has not been as orderly as the entrance of other groups of immigrants. Since Cuba and Haiti are so close to the tip of Florida, people have virtually been arriving en masse in boats. Some have lost their lives in attempts to escape.

Cuban refugees originally came to the United States to seek political asylum from the communistic Castro regime in the 1960s. Miami, Florida, has had a large Cuban population since the influx of the 1960s. In 1980 and 1981 a new influx of Cuban refugees prompted President Carter to institute an airlift program and to open three refugee processing centers at Eglin Air Force Base in Florida, Fort Chaffee in Arkansas, and Fort Indiantown Gap in Pennsylvania. Some refugees came to join their families in the United States. But some of these refugees were convicted criminals in Cuba and others were considered "undesirables." The arrival of these persons has resulted in concern that Castro has used the United States as a dumping ground for persons he wished to deport.

Haitians have also been fleeing to this country, but not as much for political reasons as for economic reasons: Poverty has prompted many Haitians to leave their country. Under the Refugee Act of 1980, the definition of refugee does not include someone's leaving his or her country for economic reasons. Instead, the Haitians might be considered to be asking for asylum. This issue is especially critical because refugees are entitled to the same social welfare benefits (AFDC, food stamps, Medicaid) as U.S. citizens. If they are considered to be asking for asylum, however, provision of welfare benefits is subject to question.[34] Welfare eligibility is an especially critical issue at a time when reduced welfare benefits and stringent eligibility requirements threaten America's poor. President Reagan has called for a policy which will "integrate refugees into our society without nurturing their dependence on welfare."[35] Mounting unemploy-ment and increased welfare costs may cause Americans to reconsider liberal immigration laws despite America's "melting pot" tradition.

SUMMARY

Sexism and racism manifest themselves in many areas of American life—education, employment, income, and political participation. The disadvantages that women and blacks endure place them in a position of being poorer than the rest of the population. Poverty, in turn, results in greater dependence on social welfare programs for these groups.

Since women won the right to vote, there have been movements to enact an equal rights bill for women. Opposition to equal rights centers on concerns that women may be forced into combat or may lose other privileges. Other arguments suggest that there are already a number of laws which prohibit discrimination in hiring and payment of wages to women workers. However, a number of existing laws also disadvantage women. Supporters of an equal rights amendment believe that a guarantee of equality should be a part of the U.S. Constitution and have vowed to continue to press the issue.

The Social Security program treats women inequitably in several ways. For example, homemakers are not entitled to Social Security payments unless they are the dependent or survivor of a worker. Many divorced women are not entitled to benefits earned by their husbands.

Women earn 59 cents for every dollar earned by men. Because women are poorer, they receive welfare payments more often than men. As a result they are also more likely to be hurt by welfare cutbacks.

Another welfare issue that concerns women, as well as men, is abortion. The Supreme Court has upheld the right of women to abortions, with the states reserving the right to place more stringent restrictions on abortions to be done later in the pregnancy. Right-to-life groups have continued to oppose abortions on moral and religious grounds while prochoice groups have defended a woman's right to abortion on demand. Another issue is that of federally funded abortions. While abortions are a legal means of birth control, the government no longer insures the right to a federally funded abortion for poor women, except in cases where the mother's life is in danger, or in cases of rape or incest.

Black Americans have faced a number of struggles in their fight for civil rights. Court decisions have struck down the "separate but equal" doctrine, stating that separate public facilities are not equal facilities. One implication of this decision has been the integration of public schools, although integration has not been achieved in many communities because neighborhood segregation continues to insure that schools remain segregated. The Civil Rights Act of 1964 addressed a number of black Americans' concerns, including equal treatment in employment. However, twenty years later, discrimination remains an issue. Even after controlling for educational level, black Americans earn less than whites. As a result, blacks are disproportionately represented on the welfare rolls.

Other minority groups also face discrimination. Native Americans are among the most severely affected. The Bureau of Indian Affairs has been criticized for its treatment of Native Americans, even though this government agency was established to assist this group. High levels of unemployment, poor health, and lack of formal education are rampant among Native Americans. Native Americans have resisted assimilation into the mainstream society that is often inconsistent with Native American culture and traditions. The Indian/and Education Assistance Self-Determination Act of 1975 was designed to restore planning power for social welfare programs to these people.

The current refugee situation has also posed problems. While Vietnamese people have immigrated to the United States as a result of the Vietnam War, recent influxes of Cubans and Haitians have arrived in boat loads in Florida without prior clearance. Cubans have sought political asylum; Haitians are seeking escape from the extreme poverty of their homeland. The United States has generally been a haven for those seeking escape from oppression, but welfare cutbacks have raised questions about the ability of the United States to support large numbers of people from other countries.

NOTES

1. U.S. Bureau of the Census statistics cited in *The World Almanac and Book of Facts 1982* (New York: Newspaper Enterprise Association, Inc., 1981), p. 250.
2. "ERA and Employed Women" in *ERA Countdown Campaign* (Washington, D.C.: National Organization for Women, 1981), p. 2.
3. "ERA Ratification Status Summary," *ERA Countdown Campaign* (Washington, D.C.: National Organization for Women, 1981), p. A.
4. Quoted in David Klein, "The ERA is Wanted Dead or Alive in Florida," *Tallahassee Democrat*, January 21, 1982.
5. These polls are summarized in "Strong Public Support for ERA" in *ERA Countdown Campaign* (Washington, D.C.: National Organization for Women, 1981), p. C.
6. This section relies on Thomas R. Dye, *Understanding Public Policy*, 4th ed. (Englewood Cliffs, N.J.: Prentice-Hall, 1978), pp. 78–79.
7. U.S. Bureau of the Census, *Statistical Abstract of the United States, 1980*, p. 60.
8. This section relies on Thomas R. Dye and L. Harmon Zeigler, *The Irony of Democracy*, 5th ed (Monterey, Calif.: Duxbury Press, 1981), pp. 263–266.
9. "ERA and Social Security" in *ERA Countdown Campaign*, (Washington, D.C.: The National Organization for Women), 1981, p. 4.
10. Ibid., p. 4.
11. This section relies on U.S. Department of Health, Education and Welfare, *Social Security and the Changing Roles of Men and Women*, U.S. Government Printing Office, February 1979, Chapters 1 and 2.
12. Dye, *Understanding Public Policy*, p. 73.
13. Ibid., pp. 56–62.
14. Chester W. Hartman, *Housing and Social Policy* (Englewood Cliffs, N.J.: Prentice-Hall, 1975), p. 136.
15. Ibid., p. 139.
16. Ibid.
17. Ibid.
18. Cited in ibid., pp. 140–41.
19. Ibid., p. 141.
20. Thomas H. Walz and Gary Askerooth, *The Upside Down Welfare State* (Minneapolis: Elwood Printing, 1973), p. 25.
21. Ibid.
22. Joseph J. Westeroreyer, "Indian Powerlessness in Minnesota," *Society* (March/April 1973): 50 cited in Ibid., p. 31.
23. June Hopps, "Oppressions Based on Color," *Social Work* 27, no. 1 (January 1982): 3.

24. Dye, *Understanding Public Policy*, p. 69.
25. Ibid., pp. 67, 69.
26. *Federal Policies on Remedies Concerning Equal Employment Opportunity in State and Local Government Personnel Systems*, March 23, 1973, cited in Felix A. Nigro and Lloyd G. Nigro, *The New Public Personnel Administration* (Itasca, Ill.: F.E. Peacock, 1976), p. 21.
27. Ibid.
28. Ibid.
29. Dye, *Understanding Public Policy*, p. 69.
30. Nigro and Nigro, *The New Public Personnel Administration*, p. 21.
31. Dye, *Understanding Public Policy*, p. 73.
32. Dye and Zeigler, *The Irony of Democracy*, p. 212.
33. Donald Brieland, Lela B. Costin, and Charles R. Atherton, *Contemporary Social Work, An Introduction to Social Work and Social Welfare*, 2nd ed. (New York: McGraw Hill, 1980), p. 404.
34. Nadine Cohodas, "Cuban Refugee Crisis May Prompt Introduction of Special Legislation," *Congressional Quarterly Weekly Report*, May 31, 1980, p. 1496.
35. Statement issued by President Reagan on July 30, 1981, in *Congressional Quarterly Weekly Report*, August 22, 1981, p. 1577.

12

Implementing and Evaluating Social Welfare Policy: What Happens after a Law Is Passed

Americans once believed that social problems could be solved by passing laws, creating bureaucracies, and spending money. Americans generally believed that if Congress adopted a policy and appropriated money for it, and the executive branch organized a program, hired people, spent money, and carried out the activities designed to implement the policy, then the effects of the policy felt by society would be those intended by the Congress. But today there is a growing uneasiness among both policy-makers and the general public about the effectiveness and cost of many social welfare programs. Americans have lost their innocence about government and public policy.

IMPLEMENTING PUBLIC POLICY

Many problems in social welfare policy arise *after a law is passed*—in the implementation process. Policy implementation includes all of the activities designed to carry out the intention of the law. Policy implementation includes (1) creating, organizing, and staffing agencies to carry out the new policy, or assigning new responsibilities to existing agencies and personnel; (2) issuing and entering directives, rules, regulations, and guidelines to

DEPARTMENT OF HEALTH AND HUMAN SERVICES

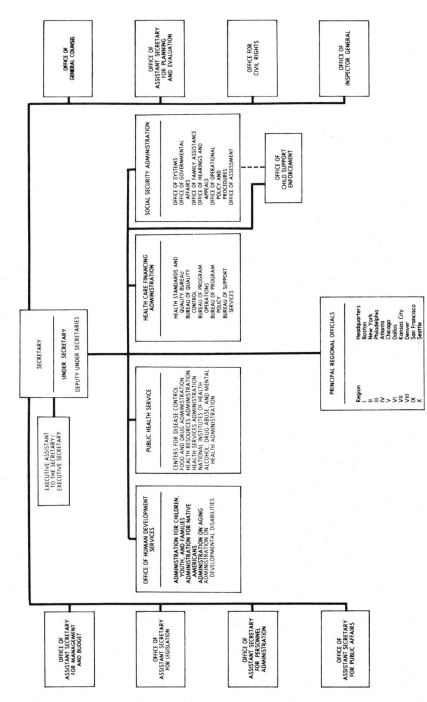

(*U.S. Government Manual*, p. 830.)

translate policies into specific courses of action; and (3) directing and coordinating both personnel and expenditures toward the achievement of policy objectives.

There is always a gap—sometimes small, sometimes very large—between a policy decision and its implementation. Some scholars of implementation take an almost cynical view of the process:

> Our normal expectation should be that new programs will fail to get off the ground and that, at best, they will take considerable time to get started. The cards in this world are stacked against things happening, as so much effort is required to make them move. The remarkable thing is that new programs work at all.[1]

THE POLITICS OF IMPLEMENTATION

What are the obstacles to implementation? Why isn't implementation a *rational* activity? Why can't policies be directly implemented in decisions about organization, staffing, spending, regulation, direction, and coordination?

The obstacles to successful implementation are many, but we might categorize them in terms of (1) communication, (2) resources, (3) attitudes, and (4) bureaucratic structure.[2]

Communications

The first requirement for effective policy implementation is that the people who are running the program must know what they are supposed to do. Directives must not only be received, but they must also be clear. Vague, inconsistent, and contradictory directives confuse administrators. Directives give meanings to policies—meanings which may not be consistent with the original intention of the law. Moreover, poor directives enable people who disagree with the policy to read their own biases into programs.

Generally the more decentralized the administration of a program, the more layers of administration through which directives must flow, and the less likely that policies will be transmitted accurately and consistently. Whatever the advantages of decentralization, prompt, consistent, and uniform policy implementation is *not* usually found in a decentralized structure.

Frequently Congress (and state legislatures) is deliberately vague about public policy. Congress and the president may pass vague and ambiguous laws largely for *symbolic* reasons—to reassure people that "something" is being done to help with a problem. Yet in these cases Congress and the president do not really know exactly what to do about the problem. They therefore delegate wide discretion to administrators, who act under the "authority" of broad laws, to determine what, if anything, actually will be done. Often Congress and the president want to claim credit for the high-sounding principles enacted into law but do not want to accept responsibility for the unpopular actions that administrators must take to implement these principles. It is much easier for political leaders to blame the "bureaucrats" and pretend that government regulations are a product of an "ungovernable" Washington bureaucracy.

For example, in the Economic Opportunity Act of 1964, Congress and President Johnson wrote into the law a provision calling for "maximum feasible participation of the poor" in community action agencies and programs supported by the Office of Economic Opportunity. But no one knew exactly what that phrase meant. How were the poor to help plan and run the programs? Did this phrase authorize poverty workers to organize the poor politically? Did this phrase mean that social activists paid by the government should help organize the poor to pressure welfare and housing agencies for better services? The policy was not clear and its implementation was confusing and frustrating. Eventually, of course, the Office of Economic Opportunity was abolished, in part because of its problems in administering an unclear mandate from Congress.

Resources

Policy directives may be clear, accurate, and consistent, but if administrators lack the resources necessary to carry out these policies, implementation fails. Resources include *staffs* with the proper *skills* to carry out their assignments, and with the *authority* and *facilities* necessary to translate a paper proposal into a functioning public service.

It is common for government agencies to claim that problems of implementation arise from undersized staffs. And many of the claims are true. Indeed, one tactic of opponents of a particular policy, even after they lose the fight over the actual policy in Congress, is to try to reduce the size of the budget and staff that is to implement the policy. The political battle does not end with the passing of a law. It continues each year in fights over resources to implement the law.

It is not enough that there be adequate funds to hire personnel to carry out a policy. In addition, the personnel must have the skills necessary for the job. Staffing is especially difficult in new programs. There are not ready-made reserves of people who are trained for the program and who know what to do. Yet there is always pressure to "show results" as quickly as possible to insure the continuation of the program the next year.

Sometimes agencies lack the authority, even on paper, to implement policy. Agencies may not be authorized to issue checks to citizens; or to purchase goods or services; or to provide funds to other government agencies; or to withdraw funds in the case of noncompliance; or to go to court to force compliance. Some agencies may have the necessary authority (for example, to withdraw federal funds from a local government agency or a nonprofit corporation), but they may be reluctant to exercise this authority because of the adverse political repercussions that might ensue. Agencies that do not have the necessary authority to carry out policy (or agencies that fear that exercising that authority may be politically risky) must rely on *persuasion and cooperation*. Rather than order local agencies, private corporations, or individual citizens to do something, higher level officials may consult with them, ask for their cooperation, or appeal to their sense of public service. Successful implementation generally requires goodwill on the part of everyone involved. Agencies or administrators who must continually resort to sanctions will probably be unsuccessful in the long run.

Physical facilities may also be critical resources in implementation. Programs generally need offices, equipment, and supplies. It is difficult to run an agency without telephones. Yet many government agencies (especially new agencies) find it difficult to acquire the necessary facilities to carry out their programs. Again, most government administrators must rely on persuasion and cooperation to get other government agencies to provide them with offices, desks, telephones, travel approvals, and so on.

Attitudes

If administrators and program personnel sympathize with a particular policy, it is likely to be carried out as the original policy-makers intended. But when the attitudes of administrators and staff personnel differ from those of the policy-makers, the implementation process becomes very complex. Because administrators always have some discretion (and occasionally a great deal) in implementation, their attitudes toward policies have much to do with how a program is implemented. When people are told to do things with which they do not agree, inevitable slippage will occur between a policy and its implementation.

Generally, social service personnel enter the field because they want to "help people"—especially the aged, poor, handicapped, and less fortunate in society. There is seldom any attitudinal problem in social agencies in implementing policies to *expand* social services. But highly committed social service personnel may find it very difficult to implement policies to *cut back* or eliminate social services.

Conservative policy-makers are aware of the social service orientation of the "welfare bureaucracy." They do not believe, for example, that welfare administrators really try to enforce work provisions of the welfare law.[3] They believe that the welfare bureaucracy has been partially responsible for the growth in numbers of recipients over the years; eligibility requirements, these conservatives say, have been given liberal interpretation by sympathetic administrators. They believe that welfare administrators are a major obstacle to policies designed to tighten eligibility, reduce overlapping benefits, and encourage work.

In government agencies it is generally impossible to remove people simply because they disagree with a policy. Direct pressures are generally unavailable: Pay increases are primarily across-the-board; promotions are infrequent and often based on seniority. Again, "selling" a policy—winning support through persuasion—is more effective at overcoming opposition than threatening sanctions. If those who implement policy cannot be convinced that the policy is good for their clients or themselves, perhaps they can be convinced that it is less offensive than other alternatives which might be imposed by policy-makers.

Bureaucratic Structure

Previously established organizations and procedures in bureaucracies may hinder implementation of new policies and programs. Bureaucratic "inertia" slows changes in policy. Administrators become accustomed to ways of doing things (standard operating procedures, or SOPs), and administrative structures have a tendency to remain in place long after their original functions have changed or even disappeared.

Standard operating procedures are routines that enable officials to perform numerous tasks every day; SOPs save time. If every worker had to invent a new way of doing things in every new case, there would not be enough time to help very many people. SOPs can be written into a manual to help less experienced workers handle cases. SOPs bring consistency to the handling of cases; rules are applied more uniformly.

However, SOPs can also obstruct policy implementation. "Once requirements and practices are instituted, they tend to remain in force long after the conditions that spawned them have disappeared."[4] Routines are not regularly reexamined; they tend to persist even when policy changes. If SOPs are not revised to reflect policy changes, these changes are not implemented. Moreover, many people prefer the stability and familiarity of existing routines, and they are reluctant to revise their patterns. Organizations have spent time, effort, and money in developing these routines. These "sunk costs" commit organizations to limit change as much as possible.

Finally, SOPs can make it difficult to handle nonconforming cases in an individual fashion. Even though particular cases may not conform to prewritten SOPs, many administrators try to force these cases into one or another of the established classifications.*

---

*Consider, for example, the conversations reported in the accompanying illustration. How often have you experienced a similar conversation yourself? How much more frustrating these conversations must be for poor or elderly people or people with less formal education.

ILLUSTRATION: BUREAUCRACY AND IMPLEMENTATION

SWITCHBOARD:	City Hall, may I help you?
CALLER:	My daughter is handicapped and needs special transportation to her therapist. Who can I speak to in the city about this?
SWITCHBOARD: (after a pause):	I think the Office of Aging handles things like that. Let me connect you.
OFFICE OF AGING:	Good morning, Office of Aging, can you hold please? (Several minutes later.) Sorry to keep you waiting; can I help you?
CALLER:	My daughter is handicapped and needs special transportation to her therapist. Usually someone in the family helps out but it's not always...
OFFICE OF AGING:	How old is your daughter?
CALLER:	She's only a teenager, but the switchboard...
OFFICE OF AGING:	I'm sorry, but your daughter isn't eligible. Our program is only for senior citizens. Ask the switchboard to connect you to the Youth Bureau. I'll connect you back. (There are several clicks and the connection is lost. The caller dials the main city hall number again.)
SWITCHBOARD:	City Hall, may I help you?
CALLER:	The Youth Bureau please.
SWITCHBOARD:	Do you want the Delinquency Program or the Recreation Program?
CALLED:	I think it must be the Recreation Program. It's my daughter. I called earlier and was cut off, but I don't think I talked to you. I just want to...
YOUTH BUREAU:	Youth Bureau, Recreation, can I help you?
CALLER:	I hope so. My daughter is handicapped and needs special transportation to her therapist. I was wondering if you...
YOUTH BUREAU:	I'm sorry; we don't have information on that kind of program. You might try the Office of Aging...
CALLER:	But I...
YOUTH BUREAU:	...or the School Board. Their number is...

Source: Reproduced by permission of the publisher from Wayne Anderson, Bernard J. Frieden, and Michael J. Murphy, eds., *Managing Human Services* (Washington, D.C.: International City Management Association, 1977), p. 193; also cited in Bruce L. Gates, *Social Program Administration* (Englewood Cliffs, N.J.: Prentice-Hall, 1980), p. 163.

The organization of bureaucracies also affects implementation, especially when responsibility for a policy is dispersed among many governmental units. There are eighty thousand governments in the United States: a national government, fifty state governments, three thousand county governments, over eighteen thousand city governments, seventeen thousand township governments, sixteen thousand school districts, and twenty-four thousand special districts. Even within the national government, various departments have responsibility for major social welfare programs: The Department of Health and Human Services has responsibility for AFDC; the Department of Agriculture administers the Food Stamp program; the Department of Labor administers job training programs and employment services.

The more governments and agencies involved with a particular policy, and the more independent their decisions, the greater the problems of implementation. Separate agencies become concerned with their own "turf" —areas which they believe should be their exclusive responsibility. Agencies may fight each other to hold onto their traditional areas of responsibility. Proponents of particular programs may insist in Congress that their programs be administered by separate agencies that are largely independent of traditional executive departments. They fear that consolidating program responsibilities will downgrade the emphasis that the larger department may give to their particular program.

Some fragmentation may be desirable. The argument for federalism—the division of governmental responsibilities between the national government and the fifty state governments—is that it allows each state to deal more directly with conditions confronting that state. Government "closer to home" is sometimes thought to be more flexible and manageable than a distant bureaucracy in Washington.

However, when programs and services are fragmented, coordination of policy is difficult. This is true whether we are talking about the fragmentation of responsibilities among different agencies of the national government, or the division of responsibilities between the national government and the fifty states. Uniformity is lost. Consider, for example, the nation's fifty separate AFDC programs. These are *state*-administered programs with federal financial assistance. The federal government pays over half of the costs of AFDC. Yet actual benefits given to AFDC families range from less than $150 per month in seven (southern) states to over $275 per month in some other (northern and western) states.

EVALUATING SOCIAL POLICY

In recent years there has been a growing interest in *policy evaluation*—in learning about the consequences of public policy. Government agencies regularly report how much money they spend, how many persons ("clients") are given various services, and how much these services cost.

Congressional committees regularly receive testimony from influential individuals and groups about how popular or unpopular various programs and services are. But *even if* programs and policies are well-organized, financially possible, efficiently operated, widely utilized, and politically popular, the questions still arise: "So what?" "Do they work?" "Do these programs have any beneficial effects on society?" "What about people *not* receiving the benefits or services?" "What is the relationship between the costs of the program and the benefits to society?" "Could we be doing something else of more benefit to society with the money and human resources devoted to these programs?"

Can the federal government answer these questions? Can it say, for example, that AFDC, SSI, food stamps, and Medicaid are accomplishing their objectives; that their benefits to society exceed their costs, that they are not overly burdensome on taxpayers; that there are no better or less costly means of achieving the same ends? One surprisingly candid report by the liberal-oriented think tank, the Urban Institute, argues convincingly that the federal government *does not know* whether most of the things it does are worth doing:

> The most impressive finding about the evaluation of social programs in the federal government is that substantial work in this field has been almost nonexistent.
>
> Few significant studies have been undertaken. Most of those carried out have been poorly conceived. Many small studies around the country have been carried out with such lack of uniformity of design and objective that the results rarely are comparable or responsive to the questions facing policy makers....
>
> The impact of activities that cost the public millions, sometimes billions, of dollars has not been measured. One cannot point with confidence to the difference, if any, that most social programs cause in the lives of Americans.[5]

POLICY EVALUATION
AS A RATIONAL ACTIVITY

From a rational perspective, policy evaluation involves more than just learning about the consequences of public policy. Consider the following definitions by leading scholars in the field:

> Policy evaluation is the assessment of the overall effectiveness of a national program in meeting its objectives, or the assessment of the relative effectiveness of two or more programs in meeting common objectives.[6]

> Policy evaluation research is the objective, systematic, empirical examination of the effects ongoing policies and programs have on their target in terms of the goals they are meant to achieve.[7]

> Evaluation research is viewed by its partisans as a way to increase the rationality of policy making. With objective information on the outcomes of

programs, wise decisions can be made on budget allocations and program planning. Programs that yield good results will be expanded; those that make poor showings will be abandoned or drastically modified.[8]

These definitions of policy evaluation assume that the goals and objectives of programs and policies are clear, that we know how to measure progress toward these goals, that we know how to measure costs, and that we can impartially weigh benefits against costs in evaluating a public program. In short, these definitions view policy evaluation as a *rational* activity.

Ideally, the evaluation of a program would include all of its effects on real world conditions. Evaluators would want to (1) identify and rank all of the goals of a program; (2) devise measures to describe progress toward these goals; (3) identify the "target" situation or group for which the program was designed; (4) identify nontarget groups who might be affected indirectly by the program ("spillover" effects) and nontarget groups who are similar to the target groups but did not participate in the program or receive its direct benefits ("control group"); (5) measure programs' effects on target and nontarget groups over as long a period of time as possible; (6) identify and measure the costs of the program in terms of all of the resources allocated to it; and (7) identify and measure the indirect costs of the program, including the loss of opportunities to pursue other activities.

Identifying target groups in social welfare programs means defining the part of the population for whom the program is intended—the poor, the sick, the ill-housed, and so on. Then, the desired effect of the program on the target population must be determined. Is it to change their physical or economic conditions in life—their health, their nutrition, their income? Or is it to change their behavior—put them to work in the private or public sector, or increase their physical activity? Is it to change their knowledge, attitudes, awareness, or interest—to organize poor neighborhoods, to pressure slum landlords into improving housing conditions, to increase voter turnout among the poor and the black, to discourage unrest, riots, and violence? If multiple effects are intended, what are the priorities (rankings) among different effects? What are the possible *unintended* effects (side effects) on target groups—for example, does public housing achieve better physical environments for the urban poor at the cost of increasing their segregation and isolation from the mainstream of the community?

In making these identifications and measurements, the evaluators must not confuse *policy outputs* (what governments do) with *policy impacts* (what consequences these government actions have). It is important *not* to measure benefits in terms of government activity. For example the number of dollars spent per member of a target group (per pupil educational expenditures; per capita welfare expenditures; per capita health expendi-

Several ideal, rational models of program evaluation have been proposed. One noted evaluation team, headed by the sociologist Peter H. Rossi, has suggested that evaluation research includes four important types of questions.

1. Program Planning Questions:

    What is the extent and distribution of the target population?

    Is the program designed in conformity with its intended goals, and are chances of successful implementation maximized?

2. Program Monitoring Questions:

    Is the program reaching the persons, households, or other target units to which it is addressed?

    Is the program providing the resources, services, or other benefits that were intended in the project design?

3. Impact Assessment Questions:

    Is the program effective in achieving its intended goals?

    Can the results of the program be explained by some alternative process that does not include the program?

    Is the program having some effects that were not intended?

4. Economic Efficiency Questions:

    What are the costs to deliver services and benefits to program participants?

    Is the program an efficient use of resources compared with alternative uses of the resources?

It is also possible to identify a "Theoretical Model of Program Development" to assist in understanding exactly what stage of the policy process is being evaluated. One such model is shown here:

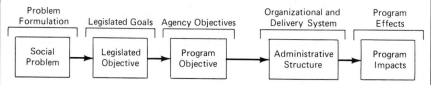

Evaluative research might be directed at any of the linkages suggested here. For example, one might want to inquire whether congressional legislation is related to the social problem, or whether the agency's objectives are consistent with the goals of Congress, or whether the program's activities have any impact on society.

See Peter H. Rossi, Howard E. Freeman, and Sonia R. Wright, *Evaluation: A Systematic Approach* (Beverly Hills: Sage Publications, 1979).

tures) are not really measurements of the *impact* of government activity. We cannot be content with counting how many times a bird flaps its wings; we must learn how far the bird has flown. In assessing the *impact* of public policy we cannot simply count the number of dollars spent or clients served, but rather we must identify the changes in individuals, groups, and society brought about by public policies.

Identifying the effects of a program on *nontarget* groups is equally important. For example, what effects will proposed welfare reforms have on social workers, social work bureaucracies, working families who are not on welfare, taxpayers, and others? Nontarget effects may turn out to be either benefits or costs.

Evaluators must also determine whether the programs' goals are long-range or immediate. When will the benefits and costs be felt? Is the program designed for a short-term, emergency situation or is it a long-term, developmental effort? Many impact studies show that new or innovative programs have short-term positive effects—for example, Head Start and other educational programs. The newness of the program, or the realization by the target group that it is being given special treatment and being watched closely, may create measurable changes (the *Hawthorne effect*). But these positive effects may disappear as the novelty and enthusiasm of the new program wear off.

Perhaps the most difficult problem confronting evaluators is the weighing of costs against benefits. Benefits may be measured in terms of bettering human conditions—improved education, improved medical care for the poor, better nutrition, steady employment, and so on. Costs are usually measured in dollars. But how can we measure the values of education, health, or self-esteem in dollars?

THE MANY FACES OF PROGRAM EVALUATION

Most government agencies make some attempt to assess the utility of their programs. These efforts usually take one or more of the following forms.

Public Hearings

This is the most common type of program review. Frequently legislative committees ask agency heads to give formal or informal testimony regarding the accomplishments of their programs. This usually occurs near budget time. In addition, written "program reports" or "annual reports" may be provided to legislators and interested citizens by agencies as a "public information" activity. However, testimonials and reports of program administrators are not very objective means of program evaluation. They frequently magnify the benefits and minimize the costs of programs.

Site Visits

Occasionally teams of legislators, high-ranking federal or state officials, or expert consultants (or some combination of all of these people) will descend upon agencies to conduct investigations "in the field." These teams can interview workers and clients and directly observe the operation of the agency. These teams can accumulate impressions about how programs are being run, whether they have competent staffs, and perhaps even whether or not the "clients" (target groups) are pleased with the services.

Program Measures

The data developed by the agencies themselves generally describe program or *output* measures—for example, the number of recipients of various welfare programs; the number of persons in work-training programs; the number of hospital beds available; the number of persons treated. But these output measures rarely indicate the *impact* these numbers have on society—for example, the conditions of life confronting a poor family, the success of work trainees in later finding and holding useful employment in the nation's workforce; the actual health of the nation's poor in terms of sicknesses, life spans, death rates, and so on.

Comparison with Professional Standards

In some areas of social welfare activity, professional associations have developed their own "standards" of benefits and services. These standards may be expressed in terms of maximum number of cases that a welfare case worker can handle effectively; or perhaps in the minimum number of hospital beds required by a population of 100,000 people; or in other ways. Actual governmental outputs can be compared with these "ideal" outputs. While this kind of study can be helpful, it still focuses on the *outputs* and not on the *impacts* that government activities have on the conditions of target and nontarget groups. Moreover, the standards are usually developed by professionals who may be questioning what ideal levels of benefits and services should be. There is really very little hard evidence that ideal levels of government outputs have any significant impact on society.

Formal Designs: Experimental Research

The "classic" research design for evaluating policies and programs employs two comparable groups—an *experimental group* and a *control group*—that are equivalent in every way *except* that the policy has been applied only to the experimental group. After the application of the policy for a given length of time, its impact is measured by comparing changes in the experimental group with changes, if any, in the control group. Initially, control and experimental groups must be identical in every possible way, and the program must be applied only to the experimental group. Postprogram differences between the two groups must be carefully measured. Also every effort must be made to make certain that any observed postprogram differences between the two groups can be attributable to the program and not to some other intervening cause that affected one of the groups as the program was administered. This classic research design is preferred by social scientists because it provides the best opportunity for estimating changes that can be directly attributed to policies and programs (see Figure 12–1 for a model of the classic research design).

Formal Designs: Quasi-Experiments

It is frequently impossible to conduct controlled experiments in public policy, because sometimes the human beings involved cannot be placed arbitrarily in experimental or control groups just for the sake of program evaluation. (Indeed, if experimental and control groups are really identical, the application of *public* policy to one group of citizens and not the other may violate the "equal protection of the laws" clause of the Fourteenth Amendment of the U.S. Constitution.) Frequently, it is only possible to compare individuals and groups that have participated in programs with those that have not, or to compare cities, states, and nations that have programs with those that do not. Comparisons are made about the extent to which the groups that have experienced the program have achieved the desired goals in relation to those groups that have not experienced the program. The problem is to try to eliminate the possibility that any difference between the two groups in goal achievement may really be caused by some factor *other than* experience with the program. For example, we may compare the job records of people who have participated in CETA training with those who have not. The former CETA trainees may or may not have better job records than other groups. If they do not, it may be because the CETA trainees were less skilled to begin with; if they do, it may be because CETA officials "creamed" off the local unemployed and trained

Figure 12-1 "Classic" research design.

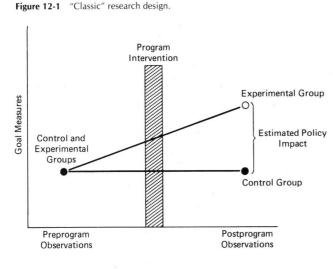

only those who already possessed good skills and job experience. Thus, quasi-experimental research designs, like most social science research, still leave room for discussion and disagreement (see Figure 12–2 for a model of the quasi-experimental research design).

Formal Designs: Time Series

Another research design is the "before and after" study—a comparison of conditions before and after a policy or program has been adopted. Usually only the target group is examined. This design is essential in jurisdictions where no control groups can be identified. When several observations are made of conditions *before* the program is adopted, and then several observations are made after the program is adopted, this is generally referred to as a *time series*. These observations are designed to show program impacts; *but* it is very difficult to know whether the changes, if any, have come about as a result of the program itself, or as a result of other changes which were occurring in society at the same time (see Figure 12–3 for a model of the time series research design).

POLICY EVALUATION
AS A POLITICAL ACTIVITY

Program evaluation may resemble scientific and rational inquiry, but it can never really be separated from politics. Let us consider just a few of the political problems that make rational policy evaluation difficult, if not impossible.

Figure 12-2   Quasi-experimental research design

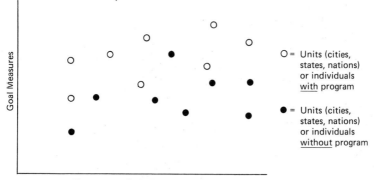

Postprogram Period Observations Only

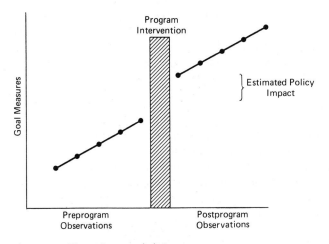

Figure 12-3   Time series research design

Unclear, Ambiguous Program Goals

Evaluators are often told to evaluate a program and yet are not informed of its goals or purposes. Reading the language of the original legislation that established the program may not be very helpful; legislative language frequently uses fuzzy words— "improve the conditions of life of the poor," "improve the health of society," "enhance the quality of life," for example. Even interviews with the original legislative sponsors (Congress members who sponsored a federal bill or state legislators who did so at the state level) may produce ambiguous, or even contradictory, goals. Often the evaluators, at the risk of offending someone, must define the goals or purposes themselves. In this way, evaluation itself becomes a political activity.

Symbolic Goals

Many programs and policies have primarily symbolic value. They do not actually change the conditions of target groups, but rather make these groups feel that their government "cares." Of course, a government agency does not welcome a study that reveals that its efforts have no tangible effects. Indeed, such a finding, if widely publicized, might reduce the symbolic impact of the program by telling target groups of its uselessness.

Unhappy Findings

Agencies and administrators usually have a heavy investment—organizational, financial, psychological—in current programs and policies. They are predisposed against findings that these programs do not work, involve excessive costs, or have unexpected negative consequences. The agency may prefer an "in-house" evaluation, over which the agency will have control. If the evaluation is to be an "outside" one, the agency may wish to decide who should get the contract for the evaluation. If a negative report is issued, the agency may adopt a variety of strategies to offset its recommendations.

Program Interference

Most serious studies of public programs involve some burdens on ongoing program activities. Accomplishing the day-to-day business of an agency is generally a higher priority in the mind of an administrator than making special arrangements for evaluation. Program evaluation also requires funds, facilities, time, and personnel, all of which administrators may not like to sacrifice from ongoing programs.

Usefulness of Evaluations

Program administrators are clearly dissatisfied with evaluative studies that conclude that: "The program is not achieving the desired results." Not only is such a finding a threat to the agency, but, standing alone, it fails to tell administrators *why* the program is failing. Evaluative studies are better received at the agency level when they include some action recommendations that might conceivably rescue the program. But even when evaluative studies show programs to be failures, the usual reaction is to patch things up and try again.

Evaluation by Whom?

One of the central political questions in evaluation is the determination of who will do the evaluation. From the perspective of the agency and its clients, the evaluation should be done by the agency or by an organizational representative of its clients. An "in-house" evaluation is most likely to produce favorable results. The next best thing, from the agency's perspective, is to allow the agency to contract with a private firm for the evaluation. A private firm that wants to win future contracts from the agency, or any other agency, is very hesitant about producing totally negative evaluations. The worst evaluation arrangement, from the agency perspective, is to have an independent office (the Congressional Budget Office, the General Accounting Office, or a state comptroller's office, for example) undertake the evaluation.

THE GUARANTEED ANNUAL INCOME EXPERIMENTS

Many policy evaluators argue that "policy experimentation" offers the best opportunity to determine the impact of public policies. This includes

Even in the face of clear evidence that your favorite program is useless, or even counter-productive, there are still a variety of administrative strategies:

1. Claim that the effects of the program are long-range and cannot be adequately measured for many years.

2. Argue that the effects of the program are general and intangible, and that these effects were not identified in the crude statistical measures used in the evaluation.

3. If an experimental research design was used, claim that withholding services or benefits from the control group was "unfair"; and claim that there were no differences between the control and experimental groups because of a knowledge of the experiment by both groups.

4. If a time series research design was used, claim that there were no differences between the "before" and "after" observations because of other coinciding variables that hid the effects of the program. That is to say, claim that the "after" group would be even worse without the program.

5. Argue that the lack of differences between the persons receiving the program services and those not receiving them only means that the program is not sufficiently intensive and indicates the need to spend *more* resources on the program.

6. Argue that the failure to identify any positive effects of the program is a result of the inadequacy of the evaluation research design and/or bias on the part of the evaluators.

selection of matching experimental and control groups, the application of the policy to the experimental group only, and careful comparisons of differences between the experimental and the control groups after the application of the policy. The argument for experimental social research is that it can save money in the long run. This is in contrast to giant public programs that are created without any prior knowledge about whether they will work. One economist writes:

> The fact is that there have been few effective ways for determining the effectiveness of a social program before it is started; indeed, in most cases it is impossible even to forecast the cost of a new program until it has been in operation for a long time.
> Clearly this situation is not conducive to sound and effective decision making.[9]

Perhaps the most well-known example of an attempt by the federal government to experiment with public policy is the New Jersey Graduated Work Incentive Experiment funded by the Office of Economic Opportunity. The experiment was designed to resolve some serious questions about the impact of welfare payments on the incentives for poor people to work.[10] In order to learn more about the effects of the present welfare system on human behavior, and more important to learn more about the possible effects of proposed programs for guaranteed family incomes, the OEO funded a three-year social experiment involving 1,350 families in New Jersey and Pennsylvania. The research was conducted by the Institute for Research on Poverty of the University of Wisconsin.

Debates over welfare reform had generated certain questions that social science could presumably answer with careful, controlled experimentation. Would a guaranteed family income reduce the incentive to work? If payments were made to poor families with employable male heads, would the men drop out of the labor force? Would the level of the income guarantee or the steepness of the reductions in payments dependent on increases in earnings make any difference in working behavior? Because current welfare programs do not provide a guaranteed minimum family income, do not generally make payments to families with employable males, and do not graduate payments substantially in relation to earnings, these questions could only be answered through *policy experimentation*. But policy experimentation raised some serious initial problems for the OEO. First of all, any experiment involving substantial payments to a fair sampling of families would be expensive. For example, if payments averaged $1,000 per year per family, and if each family had to be observed for three years, and if 1,000 families were to be involved, a minimum of $3 million would be spent even *before* any consideration of the costs of administration, data collection, analysis and study, and reporting. Ideally a *national* sample should have been used, but it would have been more expensive to monitor than a local sample and differing employment conditions in different parts of the country would have made it difficult to sort out the effects of income payments from variations in local job availability. By concentrating the sample in one region, it was hoped that local conditions would be held constant. Ideally *all* types of low-income families should have been tested, but that procedure would have necessitated a larger sample and greater expense. So only poor families with an able-bodied man between the ages of eighteen and fifty-eight were selected; the work behavior of these men in the face of a guaranteed income was of special interest.

To ascertain the effects of different levels of guaranteed income, four guarantee levels were established. Some families were chosen to receive 50 percent of the Social Security Administration's poverty-level income, others 75 percent, others 100 percent, and still others 125 percent. In order to ascertain the effects of graduated payments in relation to earnings, some families had their payments reduced by 30 percent of their outside earnings, others 50 percent, and still others 70 percent. Finally, a control sample was observed—low-income families who received no payments at all.

The experiment was initiated in August 1968 and continued until September 1972. But political events moved swiftly and soon engulfed the study. In 1969 President Nixon proposed to Congress the Family Assistance Plan (FAP), which guaranteed all families a minimum income of 50 percent of the poverty level and a payment reduction of 50 percent for outside earnings. The Nixon administration had not waited to learn the results of the OEO experiment before introducing FAP. Nixon wanted welfare reform to be his priority domestic legislation and the bill was symbolically numbered HR 1 (House of Representatives Bill 1).

After the FAP bill had been introduced, the Nixon administration pressured the OEO to produce favorable supporting evidence in behalf of the guaranteed income—specifically, evidence that a guaranteed income at the levels and graduated sublevels proposed in FAP would *not* reduce incentives to work among the poor. The OEO obliged by hastily publishing a short report, "Preliminary Results of the New Jersey Graduated Work Incentive Experiment," that purported to show that there were no differences in the outside earnings of families receiving guaranteed income (experimental group) and those who were not (control group).[11]

The director of the research, economics professor Harold Watts of the University of Wisconsin, warned that "the evidence from this preliminary and crude analysis of the earliest results is less than ideal." But he concluded that "no evidence has been found in the urban experiment to support the belief that negative-tax type income maintenance programs will produce large disincentives and consequent reductions in earnings."[12] Moreover, the early results indicated that families in all experimental groups, with different guaranteed minimums and different graduated payment schedules, behaved in similar fashion to each other and to the control group receiving no payments at all. Predictably, later results confirmed the preliminary results, which were produced to assist the FAP bill in Congress.[13]

However, when the results of the Graduated Work Incentive Experiment were later *reanalyzed* by the RAND Corporation (which was not responsible for the design of the original study), markedly different results were produced.[14] The RAND Corporation reports that the Wisconsin researchers working for OEO had originally chosen New Jersey because it had no state welfare programs for "intact" families—families headed by an able-bodied, working-age male. The guaranteed incomes were offered to these intact families to compare their work behavior with control group families. But six months after the experiment began, New Jersey changed its state law and offered *all* families (experimental *and* control group families) very generous welfare benefits—benefits equal to those offered to participants in the experiment. This meant that for most of the period of the experiment, the control group was being given benefits which were equivalent to the experimental group—an obvious violation of the experimental research design. The OEO-funded University of Wisconsin researchers failed to consider this factor in their research. Thus, they concluded that there were no significant differences between the work behaviors of experimental and control groups, and they implied that a national guaranteed income would not be a disincentive to work. The RAND Corporation researchers, on the other hand, considered the New Jersey state welfare program in their estimates of work behavior. RAND concluded that recipients of a guaranteed annual income would work six and one-half fewer hours per week than they would work in the absence of such a program. In short, the RAND study suggests that a guaranteed annual income would produce a substantial disincentive to work.

The RAND study was published in 1978 after enthusiasm in Washington for a guaranteed annual income program—or "welfare reform"—had already cooled. The RAND study conflicted with the earlier OEO study and confirmed the intuition of many Congress members that a guaranteed annual income would reduce willingness to work. The RAND study also suggested that a *national* program might be very costly and involve some payments to nearly half the nation's families. Finally, RAND noted that its own estimates of high costs and work disincentives may "seriously understate the expected cost of an economy-wide ... program."

SUMMARY

Implementing public policy can be a difficult task for administrators of social welfare programs. Implementation involves a number of activities including organizing and staffing agencies, translating policies into specific courses of action, and spending funds to operate programs. One major obstacle to successful implementation is to determine the intent of social policies which is not always clearly defined in the legislation. Other problems include obtaining sufficient resources, overcoming any negative attitudes toward a program and seeing that bureaucratic structures do not prevent the program from operating smoothly.

Americans no longer believe that social problems can be eliminated by merely passing laws and spending money for new welfare programs. We are increasingly concerned with obtaining evidence about whether social programs actually work. But policy evaluation is no less political than any other part of the policy process.

A rational approach to social policy evaluation includes identifying and ranking program goals and objectives; developing units to measure these goals; identifying target and nontarget groups that might be affected; measuring tangible and intangible program effects; and measuring direct and indirect program costs. Several types of research designs lend themselves to evaluative studies of social welfare policies and programs. These are experimental designs, quasi-experimental designs, and time series designs.

Evaluating social welfare programs is a political activity for a number of reasons. Program goals and objectives are not always clear, but evaluators must evaluate something even if everyone does not agree. Some program goals are more symbolic than tangible, and the symbolic goals are even more difficult to evaluate than the tangible. No program administrator wants to receive a bad evaluation. Negative evaluations are generally criticized, and administrators will take steps to counteract negative findings. Evaluations are disruptive to the ongoing work of the agency and take time and resources from other activities. Also, the evaluation may not provide useful information about how to improve the program. In-house evaluations tend to be positive, and outside evaluations are more likely to be critical and ambivalent about the program. The well-publicized evaluations of the Guaranteed Annual Income Experiments are examples of the politics of policy evaluation.

NOTES

1. Jeffrey Pressman and Aaron Wildavsky, *Implementation* (Berkeley, Calif.: University of California Press, 1973), p. 109.
2. This discussion relies on George C. Edwards, *Implementing Public Policy* (Washington, D.C.: Congressional Quarterly, Inc., 1980).
3. See Daniel P. Moynihan, *The Politics of a Guaranteed Income* (New York: Vintage Books, 1973), p. 220.
4. Herbert Kaufman, *Red Tape* (Washington: Brookings Institution, 1977), p. 13.
5. Joseph S. Wholey and associates, *Federal Evaluation Policy* (Washington, D.C.: Urban Institute, 1970), p. 15.
6. Ibid.
7. David Nachmias, *Policy Evaluation* (New York: St. Martins, 1979), p. 4.
8. Carol H. Weiss, *Evaluation Research: Methods of Assessing Program Effectiveness* (Englewood Cliffs, N.J.: Prentice-Hall, 1972), p. 2.
9. David N. Kershaw, "A Negative Income Tax Experiment," in David Nachmias ed., *The Practice of Policy Evaluation* (New York: St. Martins, 1980), pp. 27–28.
10. See Harold M. Watts, "Graduated Work Incentives: An Experiment in Negative Taxation," *American Economic Review* 59 (May 1969): 463–472.
11. U.S. Office of Economic Opportunity, *Preliminary Results of the New Jersey Graduated Work Incentive Experiment*, February 18, 1970. Also cited in Alice M. Rivlin, *Systematic Thinking for Social Action* (Washington, D.C.: Brookings Institution, 1971).
12. Harold M. Watts, "Adjusted and Extended Preliminary Results from the Urban Graduated Work Incentive Experiment," University of Wisconsin, Institute for Research on Poverty, revised, June 10, 1970), p. 40. Also cited in Rivlin, *Systematic Thinking*, p. 101.
13. David Kershaw and Jerelyn Fair, eds., *Final Report of the New Jersey Graduated Work Incentive Experiment* (University of Wisconsin, Institute for Research on Poverty, 1974).
14. John F. Cogan, *Negative Income Taxation and Labor Supply: New Evidence from the New Jersey-Pennsylvania Experiment* (Santa Monica, Calif.: RAND Corporation, 1978).

Index